AF600437

Critical Evaluations of Economic Development Policies

Critical Evaluations of Economic Development Policies

Edited by

LAURA A. REESE and DAVID FASENFEST

Wayne State University Press Detroit

Copyright © 2004 by Wayne State University Press,
Detroit, Michigan 48201. All rights are reserved.
No part of this book may be reproduced without formal permission.

08 07 06 05 04   5 4 3 2 1

Library of Congress Cataloging-in-Publication Data

Critical evaluations of economic development policies / edited by Laura A. Reese and David Fasenfest.
p. cm.
Includes bibliographical references and index.
ISBN 0-8143-2900-4 (cloth : alk paper)
1. Economic development projects—United States. 2. Regional planning—United States. 3. Community development, Urban—United States. 4. Local government—United States. I. Reese, Laura A. (Laura Ann), 1958– II. Fasenfest, David.

HC110.E44C75 2004
338.9'001'1—dc22

2003023876

∞ The paper used in this publication meets the minimum requirements of the American National Standard for Information Sciences—Permanence of Paper for Printed Library Materials, ANSI Z39.48–1984.

In honor of friends, this is dedicated to Cindy Bell and the Village:
Colleen Croxall and Dave Samuels; Tammy Croxall;
Mike Ziolkowski; Susan and Edwin Phillips;
and Jan and Frank Wassilak.
—LAR

To Heidi and Bernhard for their support and encouragement.
—DF

CONTENTS

PREFACE

The concept for this book stems from an earlier article, "What Works Best? Values and the Evaluation of Local Economic Development Policy," *Economic Development Quarterly* 11 (1997): 195–207, and a prior symposium Critical Perspectives on Local Development Policy Evaluation, *Economic Development Quarterly* (February 1999): 3–65. The former presented the theoretical argument for critical evaluations of economic development policies as well as an initial model for the types of outcomes such evaluations should consider. The symposium in *Economic Development Quarterly* included initial models for and, in several cases, applications of critical evaluations that explicitly considered broader social goals in the evaluation of local development policy. This volume allows for a more extended dialogue about the theoretical underpinnings of critical evaluations, how they can and should be conducted, and actual applications of such evaluations. The hope is that this dialogue will stimulate more thinking on the value of alternative development outcomes in formation, implementation, and evaluations of local economic development policy.

Acknowledgments and thanks are due to a number of individuals who supported the development of this volume. First, thanks are due to Ned Hill for supporting the publication of the initial symposium. Joe Ohren has provided both conceptual and editorial assistance. Obviously, the authors of essays in the book are due a debt of gratitude not only for their fine work but also for their cooperation and patience in getting the book done. Finally, thanks are extended to Arthur Evans and Jane Hoehner of Wayne State University Press and to the anonymous reviewers who helped bring it all together.

INTRODUCTION

This book represents a continuing effort by the editors and authors to make more explicit the often implicit values behind economic development policies and, by extension, efforts to evaluate those policies. In an earlier symposium we called for exploration of *alternative evaluation frameworks* that "expect more of our economic development policies and programs" and consciously acknowledge that, "at root, if we are spending public tax dollars on such efforts the public . . . should expect real benefits" (Reese and Fasenfest, 1999: 6). This, then, serves as another forum for presenting evaluations of economic development policies that explicitly address questions of *value* and that directly focus on what the public should expect from the expenditure of public resources. In other words, the focus is on "critical" evaluations in the purest sense of the term—analysis that leads to judgments about program merits

At the outset, it is necessary to consider more carefully what the modifier "critical" suggests about evaluations. An examination of dictionary definitions is useful. While most definitions refer to faultfinding, there are many important and telling secondary definitions of "critical." Funk and Wagnalls, for example, defines critical as "given to severe judgments and exhibiting careful judgment; analytical." Criticism is the "art of making discriminating judgments." Webster defines "critical" as, among other things, "passing judgment upon, inclined to make fine distinctions, exact, inclined to find fault or judge with severity." What is apparent is that "critical" is not simply a negative judgment. Rather, it is making fine, careful, and exacting discriminations between options and outcomes. Critical evaluations, then, in contrast with traditional evaluations, suggest that the questions asked and the standards met will be, if not severe, then at least fine and exacting. All policy evaluations are inherently an exercise in criticism. But using the term "critical evaluation" highlights the fact that evaluators and analysts of economic development can frame their studies within commonly accepted paradigms—for example, market economies that apply standards related to taxes and jobs—

or they can approach the task by challenging those paradigms and by asking less frequently addressed questions, employing alternative techniques, and considering the costs and benefits of development policies at their root. In other words, critical evaluations make explicit an inquiry into the reality of economic development policies—they entail the allocation of public revenues and resources to the private sector, a public subsidization of private interests. Critical evaluations make that "discriminating judgment" and hence ask questions about reasonable *public* expectations for program outcome. These evaluations are not just inquiries into the effectiveness of any policy in meeting stated goals but are also an exploration into whether or not those goals are appropriate or in the community's interests from the outset.

Critical versus Traditional Evaluations

Methodological Elements of Traditional and Critical Approaches

What are the goals of economic development? Traditional policy evaluations assume that goals drive the selection of economic development techniques. In other words, the presumption is that policymakers agree on a goal or set of goals, choose policies accordingly, and then implement those policies. The task of the evaluator is to determine the extent to which policies are meeting stated goals. Such goals are typically identified by consulting with public officials or examining policy statements such as enabling statutes. Indeed, Pagano and Bowman suggest that local leaders establish a "vision" for the community based on "its history, its place in its hierarchy of cities, and its aspirations to change." This vision, then, serves as a basis for selecting among economic development techniques or, indeed, determining whether economic development should be pursued at all (1995: 3–4).

However, other research has suggested that goal identification is much more problematic from the start. Beaumont and Hovey have maintained that the lack of a formal theory of economic development results in a situation whereby "state and local economic development strategies evolve incrementally without [any] underlying economic theory except that more jobs are good and less jobs are bad" (1985: 328). Bingham and Blair (1984) have suggested that much urban economic development policy has been "piecemeal," reducing the impact and limiting the achievement of stated goals. And, Kirby (1995) has pointed to a general absence of theoretical frameworks in the community development literature to guide local policy choices. Such research seems to suggest that, even given an overriding vision, absent a general theory of economic development, any connection between policy and goals is going to be accidental at best and unlikely at worst. The reality of this is rarely acknowledged within traditional evaluations.

Evaluations, then, should rest first on a specification of desired outcomes. What is the community trying to achieve? The term "economic development" has always been somewhat problematic, since scholars and practitioners have used it to mean different things: economic processes, development activities, and an economic outcome. However, the "economic" part of the concept has traditionally been used in a private, capital investment, business growth sense. There has also been an implicit understanding that "the modifier *economic* is an ideological statement meant to deflect attention from the inherently political nature of economic development (regardless of whether government is actually involved) and to act as a buffer (available when needed) between key investors and elected officials and government bureaucrats who might introduce the scrutiny and accountability of a democratic society" (Beauregard, 1994: 269).

The meaning of "development" is also open to interpretation—does it simply mean economic growth or does it require some larger systematic change, that is, "development"? Herrick and Kindleberger employ an analogy to the human organism to describe the difference between growth and development: "Growth involves changes in overall aggregates such as height or weight, while development includes changes in functional capacities—physical coordination, learning capacity, or ability to adapt to changing circumstances" (1983: 21). In a similar vein, Cernea (1991) argues that "development" is too often defined in terms of planning and market efficiency, at the expense of the more generalized improvement or development of community residents.

In the local development context, the goal of economic *growth* traditionally has meant getting the local community back to work and building the local tax base at the lowest cost to the public. Such goals have driven communities and evaluations for years. Because job creation and tax-base growth usually mean votes, and citizens expect governmental officials to attract business, emphasis has been directed toward incentive packages to attract or retain employers (Rubin and Zorn, 1985). Further, since fiscal retrenchment and funding cutbacks force communities to compete with each other in increasingly intense and destructive local and regional rivalries, the resulting incentive packages become remarkably similar (Markusen, 1987; Reese and Fasenfest, 1996). They stress "smokestack chasing" to replace lost jobs and include a variety of "supply-side" incentives, such as tax and financial inducements, infrastructure improvement, and land assembly and development (Wassall and Hellman, 1985; Eisinger, 1988; Reese, 1992; Reese and Fasenfest, 1996). In traditional evaluations, local development policy is deemed successful if it appears to have positive effects upon the business climate (Bartik, 1991), improves the economic base in terms of changes in per capita income or employment (Clarke and Gaile, 1992), or, in some cases, if projects are completed at all (Friedan and Sagalyn, 1989). Specifically, traditional evaluations focus on stated objectives without examining the selection of the particular objective or the long-term consequences of that selection.

If economic *development,* in the sense described by Herrick and Kindleberger, means the valued result of local development policies, the goals are much different, to wit: (1) increase the stability as well as the gross levels of income for the population; (2) increase local control over both market and government operations, particularly in those aspects that affect citizens in poverty; and (3) increase economic and political empowerment of all sectors of a community, including individual citizens (Brown and Warner, 1991: 37–38). Thus, a shift in goals from a traditional and narrow conception of "growth" to a broader and more critical notion of "development" increases the requirements for success in local economic development. Effective policies are no longer those that increase simple measures like the number of jobs or businesses; instead, policies must foster "structural and institutional changes which promote a more equitable distribution of new jobs and income generated by growth" (Brown and Warner, 1991: 29) and enhance a community's "capacity to act and innovate" (Beauregard, 1994: 271).

Is "development" too ambitious or unrealistic a goal for local economic development policies? Is it too much to expect that such policies should achieve results beyond job creation and tax-base growth? If society is spending public dollars on policies, strategies, and incentives to attract or create capital investment, should not the goals enhance development for the community at large? Loftman and Nevin, in evaluating local policies, conclude that "if local authorities in attempting to regenerate the economies of declining urban areas, fail to ensure that benefits are distributed equitably, and indeed compound inequality, questions have to be asked as to why the public sector should become involved in such activity at all" (cited in Loftman, 1995: 21). In a similar vein, it has been suggested that economic development strategies such as tax abatements face greater public scrutiny, including referenda, since such public expenditures represent "debt issues" and differential cost burdens and service benefits (Nunn, 1994). Issues related to equity are pivotal to the enterprise of local economic development. Indeed, in their presentation of seven "metaphors" or ways of understanding or conceptualizing economic development, Mier and Bingham (1994) included economic development as a "quest for social justice."

Traditional evaluative research certainly suggests that this is too much to expect. However, even the more narrow measures of goal attainment are problematic. The most frequently used outcome measures revolve around economic health and performance indicators, including employment levels, numbers of or growth in businesses, growth in jobs, change in occupational/industrial categories, income measures, and various indicators of value added by firms (see, e.g., Garn and Ledebur, 1980; Burchell et al., 1984; Ladd and Yinger, 1989; and Beauregard, 1994). More narrowly, many evaluations have focused almost exclusively on measures of change in local per capita income and job growth (Clarke and Gaile, 1992). On a national scale, economic development has traditionally been examined by focusing on GNP, GDP, NNP, total income, per capita income, average income, productivity, and employment change (Herrick and Kindleberger, 1983; Ross and Usher, 1986). However, such growth-based measures have several common flaws: a tendency to reflect only certain types of economic change, to overstate positive outcomes, to devalue effects on social factors in the community, and to ignore attendant negative social externalities such as crime and pollution.

Measures like local per capita income, income growth, and employment or job growth can also be misleading. Research has often confused "city economic health" with the "health of city residents." The former, measured by "the number of private jobs per resident, is closely linked to the wages and salaries generated in the city per resident, but is not the same as the economic health of city residents which is measured by their per capita income" (Ladd and Yinger, 1989: 29). Definition of goals does matter. Even measures of local per capita income can be problematic, since that may be outside the control of local governments, and local efforts may be an artifact of jurisdictional boundaries or community patterns. In a similar manner, measures of job growth may be distorted by income inequalities and increased service costs associated with higher levels of inbound workers (Clarke and Gaile, 1992). Thus, at the root, traditionally used measures of economic growth fail to make a connection between changes in individual wealth and local fiscal health. In other words, "a city can be healthy in the sense of generating many jobs per resident at the same time that its residents remain impoverished" (Ladd and Yinger, 1989: 17).

If traditional and narrow indicators of economic growth are problematic anyway, perhaps a shift in focus toward development might not be so dramatic. Indeed, to the extent that evaluations are intended to identify program improvements, a broader examination of policy outcomes and impacts, opportunity costs, distributional implications, and differential social and economic effects is clearly called for (Loftman, 1995).

Critical Evaluations

Critical evaluations of local economic development policies go beyond the simple and narrow consideration of immediate outcomes and explicitly address broader and more fundamental questions:

- To what extent do economic development policies, as public expenditures, serve public as opposed to private goals and needs?
- To what extent do economic development policies benefit those most in need within communities?
- To what extent do economic development policies build and enhance community stability as opposed to reinforcing market imperatives?
- How should conflicting interests within cities be balanced in creating and implementing development policies?
- To what extent are policy *means* as opposed to policy *ends* an important consideration in evaluating economic development policy?
- How do policymakers assess the public costs of private development incentives?
- How might policymakers systematically assess and choose among policies using "social" as opposed to purely "economic" criteria?
- Are economic development policies that are targeted toward public rather than private interests inherently less "rational," or might such policies actually address both social and economic considerations? In other words, are social and economic values inherently at odds?
- How does the selection and implementation of particular evaluation methodologies affect the results of outcome assessments? How do the methods used color the findings?

- How can qualitative considerations be taken into account in quantitative evaluations?
- What is the role of community stakeholders in evaluating economic development policies, and how might they most effectively be involved?

Policymakers and academics alike are cognizant that policy deliberation and choice among competing policies is a value-laden or "political" process. However, it has been less clear that evaluation methodologies and decision analysis techniques are similarly exercises in weighing often-competing values. The questions noted above and addressed in the chapters in this book make this abundantly clear. And, in doing so, they show how different evaluation designs embody different values and how the implementation of different evaluation designs can lead to very different conclusions about policy outcomes and "success."

That all policy evaluation is inherently normative has long been understood in the evaluation literature. But it has not always been explicitly acknowledged in evaluating local economic development policy (Gunnell, 1968; Tribe, 1972; Rein, 1976). A critical evaluation approach, however, makes the normative reality an explicit part of the research process. This renders critical evaluations unique in several respects. First, as several of the chapters here indicate, they imply different designs than more traditional policy evaluations. Identifying and choosing the level of analysis requires awareness that area, citywide, or gross policy outcomes may be very different than targeted, neighborhood, or net outcomes. Policies that may appear to "fail" at the macro level may well be successful at the micro level. In this sense a decision about level of analysis reflects a value choice requiring specification of exactly *whose* benefits serve as the evaluative criteria. The empowerment zone evaluations discussed in the Dewar chapter raise the issue of how to involve stakeholders in the design of the evaluation. In traditional evaluation designs, the "value-free" dictum requires that those with a stake in the program be as far removed from the evaluation as possible. Evaluation is thus the purview of "neutral" researchers. However, if the goal of an economic development program is empowerment, and the intent is to uncover the goals of the program from the perspective of those most closely affected, then the evaluation design requires some form of stakeholder participation.

Second, critical evaluations, because they consider social or equity outcomes, are inherently complex, particularly in the required measures or indicators. The acceptance of standard measures of growth (ever-increasing jobs and tax base, for example) as "success" has led to the assumption that economic development has to be "good." This "uncritical admiration, however, stifles a probing of the constitutive rules that structure our understandings of what economic development means and that delineate what actions and consequences qualify as valid and appropriate" (Beauregard, 1994: 267). As the authors have noted elsewhere, "creating counterfactuals (but for the economic development incentives, would certain outcomes have occurred?) and adequately measuring program outcome as opposed to processes are two of the most formidable challenges" of evaluation design. And, when the outcomes of interest shift from the relatively easily quantifiable measuring of job and tax-base growth to variables such as "income distribution, changes in poverty, job security, employment change by sector, and political empowerment," the challenges multiply exponentially (Reese and Fasenfest, 1999: 3).

Table I.1 provides a direct comparison of indicators traditionally used to measure the effectiveness of local economic development policies and logical indicators for critical evaluations that explicitly address the achievement of social goals (see Reese and Fasenfest, 1997, for a full description of this approach). The difference between the indicators in the two columns lies not only in their focus on immediate outputs as opposed to longer range outcomes but also in their inherent link to value judgments.

For example, traditional evaluations typically employ indicators of employment growth, job generation, and jobs per resident. Critical evaluations would require attention to the quality and distribution of jobs generated as well. Are the jobs in sectors appropriate to the local economy? Is the economic base diversified? Are the jobs safe? Do they provide long-term security and incomes sufficient for sustainable households? Indeed, such measures reflect more than just a call for broader notions of economic development; they also have particular implications for understanding the full impact of economic development policies. For example, though local economic development programs may generate jobs, if many of those jobs are part-time or at low wages, the net local effect may be simply to increase the number of "working poor." A shift in indicators or measures of success leads to very different conclusions about the effects of policy.

The evaluations in this book do an admirable job of either establishing models for such evaluation or illustrating how such models can be applied. And, they show how the application of evaluation models that make explicit

Table I.1

Traditional Indicators	*Indicators for Critical Evaluations*
Employment growth	Employment change by sector
Change in per capita income	Income distribution
Job generation	Job generation by sector
Private jobs per resident	Wage and non-wage employment
Change in GNP/GDP	Change in percent in poverty
New business attraction	Diversity of economic base
New business starts	Extent of citizen participation
Sales increases	Job security
Increased tax base	Pay levels of new jobs
Business expansion	Safety of new jobs
Dollars of investment capital	Quality/challenge of new jobs
	Recession-proof economy
	Value use of new products

critical expectations for public value can come to different conclusions about the efficacy of economic development policies. Most importantly, these evaluations and evaluation models highlight the continuing dialogue that needs to take place among those making and assessing local development policies. Such discussion should make explicit the values implicit in both the design and evaluation of economic development policies. Critical assessment of evaluation methodologies requires clearly identified goal expectations: Is it numbers of jobs or quality of jobs? Is it growth in jobs or who gets the jobs? Is it creation of wealth in a community or the distribution of wealth in a community? Is it private- or public-sector benefit? Is it policy to manipulate behavior or policy to empower behavior? Stimulating such dialogue can only lead to more completely informed policy development as well as evaluation of outcomes. Stone has suggested that, to govern effectively, local officials must engage in a process of "social learning." This implies that, for effective and equitable economic development policies to be implemented, a wide array of alternatives must be brought before the governing regime, and "to the extent that urban regimes safeguard special privileges at the expense of social learning, democracy is weakened" (1989: 244). Thus, through explicit discourse on *values* all stakeholders in the outcomes of economic development policy become empowered and policies more informed through "social learning" are likely to result.

The normative nature of economic development policy leads to questions beyond evaluation process and techniques. The Tao and Feiock chapter raises the more fundamental question of ends versus means and highlights that explicit and systematic comparison of the latter are as important as evaluations of the former. In this way they remind academics and policymakers that evaluation can be more than a retrospective exercise in policy outcome assessment. Truly critical evaluations of economic development strategies require a prospective analysis of the means—the policies themselves. In this chapter, two different policies lead to the same ends (targeted reduction of households on welfare), but the policies themselves are very different in both theory and implementation. One policy (enterprise zones) operates through private-sector implementation and discretion and in the process serves to strengthen private-sector resources and reduce public accountability for program failure. In this sense part of the policy outcome is embedded in implementation. Thus, even though the "end" is valuable do the means really strengthen *community* goals? The second policy (community redevelopment areas) is implemented by local governments, includes a neighborhood planning exercise that strengthens local government capacity, and even absent "economic development" outcomes, leaves neighborhoods with improved infrastructure. In this case the means lead to empowerment, neighborhood investment, and clear accountability for program success. Two different means, the same end, but in implementation very different "values" emerge. The clear lesson of this chapter and the rest of the book is that critical assessment must consider all aspects of the policy process: means or policies, process or implementation, and ends or outcomes. It is to this call that the chapters in the volume respond.

Chapter Summaries

The next chapter offers an insight into the differences in critical and traditional thinking about local development evaluation by presenting and then critiquing a traditional policy evaluation. Reviewing their national analysis of EDA's Economic Development Districts, Fasenfest and Reese present a traditional analytical approach. The chapter concludes with comments on what a critical perspective brings to such an analysis and offers insight into what would have been different in the approach to understanding the program's impact on local planning efforts, speculating on how the analysis could draw different conclusions as a result. The chapters that follow begin from such a critical perspective offering models for alternatives to traditional evaluation methodology.

To frame the rest of the critical evaluations, the chapter by Tao and Feiock asks several questions central to the aim of this book. Are citywide and neighborhood outcomes of economic development policies the same? Can policies promote economic growth but not community development? Can policies with very different ideological underpinnings (market-driven versus local government-driven/top down versus bottom up) have similar outcomes? Most importantly, the chapter illustrates the importance of how evaluations are structured—in this case whether the unit of analysis is city or area level—in determining the outcome of the evaluation. Programs may be judged ineffective at the citywide level yet have significant impact in more targeted areas. The chapter also addresses specifically the question of "values" when it comes to selection of economic development programs. If two alternatives—in this case enterprise zones and community redevelopment areas—have basically the same effects (e.g., both increase development in targeted areas), on what basis should the choice be made? Here the contrast is quite stark. The enterprise zone program allocates direct benefits to businesses and then over time benefits accrue to the targeted area in trickle-down fashion. On the other hand the community redevelopment program represents a bottom-up approach in which direct investment through an explicit planning process, development of community capacity through a local governing board, and direct government investment in infrastructure all serve to strengthen targeted areas.

If the same goals are achieved with either approach, then the choice becomes which program offers greater community "value." The answer appears to be the redevelopment area since, quite apart from any long-term program benefits, investments are being made directly to targeted areas. In other words, absent any long-term development effects resulting from the program, the community reinvestment areas are being strengthened both in infrastructure and through the community-building benefits of the planning and goal-setting process. And, if the program evaluation were to be extended to measure other broader outcomes such as community capacity, the findings might be even stronger that the reinvestment strategy has greater long-term benefits. Consideration of both means and ends provides a new way to think about economic development policy choice and new definitions of "good" policy.

The chapter by Imbroscio offers a public balance sheet as a way of explicitly considering the potential costs and benefits to the community of prospective economic development policies and programs and demonstrates its use in various applications in the literature. It directly complements the Tao and Feiock chapter by providing a systematic way of choosing between policies based on a consideration of the "social" costs of alternative courses of action. It emphasizes consideration of program costs for the community at large rather than a myopic focus on potential benefits to the private sector. It makes clear that there are real public costs to subsidies for private firms. And, the public balance sheet approach requires that actual public benefits accrue in the end. As the author notes, the public balance sheet makes very clear that policies should be evaluated in terms of "public versus private" benefits since public expenditures are involved. The chapter poses a fundamental question—what are the social costs of private-sector development? Externalities resulting from private investment or disinvestment decisions are thus internalized in the policymaking process. At the same time the public balance sheet approach allows identification of circumstances where growth is not necessarily "good," that is where it imposes significant costs on communities in the form of sprawl, infrastructure stress, environmental problems, increasing service costs and the like. Once the costs and the benefits of development or particular development policies are identified it is easier to consider value judgments about who should bear those costs—the private or public sector. Private developers can be assessed the costs of development or they can compensate the community by providing other types of public "goods" (linkage programs for example). In the context of the Tao and Feiock chapter, the public balance sheet would help assess whether the ends justified the means since the social or community benefits of the reinvestment program would be included in the calculus. Finally, as Imbroscio points out, examination of broader public benefits and costs may lead to consideration of policies that at first blush might be considered too radical, such as public ownership of private assets or public subsidy of employee ownership. Thus the type of evaluation selected can affect identification of costs and benefits, allow for a reallocation of costs, and even identify policy options that might provide a better "balance" of benefits to the community as a whole.

The next chapter, by Yin, takes a step back to consider what knowledge should optimally underpin economic development policymaking and, later, evaluation. In short, a first step in any economic development policy process is understanding the local or neighborhood economic base. An accurate assessment of preexisting conditions, barriers to development, and opportunities for investment is often assumed but not necessarily considered. To evaluate policy, scholars and practitioners must first assess existing conditions. And, as with evaluation, there are various methods for studying the local economic base, and the selection of technique influences the findings that result. Thus the traditional and widely used export base studies tend to provide insufficient or misleading information about very stressed communities. The normative effect is that many opportunities or assets are missed and policy options building on those assets forgone, and development options that further drain resources from poor neighborhoods are often prescribed. And, as pointed out in the Dewar chapter, findings and policy recommendations differ according to which groups or individuals are involved in conducting the economic base study. The community balance sheet approach incorporates stakeholders in "framing questions and performing research." The result of this participation is that residents became knowledgeable about the neighborhood economy in the same manner that individuals know their financial status when they pay bills and balance their checkbooks. This has a direct impact on goal development: goals become more realistic, based on actual neighborhood strengths and weaknesses, and emerge with the full participation of those most directly affected. In short, Yin shows that even assessing the local economic base is not an objective or neutral task.

The chapter by Dewar focuses very explicitly on the normative nature of the evaluation process using the federal empowerment zone program. The fact that resident "empowerment" is an explicit goal of the program requires that evaluations consider normative issues. However, extant evaluation designs and practice are not necessarily up to this task. Traditional methodologists teach that evaluations are to be objective and evaluators neutral observers. They are not to affect or be affected by the subjects or programs they are studying. But what happens when one goal of the program involves "empowering" zone residents, not only through participation in goal development and program implementation but also in evaluation. How are the "subjects" to become the "objects"?

As Dewar notes, there are several ways to share participation and control in evaluative research. These range on a continuum from very little to direct control. It is not surprising that most existing studies have employed methodologies that are closer to the "very little" control end of the spectrum; they are more often contractual than participatory. Having the studied participate in the study seems to violate the basic tenants of behavioral research upon which evaluation methodologies are based. Just as important, involving neighborhood or zone residents is complicated, time consuming, and expensive. It is possible, as Dewar suggests, that such evaluations may end up being too idiosyncratic and narrow for findings to be generalized to other communities.

Even so, what are the effects of choosing less participatory over more participatory styles of evaluation for the empowerment zone? The answer appears to be that not only are opportunities for empowerment lost but the findings of the evaluation are affected. In other words, consultative evaluations focusing on job or tax-base growth may indicate only limited program success, while participatory evaluations may show that the empowerment zone program has had positive effects on community participation, friendship networks and feelings of individual efficacy. If the way evaluations are framed and implemented affects the outcome, then how can evaluations be interpreted objectively? Such a question flies in the face of much of what scholars "know" about evaluations. It must be considered, however, since the way an evaluation is designed and the questions it poses can affect how resultant programs and policies are judged.

The chapter by Persky, Felsenstein, and Carlson focuses on different ways to evaluate the job creation impacts of economic development programs and incentives. More specifically, the authors show how a "job chains" approach to evaluating job creation provides a more explicit focus on the extent to which economic development policies improve the welfare of low- and medium-skilled workers. It is not enough that policies simply increase jobs—indeed, economic development programs do more than just generate discrete jobs. Each job creates "chain reactions" in the market, where residents move up and into jobs vacated by others. Thus the question of policy "success" relates to the quality of the jobs, who is getting them, and how are the jobs impacting the local labor market more generally. Job chain evaluations incorporate a more stringent definition of "success" because not all jobs are equal; in terms of their contribution to local welfare, jobs at the bottom of the chain are worth more to recipients than jobs at the top of the chain. On the other hand, jobs going to nonresidents or "immigrants" do not contribute local benefits and truncate the overall job chain.

The authors identify four hypotheses that can be tested using job chain analysis relating to the number of people affected by an economic development program, the distribution of benefits from job creation, relative increases in welfare attributable to jobs at the lower end of the chain, and connections between the length of the job chain and subsequent metropolitan growth. In short, they show how following the chain of employment can answer questions beyond simple job growth. Using a simulated application of job chain analysis they illustrate how the analysis would be implemented. But they also are able to posit that job creation at higher skill levels will not be as effective in moving lower-income and/or skilled workers up the chain because new jobs tend to be filled by workers from outside at the same job level. The lesson of this chapter is that an evaluation methodology that considers the *full* complexity of the quality of job moves within the economy can point to economic development policies that primarily increase the welfare of lower- rather than exclusively higher-skilled workers.

Finally, Leatherman and Marcouiller provide a comprehensive review of current economic modeling techniques used to simplify complex relationships and project direct and indirect costs and benefits of prospective economic development policies. As the other authors have argued, it is clear that the choice of modeling technique also has normative implications. While most common modeling methods such as input/output analysis tend to examine aggregate economic effects, others such as the social accounting matrix allow for explicit consideration of the distribution patterns of program costs and benefits. Thus, while one method obscures the question of "who gets what," the other addresses it explicitly. The authors show, in an example based on rural areas in Wisconsin, how traditional aggregate modeling techniques lead to the conclusion that economic development policies should focus on timber production rather than tourism. However, the social accounting method reveals that such an emphasis will only serve to exacerbate preexisting income inequalities. Focusing on tourism on the other hand reduces inequities since benefits are most likely to accrue to *both* low-income and high-income households.

Thus the questions that alternative modeling techniques ask are inherently different and produce different policy answers. The authors note that traditional input/output analyses "tend to focus on the interaction of production sectors and how economic growth occurs." Social accounting matrices, however, "were built to focus on the interaction between economic and social structures and how wealth is distributed." In addition to providing policymakers with explicit information on the distributive implications of economic development policies, social accounting matrices also offer another important contemporary policy benefit; they can identify development policies that reduce income inequalities. Thus, explicitly redistributive and politically unpopular policies are avoided yet the same goals are accomplished through economic development techniques that stimulate employment at the lower end of the income scale. One can easily contemplate how policymakers, armed with social accounting methodologies to forecast job creation and the job chain analyses suggested by Persky et al. to examine the beneficiaries of job growth, would be able to identify policies that generated economic growth but also targeted that growth to those most in need. In this sense economic analysis and evaluation are directly related to the normative issues of "good" policy choice.

Challenges of Critical Evaluations

All the chapters in this volume highlight, to one extent or another, the challenges and shortcomings of implementing critical evaluations of economic development policies. Each of the alternative frameworks requires considerable theoretical, conceptual, and empirical innovation. Dewar, for example, points out numerous difficulties in conducting empowerment zone evaluations that incorporate citizen input. Imbroscio's local public balance sheet requires calculating the subjective costs and benefits of preserving social communities. The challenge of "valuing" opportunity costs, social costs, and other intangibles has bedeviled cost/benefit analyses for decades. Yin's alternative base studies and Leatherman and Marcoullier's social accounting matrices both present significant methodological challenges.

There are still other important challenges associated with designing and implementing critical evaluations. From a purely technical standpoint, data on the indicators identified in the chapters here are often difficult to collect. Although changes in tax-base valuation are fairly concrete, measures of qualitative improvements in service, political empowerment, and job quality, for example, are problematic. Proxy measures of somewhat amorphous concepts are needed; they require greater skill on the part of evaluators, demand intersubjective validation of operationalizations, and offer greater challenges in collecting necessary data. Just because they are more difficult, however, is no reason to discard such evaluative approaches. Some specific circumstances in which critical approaches would be feasible come to mind. Impracticalities abound in evaluating a community's overall economic development effort, but application to specific and more limited efforts may offer an opportunity to begin. For example, evaluating a business incubator, a new workforce training effort, or a particular capital development strategy, such as a Community Development Corporation, might prove more feasible than assessing a comprehensive local economic development strategy.

Political issues also surface in efforts to include the alternative measures necessary to critical policy evaluations. First, practitioners tend to be judged on immediate outputs by both political actors and the public; judging their efforts on long-term outcomes is likely to be threatening, unwelcome, and a change in orientation from past practice. For elected officials, with a short-term perspective dictated by election cycles, consideration of long-range policy outcomes and impacts may lie beyond their frame of reference. Although the latter problem is intractable, academic evaluations are clearly not as bound by such political considerations and could more easily move toward broader conceptualizations of valued outcomes.

How to get such evaluations used is another challenge. However, local legislation could incorporate requirements for evaluations, as could state enabling legislation; greater public involvement might well increase the demands for evaluation; and job expectations for economic development professionals could be redefined, to name a few possibilities. Indeed, citizen pressure, current calls for "reinventing" government, and performance-based resource allocation may coalesce to foster political environments in which local leaders become much more interested in broadly based evaluations, both to meet constituent concerns and, admittedly, to support desired programs.

Yet another "political" issue deals with "weighting," or prioritizing, various policy objectives. All policy decisions and public-sector investment decisions involve, whether explicitly or implicitly, trade-offs among competing projects under conditions of limited resources. Further, business relocations that increase jobs and tax base and even equalize incomes may also increase pollution and traffic congestion, perhaps thereby decreasing overall quality of life. Shadow pricing schemes are commonly used to "value" intangibles and forgone alternatives in cost/benefit analyses. Although such calculations are cumbersome and expensive, local governments can undertake something akin to what the business world calls "sensitivity analysis" of prospective projects. This provides a range of circumstances and situations under which expected revenue and outcome streams will be forthcoming—and thereby serves as a guideline for conditions to impose so as to ensure that public investments provide public benefits (Fasenfest, 1986; Fasenfest and Ciancanelli, 1988). Furthermore, an analysis that weighs and monetizes outcomes permits the imposition of social values and community concerns similar to shadow pricing. Including a broader array of indicators and more normative goals, plus evaluation requirements to identify successive outcomes, enhances the identification and assessment of differential policy effects. Again, how these are weighted will likely and most appropriately be determined "politically." However, the value of critical evaluations is that they facilitate and foster explicit examination of the spectrum of policy effects.

Another central concern is the extent of the effect local governments have—or can be expected to have—on some of the indicators contained within the evaluation approaches presented in this volume. The point could be made, for example, that income distribution, poverty, job security, safety and quality, and even economic base diversity, are beyond the control of local entities. Although this is largely the case, local policies can make a difference to the local political economy; for example, local property tax abatements could be given to firms producing cigarettes or to those baking bread, to firms that are unionized or not, to firms that have safe working conditions or those with high injury rates, to firms that have comprehensive health care plans or firms that do not, to firms that pollute the environment or firms that do not, to footloose multinationals or local entrepreneurs—and the list goes on. Cities obviously have choices in distributing benefits to enterprises that either meet social goals or do not. By allocating incentives to employers based on wage rates, health care plans, job safety, or quality of employment, cities can have some influence on the distribution of income for residents and, ultimately, the quality of life. Thus, though there are many external factors and dynamics that affect these larger social and economic issues, local economic development policies can either be used to mitigate or exacerbate such trends and should be judged accordingly. The key is to get an explicit set of criteria, and through critical evaluations, to expand the repertoire of policy outcomes the public can expect from development programs

Related to the issue of "sphere of influence" of local efforts is a more theoretical concern regarding causality: specifically, can it be logically posited that economic development strategies should cause the sorts of broader societal changes identified in the models presented in the chapters? On the one hand, the complexities inherent in the development process, uncertainty regarding causal relationships, and constraints on data availability and evaluation design technology, as noted previously, suggest that the answer is "no." Further, a positive response would fly in the face of everything that is known about realistic limits of public policy.

Still, as suggested above, this need not be a reason to discard critical evaluative approaches. To the extent that such causal connections are explored through incorporation into economic development policy evaluations and introduced into debates about policy alternatives, the ties between public policies and long-term impact can begin to be explored. If the most pressing urban problem is homelessness, for example, such assessments can begin to address issues of trade-offs: should we spend public dollars on business incentives or shelters?

Conclusion

As suggested by Tao and Feiock, economic development policies themselves represent alternative "roads" toward the presumed goal of greater development for local communities. Clearly, some paths are more worn than others. The literature has repeatedly indicated that supply-side strategies such as tax abatements, other financial incentives, infrastructure improvements, loan arrangements, and marketing are the dominant economic development policies (see Wolman, 1996, and Reese and Fasenfest, 1997, for summaries of this literature). Other roads to economic development, variously labeled demand-side, progressive, Type II, or emergent, depending on the author, have been suggested as offering more promise for the achievement of alternative social values such as those identified in the chapters in this book (see, e.g., Elkin, 1987; Eisinger, 1988; Goetz, 1990; Reese, 1998; and McGuire, 2000). Policymakers and policy evaluators are offered Robert Frost's proverbial forks in the road at a variety of points along the journey: choices among alternative means, some more or less familiar, as well as choices of evaluation methods, measures, and outcomes. The authors in this collection of essays clearly show how the path taken as well as the consideration of the results of that choice *matter* in that they lead to very different questions and answers. But perhaps even more importantly, critical evaluations redirect us from thinking about what has happened and ask us to think about what could or should be happening. The language of economic development policy, the definition and discussion of valued outcomes, how policies are implemented and evaluated, and the standards to which public policy are held all make the critical "difference."

Notes

Some of the basic arguments presented here have been included in Reese and Fasenfest 1997, reprinted in Blair and Reese, ed., 1999; and Fasenfest, Ciancanelli, and Reese 1997.

ONE

Planning for a Change: An Assessment of EDA's Local Planning Initiatives

David Fasenfest and Laura A. Reese

The past century has been a chronicle of the tension within the American economy between the unplanned marketplace and public-sector intervention. As a response to the ravages of the Great Depression, seen as the byproduct of uncontrolled and unrestrained market activity coupled with some extraordinary natural calamities, came the New Deal and all its governmental intervention. World War II brought price control boards and transformed the public works projects of the 1930s into a nationally planned economy geared up for war production. The aftermath of the war and the great economic boom that followed, as well as the increasing disparity between rich and poor, brought Keynesian policies to the fore as programs like the Great Society and agencies like Housing and Urban Development (HUD) and others were carved into the public landscape to shape and focus market economies toward socially desirable objectives.

These changes did not come without the opposition of those who argued for both political and theoretical reasons that governmental intervention distorted the marketplace, a mechanism for good or ill that allocated resources most efficiently and maximized the overall welfare of society's citizens. These arguments notwithstanding, governments at all levels continued to seek a balance between intervention and laissez faire market forces. By the middle of the 1960s the Economic Development Administration (EDA) sought to improve those communities that did not fare well under market conditions. Mindful of agencies like HUD, whose mission was to help develop America's cities, the EDA embarked on a non-urban agenda to promote local development. The Economic Development District (EDD) program allowed states to identify areas that had some combination of below-average income, above-average unemployment, and other measures of persistent economic distress, and to designate agencies or organizations that would serve as the federally designated EDD for that area to coordinate cooperative efforts at local development. Were those efforts successful? Can government action promote market activity and coordinate development in areas that experience so-called market failure? What can governments do when the market creates disparities across regions, when solutions can be mobilized only by cross-jurisdictional efforts?

In the local development evaluation context, success at economic growth traditionally has meant getting the local community back to work and building the local tax base at the lowest cost to the public. Such goals have motivated communities and been the basis of evaluations for years. And the "economic" part of the concept has traditionally been used in a private, capital investment, business growth sense. There has also been an implicit understanding that "the modifier *economic* is an ideological statement meant to deflect attention from the inherently political nature of economic development (regardless of whether government is actually involved) and to act as a buffer (available when needed) between key investors and elected officials and government bureaucrats who might introduce the scrutiny and accountability of a democratic society" (Beauregard, 1994: 269).

This chapter represents a contribution to the empirical economic development evaluation literature by providing an evaluation of a federal planning program implemented at the regional level. Implicit in this evaluation are the questions of whether the planning efforts were successful and who, if anyone, benefited from these efforts. The examination extends the evaluation literature by incorporating an assessment of process, outputs, and outcomes, using both survey and case study methodologies. Since the program evaluated here is essentially an economic development planning program, the measures of success applied are somewhat different from traditional evaluations that focus primarily on job growth or tax-base enhancements. Rather, program outcomes, as defined in program enabling documentation, include the enhancement of technical assistance and capacity for regional coordination as well as the extent of representation of groups typically marginalized in the planning process—such as neighborhoods, citizens, minority groups, and poverty groups. Thus the goals evaluated here address concerns in the literature that the success indicators used in current evaluations are far from perfect in what they measure and are noteworthy for what they miss (Reese and Fasenfest, 1997). As a traditional evaluation contracted for by the EDA, the analysis rests primarily on perceptual measures of program process and success as opposed to actual measurement of economic data.[1] While this effort clearly contributes to knowledge about "what works" in building capacity and stimulating economic development, this evaluation includes some of the shortcomings described in the introduction and present in many economic development evaluations. Still, the evaluation findings presented here contribute significantly to an understanding of the importance of coordination, capacity building, planning, and representation—factors often overlooked within the traditional economic development evaluation literature.

The remainder of this chapter presents the highlights and findings of the more traditional evaluation of a locally implemented but federally financed economic development program. The approach is concerned with the question of what was accomplished by the program as a whole and not whether any particular EDD successfully managed regional planning in search of local development. As such the evaluation is not a case-by-case assessment of what happened in any particular EDD. Rather, it looks at the system of practices and tries to ascertain whether the structure created fosters local development, even as particular combinations of factors may make it more or less likely individual agencies succeed. Furthermore, it does not offer a formula for success—the absence of some positive conditions in a given locality does not necessarily result in planning disasters, and the presence of negative externalities does not necessarily mean coordinated efforts will fail. The chapter concludes with a discussion about how a critical evaluation poses different questions than those posed in traditional evaluations. In doing so a critical evaluation broadens the focus of what is meant by "local," by "economic," and by "development," and seeks to reconceptualize the criteria for successful local development.

Program Description

The Economic Development Administration operates a number of programs in pursuit of their mission to generate and retain jobs and stimulate economic growth in distressed areas. To receive support and attain federal designation as an Economic Development District agencies are required to have and maintain a Comprehensive Economic Development Strategy (CEDS[2]). The EDA supports 325 EDDs across the country charged to facilitate strategies for economic development by providing funds for planning and by establishing guidelines that direct development via the CEDS process.

Total EDA program funding allocated to this effort has remained relatively static, from about $15 million at its inception in 1967 to a little over $18 million in 2001, even as the number of EDDs has increased over time (see table 1.1). These funds are primarily used to prepare and update the CEDS, "hold planning meetings, design and develop projects, and provide technical assistance to their local governments" (Corporation for Enterprise Development, 1999: 12).

The specific objective of the CEDS process is to "help create jobs, foster more stable and diversified economies, and improve living conditions. It provides a mechanism for coordinating the efforts of individuals, organizations, local governments, and private industry concerned with economic development" (Economic Development Administration, 2000). The CEDS document is to be updated regularly and should include the following components (Economic Development Administration, 2000):

- Analysis of economic and community development problems and opportunities;
- Background and history of economic development in the EDD area;
- Discussion of the level of community participation in planning efforts;
- Goals and objectives that correspond to the problems and opportunities previously identified;
- Action plan to achieve goals and objectives that includes the identification of suggested projects; and,
- Performance measures to evaluate goal attainment.

Table 1.1 EDD Funding Trends

Fiscal Year	*Number of EDDs*	*Average EDD Grant*[a]
1967	95	157,341
1977	200	147,112
1987	286	88,904
1997	319	61,492
2001	325	56,508

[a]in constant 2001 dollars (EDA, 2001)

Thus the CEDS should guide, coordinate, and focus local actors as they pursue economic development. Done properly, the CEDS process should "lead to the formulation and implementation of a program that creates jobs, raises income levels, diversifies the economy, and improves the quality of life, while protecting the environment" (Economic Development Administration, 2000: 3). Obviously, these are lofty goals given the shrinking support received by each EDD. However, the intent of the CEDS process is to develop cooperative relationships and organizational capacity. It is by facilitating coordinated effort that EDDs are to promote local development and growth. The evaluation presented in this volume[3] was designed to assess the EDD planning process and the resulting CEDS document.

Methodology

Surveys were sent in the fall of 2000 to the directors of all EDD offices based on a list provided by the EDA. Overall, 205 of 325 EDDs responded to the survey for a response rate of 63 percent; based on expectations that there is relative consistency among EDDs, the sample should have a margin of error of +/- 3.9 percent at the 95 percent confidence level (see appendix 1.A).[4] Along with the survey, the EDDs were asked to provide information about the composition of their CEDS committee or to be sure that the informa tion was included in the CEDS document, also requested. The CEDS documents were subjected to a content analysis, coded by a single analyst on the following attributes: overall emphasis (natural resources, job generation, economic base diversification); the nature of the area descriptions (detail, currency, nature of strengths and weaknesses); goals (level of detail, extent to which particular categories of goals are presented—infrastructure, quality of life, job generation, poverty alleviation); strategies (detail, category); and projects (detail, geographic location, problems they are to address). While the coding was driven by a preset coding sheet developed for the evaluation, there is obviously room for some subjectivity in the interpretation of the CEDS documents.

During the spring of 2001 a second survey was sent to sixty EDDs. Selection of the second sample was based on information gathered in the first survey and site visits to eight EDDs.[5] The purpose of this second instrument was to gain a better understanding of the scope of planning and extent of participation as well as an assessment of process and program effectiveness. Questionnaires in the second round were sent to three different sets of stakeholders: EDD staff, CEDS board members, and external community representatives. Thus, while the first survey was designed to obtain a descriptive portrait of the EDDs, the second survey was evaluative in nature and designed to secure assessments from differing groups of respondents.[6]

The EDDs surveyed in the second round were selected by applying several constraints. First, the EDD had to have responded to the first survey. Selecting from respondents to the initial survey provided a common set of information to guide the subsequent selection process and to inform the analysis of the data. A second constraint was that all regions were to be equally represented; consequently ten EDDs from each of the eight regions were targeted. Finally, selection for the second survey was also based on information from the first survey on two variables, the EDD budget and the nature of the policies implemented by the EDD.[7]

Ten surveys were sent to each of the selected EDDs: two to EDD staff, six to members of the CEDS committee, and two to key stakeholders not on the CEDS list. Of the two staff surveys, one was to be completed by the executive director and the other by the staff person who was most knowledgeable about the CEDS process and the operations of the EDD. A total of 89 staff surveys were returned, representing 55 of the 60 EDDs surveyed.[8] A total of 312 surveys were sent to six CEDS committee members for each of the 52 EDDs. A total of 105 responses representing 49 EDDs were received. Finally, 120 community stakeholder surveys (that is, non-CEDS committee members) were sent to members of the local chamber of commerce and the mayor (or some other appropriate identifiable public official), of which 28 were returned. Data collected in the second survey represent all but three of the EDDs originally selected.[9]

Evaluation Design

The traditional portion of this evaluation follows standard methodological practice by identifying and assessing four aspects of the policy process; inputs, process, outputs, and outcomes. *Inputs* are widely understood to be the resources and efforts directed at accomplishing a goal, and also include the objective conditions of the community that set the stage for how easily goals may be met and conditions changed. *Process* evaluations focus on the activities that are to be conducted in order to implement policies such as meetings, citizen participation or community input, the quality of planning efforts, and so on. *Outputs* are the specific activities that directly result from inputs, such as the implementation of a plan or direct program activities. *Outcomes* refer to direct consequences or results that follow from an activity or process; outcomes are the direct results of a program in the short term.

In traditional economic development evaluations, inputs would include the resources (budget, staff time, personnel) allocated; process factors might include the extent that neighborhood groups participate in the planning process; and outputs are the activities that result, such as the creation of a Downtown Development Authority, visits to local businesses, the production of a brochure, or the development of new water lines. It is the relationship between inputs and outputs that is considered in assessing the efficiency of development efforts. Development outcomes are the resulting change in conditions; for example, businesses move to the community, foot traffic increases in the downtown, or new firms are created. If effectiveness is the major criteria then inputs must be related to outcomes.

Table 1.2 outlines the specific inputs, process factors, outputs, and outcomes that are considered in the traditional portion of this evaluation exercise. There are a number of *inputs* that support the economic development activities of the EDDs; the staff devoted to economic development and the budgets of the EDD and the larger organization of which it is a part are important resources. Further, the age of the organization, indicating stability and institutionalization, and the length of EDA designation and funding represent important organizational capacities. Characteristics of the EDD staff itself—including years of experience, education, and diversity—contribute to the operations of the EDD. Finally, the environment external to the EDD can either facilitate or hinder economic development efforts. A growing economy with low poverty and unemployment obviously make the development tasks of the EDD far easier.

Process, output, and outcome measures included in table 1.2 are derived from the goals of the EDA CEDS program. Many aspects of the planning and implementation process need to be considered. Examining policy processes are particularly salient for a program whose main goal is to facilitate planning through the development of a CEDS document. Therefore the surveys included a number of questions that focused specifically on process elements: the extent that the planning process is representative of the community at large; the extent that all groups have input into decision-making; and ultimately, the extent to which the needs and goals of all stakeholders are

Table 1.2

Inputs	*Process*	*Outputs*	*Outcomes*
Age of Organization	Meeting Attendance	Extent of Program Activity	CEDS Increases Communication
Length of EDA Funding	Staff Responsiveness	Extent Plan is Implemented	CEDS Increases Cooperation
Budget	Needs/Goals Reflected	Technical Assistance Meets Needs	Technical Assistance Fosters ED
Staff Size	Extent Politics/Conflict	Extent Programs are Innovative	EDD Increases Cooperation
Respondent Education	Group Representation	Quality of CEDS Document	EDD Increases Capacity
Respondent Tenure	Nature/Quality of Planning Process		EDD Creates New Organizations
Unemployment	Extent of Community Input		
Poverty	Extent of Rationality		
Economic Growth	Plan is Reevaluated		
Population Change			
Staff Diversity			

incorporated into the CEDS process and document—for example, attendance at meetings and whether EDD staff are responsive to attempts at community input. The nature of the local planning process is also important, and questions focused on the extent to which it was rationally based and led by EDD staff, or whether options and ideas were more likely to percolate up from the groups participating in the process. Whether the process was conflictive, "political," and in the end resulted in a full reevaluation of the plan were also considered.

Outputs were most directly measured by survey questions asking respondents to indicate what types of economic development program activities they conduct and with what intensity. However, the immediate output of the CEDS planning process is the production of a high-quality CEDS document followed by the implementation of the CEDS plan. Providing technical assistance that meets the needs of constituency groups and conducting innovative programs are also included as relatively short-term policy results.

Finally, program *outcomes* are the longer-range effects of EDD activities. Since legislative goals of EDA's funding process include increased communication and cooperation in the region as a result of both the CEDS process and EDD activities, these are primary outcome measures. Further desired outcomes of the EDD programs include providing technical assistance that fosters the economic development capacities of organizations and the region as a whole, creating new capacities for economic development, and creating and fostering new organizations for development in the region.

Traditional Evaluation

Policy Inputs

Respondents

Over half of all respondents to the first survey were the director or deputy director of the EDD or the larger organization of which it is a part. The rest were the economic development director or specialist, a planner, or some other special services manager. Respondents have an average tenure in any EDD of fourteen years, with the longest serving forty-seven years.

Respondents to both waves of surveys, whether staff, CEDS participants, or stakeholders, tended to be very well educated; only 16 percent had less than a college education. Most respondents in all groups were male (78 percent) and most were Caucasian (74 percent). EDD staff were significantly more likely to be Caucasian, suggesting greater racial or ethnic diversity among community stakeholders and CEDS participants.

EDD Organizations

While freestanding, most EDDs are part of a larger regional organization such as a council of government or other regional planning body, and both the EDDs and their larger organizations have long histories. The organizations of which the EDDs are a part have been in existence for an average of forty-seven years, while, on average, the EDDs have been receiving EDA funding for twenty-three years. For the EDDs, annual budgets have grown from an average of $440,340 to $1,014,773 over the past five years. For the larger organization, budgets have increased on average from $2,626,296 to

$3,272,969. Since EDA funding has been stable over time this increase in funding indicates a substantial ability by the EDDs to leverage funds in support of their activities. On average, four full-time staff worked exclusively within the EDD, with three more working part-time.

Characteristics of EDD Coverage Areas

Most of the responding EDDs have moderate (41 percent) or low (37 percent) levels of unemployment. Still, unemployment is seen as the most significant problem facing EDDs. Sixty-seven percent of respondents indicated that the level of unemployment was an important consideration in making economic development policy. Poverty appeared to be a larger objective challenge, with 58 percent of the EDDs reporting moderate and 33 percent high levels of poverty. However, 56 percent of respondents indicated that reducing poverty levels was a very important consideration when making economic development policy decisions.

It should be noted, however, that each EDD is quite diverse, so while most do not have high unemployment or have only moderate poverty, many tend to have pockets or areas within their operational boundaries where these pose significant challenges. The survey responses indicate that 88 percent had some areas with high unemployment and 88 percent had areas with high poverty. Population growth has been more of a challenge than population loss for most of the EDDs. Almost 60 percent have experienced an increase in population, while only 27 percent reported a population decline. Population changes (growth or loss) were reported to be not as important as unemployment or poverty when making economic development decisions.

The overall economy of the EDD areas appears to be stable or growing, both over the past five years and projected into the future.[10] The weakest economic growth reports were for the most recent year (1999): 41 percent indicated a stable economy and 43 percent indicated at least 5 percent growth. On average, for a ten-year period from 1995 to 2005, over half indicated at least a 5 percent growth rate in the local economy and 10 percent expected a decline in their local economy. Thus, while each area has significant pockets of poverty and unemployment, as a whole, the local economies have been growing along with the rest of the country.

Input Assessment

Overall, the inputs or resources supporting the CEDS process appear quite strong. The staff are well educated and experienced in implementing EDA programs. The larger organizations of which they are a part are also well institutionalized. While slightly less educated than EDD staff, community stakeholders involved in the process are also well educated. EDD budgets have been growing, evidence that they have been able to leverage EDA funding to gain other sources of support—one of the goals of the CEDS program. And while four staff members devoted to economic development may not seem generous, it is almost double that of most local development organizations (Reese et al., 2002). On the other hand, these staff must support regional as opposed to exclusively local economic development efforts.

The composition of the responding EDD staff and CEDS participants is not very representative of the larger population; they are predominantly male and Caucasian. While it is clear that CEDS members are more diverse then EDD staff, the composition of CEDS committees does not appear to meet EDA diversity goals and this raises concerns about the representativeness of the process.

Finally, it appears that the environmental conditions present in most EDDs are fairly conducive to program implementation. Unemployment has been moderate to low, while the population and the general economy are growing modestly. On the other hand, poverty appears to be a concern and most EDDs contain pockets of high poverty and unemployment.

This raises two considerations. First, the size and diversity of most EDDs makes planning and programming for the whole a challenge. It is difficult from the outset to address all needs and concerns of diverse localities. Second, though poverty appears to be a significant objective problem, EDD staff appear to be more concerned with reducing unemployment.

Policy Process

Meeting Attendance

Questions about attendance provide a perspective on the level of participation in the process as well as indicating ways that participation might be increased. Attendance at meetings appears to be relatively good; two out of three CEDS committee members indicated they attended most or all committee meetings. On the other hand, 21 percent indicated that they attended very few committee meetings, with half of those explaining that they had simply too many meetings. For some "the meetings did not really address the needs of my organization" (34 percent), "my input was not used" (32 percent), and "the meetings are held too far away (15 percent)." It appears that the main reason for non-attendance is simply the complexity of most CEDS participants' lives.

Needs, Goals, and Representation of Stakeholders

A series of questions were asked to assess aspects of the CEDS process, ranging from the way the process was conducted to the extent to which the plan was implemented. Responses to questions were presented along a 7-point scale from strongly disagree to strongly agree. For most items, respondents gave the EDD organization, the CEDS process, or the EDD staff a positive assessment, though responding EDD staff were more consistently positive throughout. While the non-CEDS stakeholders were consistently less positive, more than half were unable to answer questions because they were not sufficiently familiar with the process. Thus the less positive responses of stakeholders could be the result of lack of awareness of the CEDS process. Several of the questions (see table 1.3) focused specifically on the extent to which participants in the CEDS process and community stakeholders felt that the needs of their constituents had been well represented.

CEDS committee members were very positive regarding the responsiveness of EDD staff to their ideas and input (statements 4 and 5 in table 1.3). CEDS participants were also extremely positive about the extent to which their constituencies or "home" organizations were represented in the needs, goals, and projects identified in the CEDS documents. Overall 88 percent of all respondents felt that the needs identified in the CEDS accurately reflected the needs of their constituents, 76 percent felt the goals in the CEDS reflected the needs of their group, and 67 percent felt that the projects identified in the CEDS reflected the needs of their constituents. Thus the congruence between constituency needs of CEDS participants and the CEDS document is very high. However, community stakeholders not on the CEDS committee were significantly less positive that the CEDS accurately reflected their constituent needs, if they were even aware of the CEDS process.

Respondent groups differed somewhat in the extent to which they felt the needs, goals, and programs identified in the CEDS accurately reflected the needs of the EDD region as a whole. While EDD staff and CEDS participants are similar in their responses and uniformly positive, community stakeholders were significantly less positive. Just over 20 percent indicated that the CEDS matched regional attributes, with nearly 70 percent of the community stakeholders indicating that they did not know enough to answer the question.

Table 1.3

Survey Statement	*Percentage Agreement*		
	Staff	*CEDS*	*Stakeholders*
1. The needs identified in the CEDS document accurately reflect the needs of the EDD as a whole.	94	81	23[a]
2. The goals listed in the CEDS accurately reflect the needs of the EDD as whole	95	81	25[a]
3. The programs and projects included in the CEDS address the needs of the EDD as a whole.	94	89	92
4. The EDD staff was responsive to my ideas and suggestions.	NA	78	NA
5. The EDD staff was responsive to the ideas and suggestions of most CEDS Committee members.	NA	84	NA
6. There are some important local groups that are not well represented in the CEDS process.	25	32	25[a]
7. There are some groups that disproportionately control the CEDS process.	17	25	14[a]

[a]significantly different at the .05 level

A final question asked respondents to identify any local groups or constituencies left out of the CEDS planning process. CEDS committee members were more likely than EDD staff to indicate that some important local groups are not well represented in the CEDS planning process (32 percent) and that some groups disproportionately control the CEDS process (25 percent). Among community stakeholders able to respond, only 25 percent felt that some groups were left out and 14 percent indicated that the process was "controlled" by a few groups.

The examination of the composition of the CEDS committees also assessed the extent of stakeholder representation in the CEDS process. These committees are overwhelmingly male and most members are Caucasian. Organization affiliation is also telling: CEDS committee members are most likely to represent counties (29 percent), other units of government (26 percent), and business interests (19 percent). Another way of understanding the makeup of CEDS committees is to examine whom the members represent. For example, 11 percent of the CEDS committees are comprised of more than 50 percent business members. On the other hand, only 1 percent are composed primarily of community representatives. The largest portion of CEDS committees (22 percent) is made up mostly of county officials. Four percent have significant representation of economic development officials and 18 percent are primarily composed of officials representing other units of government. There are no CEDS committees composed of at least 50 percent professional, educational, or diversity members. Of greater concern, 62 percent of the CEDS committees have no community members at all, 72 percent have no diversity in membership, 60 percent have no representation from educational organizations, 67 percent have no economic development professionals, and 75 percent have no members from other professions.

Nature of the Planning Process

Two-thirds of EDD staff and over half of CEDS participants agree that the annual updates of the CEDS process led to an effective reevaluation of local needs. Yet, roughly a third of both groups indicated that the updates do not actually lead to such a full reevaluation of local needs. There was some disagreement about the extent to which the CEDS process is "political" as opposed to "rational." For example, community stakeholders were significantly more likely to agree that the CEDS process is heavily driven by the political needs of participants (42 percent), while CEDS committee members and EDD staff were much less likely to agree (32 percent and 24 percent, respectively). The groups also differed in the extent to which they viewed the CEDS planning process as being conflictual. EDD staff were significantly more likely to feel that the process was conflictual (12 percent) when compared to CEDS committee members (6 percent) or community stakeholders (4 percent).

Beyond this, there is a clear pattern of agreement between staff and CEDS participants on all but three questions about the nature of the planning process; the extent that the CEDS process was primarily driven by the CEDS committee, whether all area groups are well represented in the process, and whether some groups disproportionately control the CEDS planning process (see table 1.4). Both groups feel that the projects selected as a result of the CEDS process were based on the needs of individual communities as well as the region more broadly defined. Both feel that research and analysis was used to support all project decisions. And, both groups agree that projects are selected by analysis rather than being driven primarily by funding availability.

A number of questions sought to identify whether EDD staff or CEDS participants had the greatest influence over the planning process. There

Table 1.4

Statement	*Percentage Staff Agreement*	*Percentage CEDS Agreement*
Planning process is project-driven	62	46
Projects selected based on funding	56	55
Staff organized discussion	80	62
Staff provided list of potential projects	61	52
Decisions were based on research/analysis	84	68
Goals/objectives/strategies identified by committee	80	77
Process mostly driven by staff	63	48
Process mostly driven by committee	41	66[a]
Decision made with consensus	82	64
Decision made with conflict	9	10
Committee identified projects	57	66
Little discussion about goals	40	17
Committee members worked toegher	70	68
Committee focused on big picture	60	48
Projects based on community needs	86	76
Projects based on regional needs	75	78
Some groups not well represented	25	32[a]
Some groups control the process	17	25[a]
Reevaluation of needs takes place	63	53

[a]attitudes significantly different at the.05 level

appears to be no clear pattern in the responses to these questions, suggesting that staff and the CEDS committee largely share the decision-making locus (or think they do). For example, majorities of both groups agreed that EDD staff organized the discussion by presenting draft goals, objectives, and strategies and that staff provided the initial list of potential development projects. And while EDD staff were more likely to agree that the CEDS process is largely driven by staff, this difference was not statistically significant. On the other hand, majorities also agreed that goals, objectives, and strategies were identified by CEDS committee members, that the committee identified and then discussed projects for implementation, and CEDS participants are significantly more likely to feel that they control the planning process as opposed to EDD staff.

There was also agreement on the general nature of the planning process. Again, majorities of both groups agreed that decisions about goals, strategies, and objectives were made collectively and with consensus, that there was little conflict during the process, that CEDS committee members worked together to agree on economic development projects with a commitment to implementation, and that there was significant discussion and debate about broad goals and objectives. EDD staff were somewhat more likely to indicate that the CEDS process was driven by projects as opposed to needs and that CEDS committee members tended to focus on the big picture with less emphasis on detailed projects. As before, these differences were not statistically signficant.

Finally, respondents were asked to characterize which of several planning models they used in the CEDS committee (see Alexander, 2000, for a more detailed discussion of these models). The following were provided as alternatives:

- Rational Planning Model: Participants are asked to react to goals, objectives and strategic actions with some opportunity for discussion or dialogue. Commonly, staff would have already articulated options or alternatives with a focus on specific action/project statements.
- Communicative Planning Model: Participants are involved in a continuing dialogue with EDD staff over development of goals, objectives, actions and projects. There would be a presumption of collective decision-making shared between stakeholders.
- Coordinative Planning Model: participants are part of a network of stakeholders committed to collective action steps. Involvement in the process would emphasize implementation and action within an agreed set of strategic policies.
- Frame-Setting Model: participants are involved as stakeholders bringing individual political and agency interests to the planning process. There is an appreciation by EDD staff of differences between stakeholders with a desire to set the context(s) for change rather than determine specific goals and action steps.

Most often staff and CEDS participants identified with the communicative planning model (37 percent of staff and 33 percent of CEDS committee members). However, CEDS committee members were much more likely than EDD staff to identify the planning process as frame-setting (31 percent of committee members versus staff at 7 percent), while staff were more likely to see the process as rational planning (31 percent versus 23 percent) or coordinative planning (25 percent versus 14 percent). The difference in views about the overall process is significant. The fact that the majority of respondents identified both EDD staff and CEDS committee members as leading and participating in the process in previous questions is reinforced here by the plurality of both groups who see the process as being "communicative." Beyond that, however, CEDS committee members appear to view the planning process as one where various stakeholders come to the table, representing their own group interests, and EDD staff act in a coordinative rather than a directive capacity. EDD staff, on the other hand, are more likely to see the process as being one where a more "rational" or dispassionate analysis of needs and goals drives project selection. These differences are understandable given the different roles of participants in the process. EDD staff, largely trained as planners, are more likely to view the process as rational planning. CEDS participants, having been chosen by the community to represent certain interests, see the process as pluralist, where groups come together to discuss and reach consensus on goals and projects.

Process Assessment

The overall assessment of the CEDS planning process is mixed with both positive and negative aspects. On the positive side it appears that meetings are well attended and CEDS committee members are participating in the process. Missed meetings do not appear to be the result of any EDD staff action or inaction. EDD staff and CEDS participants agree that constituent and area needs are accurately represented in the CEDS, that most groups are represented in the process, and that CEDS participants feel like staff respond to their input. Overall, it appears that most participants in the CEDS process feel that it is deliberative, consensual, and cooperative, that most community and regional stakeholders are represented, and that there is a good balance of EDD staff direction and CEDS committee input.

There are some concerns, however. First, because stakeholders not on the CEDS committee were far less positive about the representativeness of the CEDS committee, it could be concluded that the CEDS process leads to representation of constituent needs as long as the constituency is represented on the CEDS committee. From the analysis of the composition of the CEDS committees themselves, it appears that EDDs have not been completely successful in ensuring that CEDS committees are fully representative of their communities. Business and government interests are well represented, while community and diversity interests are much less so. Both EDD staff and CEDS participants answered an open-ended question asking respondents to identify groups not represented in the process by mentioning human services, minority groups, labor, low-income groups, and community or neighborhood groups.[11]

Beyond representation issues, there are other concerns. About one quarter of the participants in the CEDS planning process did not feel that it resulted in a full reassessment or evaluation of local needs and goals. And while process participants generally felt that there is a good balance of staff and committee participation, staff tended to see the process as more rational, with staff in a lead role. CEDS participants are more likely to see the process as frame setting where participants represent specific group needs. These differing worldviews are somewhat at odds and may lead to different expectations and hence satisfaction levels with the results of the process. While there is widespread agreement that needs and goals represented in the CEDS is an accurate reflection of the EDD as a whole, there is less agreement that programs identified in the CEDS actually match regional needs. This will be discussed more fully in the next section.

Policy Outputs

Quality of the CEDS Documents

As part of the survey process, all EDDs were asked to send their most recent CEDS document. These were then content analyzed to assess various aspects of the quality and nature of the CEDS. This assessment included an examination of the area descriptions and the identification of needs and the nature and detail embodied in the goal statements, descriptions of strategies and discussion of projects. Finally, the extent to which needs, goals, strategies, and projects logically corresponded to one another was considered.

Based on an assessment scale developed for the evaluation, 45 percent of the CEDS documents have very detailed descriptions and 35 percent have somewhat detailed descriptions, while 20 percent have area descriptions that are not detailed at all. This suggests that most EDDs are doing a good job of presenting the challenges in their service area. Further, two out of three area descriptions are less than a year old.

Overall, the needs identified in the area descriptions in the CEDS match the stated goals very well. In only 10 percent of the cases is there a poor match between needs and goals. Thus the goals depicted in the CEDS fairly accurately reflect the needs of the EDD. There is some variation in the detail in which goals are presented, however. For about half the CEDS, goals are provided with a high level of detail, while in 34 percent of the CEDS, goals are only somewhat detailed. The CEDS appear to contain very detailed descriptions of area needs and identify goals that appear to address those needs. The extent of detail with which goals are described could be improved, however.

Strategies appear to be more detailed than goals in the CEDS documents, and strategies match stated goals quite well. In 63 percent of the documents strategies are very detailed and in 75 percent there is a very good match of strategies to goals. Strategies also have a strong correspondence to descriptions of need.

There is some disjuncture between needs/goals/strategies and the projects actually implemented by the EDDs. Factor analysis was performed on all CEDS traits to determine if all aspects of the CEDS loaded on a single factor that might represent "quality" of the document. Two distinct factors or concepts emerged, however; one is related to the quality of need, goal, and strategy statements while another reflected the quality of project descriptions and match of projects to needs and goals. And, the two factors are not significantly related to each other. In short this means that the nature of needs/goals/strategies is inherently different that the nature of development projects.

Obviously, while the quality of the CEDS plan is important, the real output question is the extent to which it has been implemented. The majority of respondents to the survey indicated that it had; 91 percent of staff and 73 percent of CEDS participants felt that the plan had been effectively implemented and 25 percent of community stakeholders agreed (50 percent did not know).

Extent of Program Activity

The more direct measure of program output is the extent to which EDDs focus on a number of alternative planning and development activities. As can be seen in table 1.5, the focus of EDD efforts is clearly on technical assistance, economic development, and planning. Community development and infrastructure planning and projects closely follow these activities. Moderate numbers of EDDs engage in transportation, small business development, land-use planning, housing, workforce development, and planning and services for the aged. Far fewer EDDs focus on environmental activities such as flood management, agriculture, coastal zone management, and soil conservation.

Economic development planning and programming has the lowest standard deviation, indicating that not only do the largest percentage of EDDs

Table 1.5

Policy Area	*Percentage Very Involved*	*Standard Deviation*
Technical assistance	90	0.43
Economic development planning	86	0.35
Planning	81	0.49
Community development	73	0.74
Infrastructure	73	0.55
Transportation	52	1.08
Small business development	43	0.95
Land-use planning	35	1.06
Housing	33	1.10
Workforce development	28	1.06
Planning and services for the aged	25	1.18
Natural resources	24	1.03
Flood management	10	0.95
Agriculture	6	0.89
Coastal zone management	5	0.76
Criminal justice	4	0.80
Soil management	3	0.81

focus on it but also that there is relatively uniform activity across the EDDs. Other activities where there is little variance are technical assistance, infrastructure planning and development, and general regional planning. The activities with the highest standard deviations are general planning and services for the aged, housing, transportation, workforce development, land-use planning, and natural resource management. Although services for the aged and natural resource management activities are not the focus of most EDDs, there are some that are very active in these areas. Conversely, while transportation is a focus for over half of the EDDs, there are some that do not concern themselves with it at all.

Technical Assistance and Program Innovation

One of the key outputs of the EDDs is to provide technical assistance for local economic development activities. The survey included questions about whether the respondent's organization or constituency had received any technical assistance from the EDD and whether that assistance met organizational needs. Most CEDS members (55 percent), but fewer stakeholders (40 percent), had received technical assistance though the difference is not statistically significant. The majority of staff (74 percent) and CEDS participants (65 percent) agreed that the EDD had been able to meet most requests for technical assistance. Community stakeholders were significantly less positive about the EDD technical assistance record (53 percent), though many were uncertain whether assistance was actually provided by the local EDD (over 40 percent). Of more concern is the extent to which the EDD had introduced innovative economic development programs. EDD staff (74 percent) are quite positive on this issue, feeling they have launched innovative programs. CEDS committee members are not as sure, with only 40 percent in agreement, and community stakeholders (24 percent) are even less positive.

Output Assessment

The overall quality of the CEDS documents appears high. Area descriptions are very detailed and there is high correspondence between needs, goals and strategies. There is some variation in the detail provided in goal statements, however. The greater concern is that projects do not appear to match needs and goals as closely as would be desired. This appears to be the case at least in part because the availability of funding drives project selection more than abstract goals. While this makes sense from a pragmatic perspective, it suggests that actual projects are not fully guided by the planning process.

EDD program activity is heavily focused on technical assistance, economic development projects, planning, community development, and infrastructure. Since these are all program areas contained within EDA guidelines and goals for the CEDS program, most EDDs are focusing on program activities central to national goals. Community respondents were in agreement that the technical assistance activities met the needs of their constituents, but unlike EDD staff, were less positive about the extent to which EDD programs are actually innovative.

Policy Outcomes

Several outcomes are the ultimate goal of the CEDS process and EDD activities. The planning process to develop the CEDS is expected to increase cooperation and communication among economic development actors and interests within the region. Respondents appear quite positive about the extent to which the CEDS process met these goals. Seventy-three percent of EDD staff and 66 percent of CEDS participants indicated that there is increased cooperation among actors, and 79 percent of staff and 75 percent of CEDS participants thought that regional communication had increased as a result of the CEDS process.

Respondents are also quite positive about the effects of the technical assistance provided by the EDD, though in this case there were some significant differences among groups of respondents, with community stakeholders less positive. Ninety-six percent of EDD staff and 76 percent of CEDS participants agreed that the technical assistance provided by the EDD had increased regional capacity for economic development. Similarly, 96 percent of staff and 72 percent of CEDS committee members felt that the economic development capacities of individual regional organizations had been increased. Stakeholders were not as enthusiastic, agreeing only 47 percent and 40 percent of the time, respectively. It should be noted again that there were high levels of uncertainty among non-CEDS stakeholders about all aspects of the CEDS process and its outcomes. Indeed, an average of 40 percent of these respondents indicated that they "did not know" enough to respond to questions about EDD program effectiveness.

A final series of questions asked each of the three groups of respondents about the overall effectiveness of the EDDs, and responses were once again very positive, particularly among EDD staff and CEDS participants. Ninety three percent of staff and 79 percent of CEDS committee members felt that the EDD had been effective in promoting cooperation for economic development. Similarly, 93 percent of staff and 75 percent of CEDS participants felt that the EDD had served to increase regional capacity for economic development. Community stakeholders were less positive, but the difference is statistically significant only for the question about increasing regional cooperation.

Of more concern were the responses to questions about the extent to which the EDD had helped to create new economic development organizations in the region. Predictably EDD staff were again quite positive on these issues; 75 percent felt that the EDD had created new organizations. CEDS committee members were less positive (45 percent) and community stakeholders even less positive still (24 percent).

Outcome Assessment

There were high levels of agreement among the different groups of respondents that the CEDS process and EDD activities were effective. Most respondents felt that the CEDS process had been instrumental in increasing cooperation and communication within the region. They were also very positive that activities of the EDD contributed to building regional cooperation and capacity for economic development.

Committee members and stakeholders were less positive than EDD staff that the EDD was effective in creating new development organizations. Because site visits indicated significant organizational development on the part of the EDDs visited, this may be due to a lack of awareness and familiarity with organizations and structures promoting economic development. This points to an important concern: beyond EDD staff and CEDS participants the community is largely unaware of or uncertain about EDD activities leading to more negative assessments of process and outcome. The fact that CEDS participants are much more positive about all these aspects than are community stakeholders strongly suggests that in this case familiarity breeds satisfaction rather than contempt.

Connections between Evaluation Attributes

To this point each aspect of the CEDS program has been evaluated individually, with particular strengths and weaknesses identified. To summarize, it is useful to explore the connections between the various aspects of the policy process—inputs, process, outputs, and outcomes. Presumably, greater inputs should lead to better processes (though this link is perhaps the most speculative), and better processes should be related to either the quality or quantity of outputs and outcomes. Because there were so many individual variables representing each of the four evaluation elements, factor analysis was employed to reduce the data to fewer, more manageable indexes.

All of the *outcome* variables loaded on one factor to create a single index of program effect (see the appendix for all factor analysis results).[12] A higher score on the outcome index represents more effective perceived long-term effects of the EDD programs. *Outputs* were measured in two ways. First, an additive index of program activity was created. A higher score on the activity output index indicates that an EDD is more active in policy areas across the board. A separate index gauges the perceived quality of these activity outputs. The planning *process* questions loaded on two factors, one representing inclusive planning processes and the other representing more narrow and perhaps less effective modalities. The *input* variables were largely independent of each other though the traits of the EDD environment loaded on two factors. One resulting index represents EDDs with healthy economies (population growth and economic expansion), while the other reflects economic stress (high unemployment and poverty).

A summary of the connections between the various program elements is portrayed in correlation coefficients provided in table 1.6. Working backward from outcomes to inputs suggests that the program elements tie together in an expected manner, that is for the most part positive inputs lead to better outputs and outcomes. Thus, EDDs with higher scores on the outcome index were significantly more likely to have higher scores on the output quality index as well as more policy activity. "Good" or inclusive planning processes are also positively correlated with more positive outcome assessments. Inputs do not appear to be directly related to outcomes.

It is interesting to note that higher scores on the output activity index are not correlated with scores on the output quality index. This implies that high levels of activity alone do not necessarily lead to more positive assessments of those activities. To examine this dynamic more closely the output activity index was separated into five component parts. Again, based on factor analysis it appears that there are actually five conceptually different types of EDD activities: physical environmental policy, social infrastructure, development projects, long-term development planning, and local community policy.[13] Several of the individual policy indexes are significantly related to evaluations of output quality. For example, a greater emphasis on local community policy activity appears to lead to more positive output assessments. On the other hand an emphasis on long-term development planning

Table 1.6

	Outcome	*Output activity*	*Output evaluation*	*Good process*	*Bad process*	*Staff*	*Budget*	*Healthy*	*Weak*
Outcome	1.00	0.28[a]	0.74a[a]	0.85[a]	–0.15	0.02	–0.02	0.02	–0.06
Output activity		1.00	0.17	0.19	–0.21[a]	0.49[a]	0.11	0.06	–0.08
Output evaluation			1.00	[a]	–0.09	–0.21	–0.27[a]	–0.18	–0.06
Good process				1.00	–0.35[a]	0.05	0.15	0.02	–0.04
Bad process					1.00	0.02	–0.03	0.05	0.08
Staff						1.00	–0.12	–0.05	0.10
Budget							1.00	0.26[a]	0.11
Healthy								1.00	0.08
Weak									1.00

[a]Correlations significant at the.05 level

appears to be related to more negative assessments. The other policy indexes are not significantly associated with the output evaluation index. Thus, it can be concluded that EDDs that emphasize activities that focus on the local community are assessed more positively while those that focus on long-term development planning are assessed more negatively. This may well be due to the fact that there are more short-term visible outputs emanating from the former than the latter. The nature of the planning process is also significantly related to the level of activity outputs; "bad" or less inclusive processes appear to reduce overall program activity.

There are also some relationships between inputs and outputs. First, it should be noted that the general economic health of the region is not related to any of the process, output or outcome indexes. The only case where the larger economy appears important is in relationship to the size of the larger organization's budget; budgets are positively correlated with healthy economies.

Larger staff allocations, however, appear to significantly increase program activity; obviously, more staff allows the EDD to be more active in providing a variety of programs. A more surprising relationship is the negative correlation between organizational budget and the evaluation of EDD outputs. Several reasons for these relationships can be posited though they are speculative at best. First, there are no relationships between EDD budget and any of the indexes—clearly, staffing is more critical than overall budget. Second, the budget of the larger organization of which the EDD is a part may have no inherent connection to either EDD program activity or the quality of that activity. The larger organization could be allocating budgets toward other activities with less focus on EDD activities specifically.

Overall Assessment

The evidence fairly clearly supports the contention that for the past thirty-five years the Economic Development Administration, through its support for the EDDs throughout the country, promoted and fostered local development planning. Each EDD was designated precisely because it served a community defined and certified by local and state government agencies as containing below-average income, above average unemployment and some indication of long-term economic distress.

Armed with a mandate to make changes, and supported with resources (albeit ever-decreasing) to fund and staff those efforts, EDDs brought a range of local stakeholders together to participate in a planning process. Communities undertook coordinated reviews of local conditions to highlight problems and establish needs, set priorities to identify goals and objectives, and promoted projects designed to address and alleviate these needs. In other words, the outcomes were consistent with a program designed to foster local development planning in the face of market failures within the community. In short, successes can be summarized as follows:

- The resources supporting the CEDS process are strong; staff are well educated and experienced and EDDs have been able to leverage EDA funding to secure other sources of support.
- Environmental conditions in most EDDs are conducive to program implementation.
- CEDS meetings are well attended with committee members fully participating in the process.
- Constituent and area needs are accurately represented in the CEDS, most groups are represented in the process, and CEDS participants feel that staff respond to their input.
- The overall quality of the CEDS documents appears high; area descriptions are very detailed and there is strong correspondence between needs, goals and strategies.
- EDDs are focusing on activities central to national goals; technical assistance, economic development, planning, community development, and infrastructure.
- Technical assistance activities appear to meet the needs of EDD constituents.
- There are high levels of agreement among the different groups of respondents that the CEDS process and EDD activities are effective in increasing cooperation and communication within the region.

There are, however, some concerns about the effectiveness of the CEDS process, though these are obviously outweighed by the successes listed above:

- EDDs have not been completely successful in ensuring that CEDS committees are fully representative of their communities; business and government interests are well represented while community and diversity interests are much less so.

- Policies outlined in the CEDS do not appear to match needs and goals as closely as would be desired because the availability of funding drives project selection more than abstract goals.
- Committee members and stakeholders were less positive that the EDD was effective in creating new development organizations.
- The community beyond EDD staff and CEDS participants is largely unaware of or uncertain about EDD activities, which appears to lead to more negative assessments of process and outcome.

Critical Evaluation

Critical reasoning was the Enlightenment's great gift to humanity. Emerging in opposition to absolutist rule and the divine right of monarchies and the church, the enlightenment was an intellectual restatement of the relationship of individuals to their god, to their state, and to themselves. No one owns critical reasoning, and all who use it are obligated to simple rules: use logic to frame thought and discussion; maintain a vision of humanizing progress; and approach with doubts the arguments and "certainties" of the powerful.

What then might a critical evaluation of the EDD program look like that would alter the frame and content of the traditional one posed above? To begin with one would ask a simple question: Do we know a good thing when we see it? As the authors have argued elsewhere (Fasenfest, Ciancanelli, and Reese, 1997; Reese and Fasenfest, 1997) there are great gray areas when determining what works best, and what criteria one uses to make that determination. In trying to answer that question, other subordinate questions arise: Good and best for whom? What are the outcomes and from whose perspective? What are the implicit expectations of the program that shape the expectations of the evaluator or even of the actors involved in the process?

Employing a critical perspective raises doubts about the answers to these questions. Local development projects themselves are constant reminders that those benefiting from some course of action are almost inherently not the best ones to be the arbiters of what is the right way to proceed (Fasenfest, 1993), and that even the public sector may be blinded by a selective inclusion of stakeholders to limit the scope of consideration and become predisposed to act on the basis of no coherent (that is heard) opposition (Fasenfest, 1986). As the evidence from the case studies and surveys suggests, the set of social actors may not have been as inclusive as is necessary to ensure that the needs identified, goals established, and projects pursued served the interests of all segments of each community. Furthermore, given that some threshold of dispossessed and disenfranchised within the community served was a prerequisite for the establishment of the EDDs, there is a surprisingly sparse representation of those very same constituents on the CEDS committees. This fact alone at least gives reason to pause when addressing the question of what the planning process has accomplished.

The traditional evaluation presented above clearly showed that there was a coherent and coordinated planning process in place, but is the process sufficient to decide in favor when evaluating the EDD program? How is this process itself to be evaluated? It is common for articles on economic development policy and process to acknowledge the general paucity of evaluations of economic development processes or strategies. There are many examples of the obligatory reference to the lack of evaluation research. Consider the following: "Evaluation has been labeled one of the "big questions" in planning and public management . . . in practice job creation often remains the sole measure of many economic development programs" (Hill, 2000: 265); and "When it comes to economic development in general, scholars have paid scant attention to evaluative issues" (Wilkinson, 1999: 172). Though dated, in his meta-analysis of economic development evaluations, Bartik (1991) found only sixteen scholarly evaluations of economic development policies conducted within a seven-year period from 1984 to 1991. The rate of economic development evaluations may have escalated somewhat since then; Bartik and Bingham identified sound examples of a number of different types of evaluations including process, before-and-after, survey, firm behavior, non-randomized comparison group, random control group, and community impact evaluations in a later assessment (1997: 256–66).

Another perennial theme in the development evaluation literature is bemoaning the quality of extant efforts. Bartik and Bingham noted, "the reality is that the vast majority of existing evaluations are process evaluations" (1997: 267). Further, they found only one evaluation that employed a control group drawn from unsuccessful program applicants (Holzer et al., 1993) and one that used a randomly selected control group (Benus et al., 1994). Several reasons have been suggested for the paucity of good empirical evaluations of economic development policies:

- Robust evaluations are extremely hard to design and conduct;
- Evaluations are time and resource intensive and are often the first activities to go in periods of public-sector fiscal retrenchment;

- Randomized control groups in particular raise political and ethical concerns;
- Extant evaluations typically do not suggest how programs can be improved so are of little practical use to policymakers;
- Public-sector auditing agencies that often conduct evaluations do not tend to use rigorous methodologies; and, probably most important,
- Policymakers fear the political repercussions of a possible negative evaluation (Bartik and Bingham, 1997).

Other authors concur that efforts to evaluate economic development policies have become "a quagmire of good intentions and bad measures" (Clarke and Gaile, 1992: 193) compounded by the fact that there is little agreement on measurement techniques as well as policy goals. Effective performance on traditional outcome measures, like jobs created, may not indicate real economic development as distinct from economic or fiscal growth (Eisenschitz, 1993; Reese and Fasenfest, 1997), making it difficult to distinguish real program failure from an absence of positive results due to aspects of the evaluation design or the indicators employed. As a result, policies may be deemed successful if projects are completed at all (Friedan and Sagalyn, 1989).

As indicated earlier, the purpose of this evaluation was to address specific questions raised by the Department of Commerce[14] in a manner traditionally accepted and understood to be a program evaluation. Had a critical evaluation been undertaken questions about the choice of projects selected would have been pursued, data about who benefited from and who paid for these projects would have been gathered and analyzed and more attention would have been paid to whether the projects that were selected were in fact the best solution given alternatives or perhaps simply the best constrained solution if not all voices were included in the determination of that project.

Furthermore, a determination would have been made, at the start of the evaluation, of what a community needs to do to promote development, and whether all forms of planning are equal toward that endeavor. Evaluators would want to decide what was the measure of success, would wonder about when failure is tangible, and would ask under what conditions given outcomes are not enough to address a wider need. There is a story in development circles that perhaps best illustrates the tensions and dilemmas raised between traditional and critical evaluations. Consider a village at the edge of a cliff with a hospital at its base. Villagers fall off the cliff and break bones, quickly overwhelming the hospital's capabilities to serve the village. The traditional (in this case the modern medical) assessment results in efforts to expand the hospital and increase its capacity to serve the community. A more critical evaluation may determine that the real beneficiaries of such a solution are those in the medical professions making more for services provided, when what is really needed is a fence at the top of the cliff to prevent more accidents. From whose perspective are the solutions posed and benefits accrued to be assessed?

The chapters that follow are explicitly critical investigations into some aspect of economic development. They are intended to shed light on how alternative approaches to common questions may reveal answers that serve the dispossessed. The chapters frame their thought and discussions logically, are guided by a vision of humanizing progress, and doubt the arguments and certainties of those in control of the process in ways that traditional evaluations such as the one presented here simply cannot.

Notes

This research has been funded by the U.S. Department of Commerce Project Number #99–07-1309, 2000–2001.

1. For the complete evaluation, see Fasenfest and Reese, 2002. The report is also available on the Wayne State University Center for Urban Studies website at http://www.cus.wayne.edu under the publication section.

2. These documents were formerly referred to as an Overall Economic Development Program (OEDP) document.

3. An earlier and more comprehensive discussion of the evaluation can be found in Reese and Fasenfest, 2003.

4. Several methods were used to ensure the highest response rate possible. All non-responding EDDs were contacted by phone and sent second surveys if necessary. Further, in early 2001 the Regional Directors were asked to contact non-responding EDDs in their regions and remind them to answer the survey. Additional surveys were also supplied at that time.

5. Eight EDD sites were selected based upon purposive criteria and each was visited over a two-day period. The purpose of the site visits was to gain background information to develop the surveys (some were conducted before the surveys) and to better understand survey responses (most were done after the first survey).

6. The three surveys used in the second round were slightly different because of the varying perspectives of the three groups. In general, the items included some qualifying questions, items about meeting attendance, reasons for missing meetings, a series of items about the CEDS process, a series of items about the nature of planning in the CEDS committee, items about the provision of technical assistance, mea-

sures of the effectiveness of the EDD, and demographic items. Stakeholders who did not participate in the CEDS sessions were not asked about the details of the process. Staff were not asked items that involved their own performance.

7. A simple distribution led to the creation of a four-level filter based on whether the relative EDD budget was less than 1 percent of the larger budget; between 1 and 20 percent; between 20 and 99 percent; 100 percent of the budget. Second, a composite measure was created reflecting strong policy activity in various areas as indicated by EDD staff in the first survey. Based on the responses to seventeen program initiatives, four policy areas were identified: Business and Workforce, Social Services, Economic Activities and Natural Resources. Each of the responses within the four policy areas was summed (responses were 0 for not utilized to 4 for very utilized), and an EDD was considered to score "high" on a particular policy area when all activity category responses were 3 or 4, with the exception of the Economic set since 50 percent of the EDDs were 4 on all 5 measures. A grid of six quadrants (one for each region) was created with five columns reflecting the five levels of policy activity (whether an EDD was high on 0, 1, 2, 3, or all 4 dimensions) with each quadrant having four rows, one for each budget ratio (defining 20 cells per quadrant). All EDDs were allocated to their appropriate cell within regions, and ten EDDs from each quadrant were selected to ensure balance along the two dimensions within quadrants.

8. Responses were received from at least one of the two staff from all but five of the sixty EDDs. Follow-up attempts to increase responses included both phone calls and emails; two to four attempts were made to each EDD that had not responded.

9. Responding EDDs represent every region and all constituents, and provide a representative sample of all EDDs in this study. Problems getting accurate and complete addresses for the CEDS committee members, and at times getting current lists of those serving on the CEDS committee, prevented the researchers from sending questionnaires to the members of CEDS committees in eight of the EDDs. However, the pattern of missing addresses was random and does not indicate a bias in the responses. The low response rate of the non-CEDS stakeholders was to be expected. These were sent to individuals who might arguably have more detailed knowledge of the planning and development initiatives of the EDDs. Specifically, elected officials or members of local chambers of commerce within the district were asked for external comments on the process. Though there was a relatively low response rate (about 23 percent), the data were mainly meant to provide a context for items like whether there were underrepresented groups or stakeholders in the district or whether the activities of the EDD were widely known.

10. Since the surveys were conducted in late 2000 and early 2001, the national economy had not yet experienced a significant downturn. Future projections were likely more optimistic as a result.

11. While non-CEDS community stakeholders felt that not all groups were well represented they were not able to identify particular examples of which groups needed to be included in the process.

12. In all cases the factor analysis employed principle-component analysis and verimax rotation. The variables loading on each identified factor were combined to

create a single index variable; f-score values are the basis of each index to standardize units of measurement across components. While it is common to restrict inclusion of a component in the index to those variables with a factor loading greater than 0.5, in the case of the policy activity variables all policy areas were used thereby including two with low factor loadings.

13. It is useful to note that several of the policy activity indexes are related to each other. EDDs that engage in greater physical infrastructure programs are also more active in community development and social infrastructure. EDDs that focus more highly on strategic planning also tend to engage in more community development and more long-term planning.

14. The opinions and conclusions drawn both in this chapter and in the larger evaluation report are solely those of the authors and do no represent the thinking or opinions of the Department of Commerce or the Economic Development Administration.

Appendix 1A

FACTOR	*LOADINGS*
Policy Outcomes	
CEDS increased regional cooperation	0.83
CEDS increased communication among development groups	0.79
Technical assistance improved capacity in region	0.87
Technical assistance improved capacity in your organization	0.52
EDD has increased regional cooperation	0.89
EDD has increased capacity for economic development	0.89
EDD has created new organizations to foster development	0.71
Policy Outputs	
CEDS plan effectively implemented	0.69
EDD met needs for technical assistance	0.59
EDD created innovative programs	0.65

FACTOR	*LOADINGS*
Physical Environment Policy	
Soil conservation planning/management	0.74
Land-use planning	0.71
Natural resource planning	0.70
Coastal zone management	0.69
Flood plain management	0.68
Transportation planning	0.58
Local Community Policy	
Housing policy/development	0.70
Community development	0.70
Technical assistance to member localities	0.68
Development Projects	
Small business development	0.76
Economic development projects	0.70
Infrastructure planning and development	0.47
Social Infrastructure Policy	
Services and planning for the aged	0.74
Criminal justice coordination and planning	0.72
Workforce development	0.61
Long-term Development Planning	
Agricultural development planning	0.84
Economic development planning	0.36

continued

FACTOR	*LOADINGS*
Inclusive Planning Process	
EDD staff responsive to my ideas	0.62
EDD staff responsive to all ideas	0.72
Needs in CEDS match needs of organization	0.85
Needs in CEDS match needs of region	0.87
Goals in CEDS match needs of organization	0.82
Goals in CEDS match needs of region	0.86
Goals, objectives, strategies identified by CEDS participants	0.74
CEDS members discussed and selected projects	0.70
CEDS process driven by CEDS committee	0.65
CEDS committee worked together to get agreement	0.73
Decisions made collectively	0.70
CEDS committee focused on big picture	0.45
Projects selected based on community needs	0.58
Projects selected based on regional needs	0.70
Decisions based on research and analysis	0.76
Poor Planning Process	
CEDS process driven by political needs of participants	0.55
Annual updates do not lead to reevaluation	0.60
Some groups not well represented	0.50
Some groups disproportionately control the process	0.64
CEDS process driven by EDD staff	0.58
Little discussion about goals, objectives	0.56
CEDS process highly project driven	0.61
Projects selected based on availability of funding	0.57

TWO

Do the Ends Justify the Means? Frost, Machiavelli, and Distributive Outcomes for Local Economic Development

Jill L. Tao and Richard C. Feiock

Local economic development policies have provided a unique challenge to researchers by presenting what appear to be simple issues within a framework of action that sometimes defies analysis. Even when the goals of such policies are seemingly straightforward, such as betterment of the lives of city residents through the provision of economic opportunity, economic development requires choices among goals and choices among policy instruments to realize those goals. Thus when there is consensus on the specific goals or ends for economic development policy, the means chosen by local governments to achieve these goals can be as divergent as Frost's proverbial paths within the wood. This poses a dilemma for anyone interested in evaluating the effectiveness of local development efforts. A multitude of approaches raises the question of comparing cases that do not necessarily represent the same constructs and may not therefore be expected to effect the same types of outcomes. As Reese and Fasenfest (1999) have argued, "Robust evaluations of economic development policies are extremely difficult to design and conduct. . . . The challenge of incorporating alternative or social economy indicators further limits the number of extant evaluation techniques" (3–4).

Do the means matter? Has the path chosen "made all the difference"? Or are Machiavelli's observations of the tenuous nature of means a more apt predictor of policy outcomes? In outlining the vagaries of fortune and the havoc visited on both the deserving and undeserving, Machiavelli advises, "that two persons, working differently, chance to arrive at the same result; and that of two who work in the same way, one attains his end, but the other does not" (Machiavelli 1964: 175). Sometimes referenced as the ultimate political pragmatist, Machiavelli offers the cautionary note often ignored in studies of public policy; politics matters because it is unpredictable. We have examined some of these issues through an evaluation of two types of targeted economic development programs in the state of Florida. In an extension of previous research (Tao and Feiock, 1999), we look at the ways in which local governments apply policies to address problems of urban decline at both the city and targeted area level. In this way, we force a confrontation between this competing set of ideas, thus seeking to rectify some of the shortcomings of previous work and to answer more definitively the question of whether the means matter when the expectation of outcomes is arguably similar.

Choice of Development Ends

The first problem faced in answering such questions lies in the definition of development ends. At the local level, there is little consensus over the meaning and goals of "development policy." At both the state and local level, local economic development is typically defined in an inclusive manner. This lack of precision is reinforced by the lack of agreement on appropriate measures for development and the reliance on aggregate indicators. To overcome this difficulty, most evaluations of economic development have defined program goals narrowly to include only economic growth at the citywide level. Studies that define development in terms of economic growth typically operationalize economic development as aggregate economic, income, or employment growth (Bartik, 1991).

While evaluations of economic development typically assume that the goal of these policies is to increase economic growth on a citywide basis, we argue that in practice, development policies are directed to specific goals that at times include community development as well as economic growth, and that they are often intended to direct benefits to areas of economic need. As outlined in the work of Eisenschitz (1993), Laura Reese and David Fasenfest (1997), the necessity of differentiating community development goals from economic growth goals in evaluations of policy effectiveness is key. When the goal of economic development programs is community development, success is no longer "merely the increase in jobs or business; instead, policies must foster structural and institutional changes which promote a more equitable distribution of new jobs and income generated by growth"

(Reese and Fasenfest, 1997). Tendler (1987) suggests that measurement of economic development must measure the well-being of residents including the redirection of resources to the poorest segments of the community (Tendler, 1987). Thus it would seem that policies that call for redistribution of resources (e.g., jobs, business opportunities, education) would be the logical starting point for an examination of the effectiveness of both economic and community development efforts.

There are numerous dimensions that could be used to try to classify the type of development pursued by cities. In keeping with the preceding discussion, two of the most salient dimensions for policymakers are whether the focus of policy is on economic growth or community development, and whether aggregate citywide level development is sought or whether targeted development of areas of decline or economic need is sought. We have argued (Tao and Feiock, 1999) and found some support for the thesis that policies focusing on targeted development are more likely to be viewed as redistributive in nature by local policymakers. This is due in part to the restriction of policy benefits, such as tax or revenue expenditures, to a targeted area. Conversely, we found that policies focusing on citywide growth were more likely to be viewed as developmental, thus expanding somewhat the typology of local policies outlined by Peterson (1981). However, such distinctions leave questions of means by the wayside while instead using levels of analysis as proxies, to some extent, for whether the focus of policy is community or economic development.

Surveys of city council members regarding the purpose of development programs confirms that some development programs often have redistributive goals in the eyes of local policymakers and seek to promote community development by targeting needy areas (Clingermayer and Feiock, 1995). The distinction between economic and community development, however, remains one of semantics in the literature. This condition highlights the difficulties outlined by Reese and Fasenfest: evaluation of the effectiveness of development policy must be able to distinguish separate processes or goals in order to pass judgment on whether a given policy has performed well. Unbundling combinations of policies so that more direct matching of means and ends can be made, and for that matter, determining whether community development rather than economic development has occurred can be problematic.

The consequence of ignoring the redistributive nature of economic development programs in evaluation studies is that little can be concluded at the end of the day about the living quality of local conditions. Less can be said about which types of development tools create the best opportunities for local governments to deal with the problems of poverty, blight and quality of life. An additional consequence of segregating analyses of economic and community development policies is that community development is sometimes considered a natural consequence of economic growth (Rowe et al., 1999; Leatherman and Marcouiller, 1999; Guest, 2000). Such assumptions can preclude genuine investigations of the questions we pose above. A common theme in the literature on economic development is the examination of the supply side factors as if they are actually demand factors. For example, Michael Porter (1997) offers an assessment of why distressed urban communities have not flourished as hoped under existing development policies:

> The inner city's disadvantages as a business location must be seen as an economic problem and addressed as part of an economic strategy. Too often, addressing weaknesses such as a poorly trained workforce or deficient logistical infrastructure is approached with only the social welfare of residents, not the needs of business, in mind. For example, inner-city training programs often fail to screen applicants—and even give priority to the least prepared residents in the name of fairness. Employers are then disappointed with the graduates. (18)

When, as demonstrated here, small businesses are perceived as the desired beneficiaries of development policies, the problem of urban decline is substantially narrowed to be redefined as a problem of business attraction. The role of government, if any, is that of facilitator of existing market forces. This view highlights much of the philosophy behind the development of market-based policy tools in the early 1980s, and as such, serves as a succinct example of how defining the problems of urban decline as only a problem of economic development changes the nature of policy expectations.

From a political perspective, this is a remarkably naive conception that belies many decades of documentation of the failures that usually follow such narrow definitions of policy problems in troubled urban areas (see Pressman's and Wildavsky's classic 1984 assessment of Oakland, California, as well as the apt critiques offered of Porter's approach by Harrison and Glasmeier, 1997, and Bates, 1997). Such a narrowed perspective relegates the problems of urban residents to afterthought, where (if they're lucky) programs deliver enhanced overall economic growth, and targeted community development impacts follow. However, such market-based approaches are not the only tools in the arsenal of a local government seeking to better the circumstances of its troubled areas.

Choice of Development Means

Even where there is agreement on the goals or ends of development policies, there may be more than one means to that end. Often there are multiple policy instruments available to pursue economic or community development. Much of the difficulty in evaluating the impact of policy adoption lies in separating out the goals of different policy instruments. In recent years, the policy and welfare economics literatures have directed attention to the specific policy instruments that governments choose to pursue policy goals (Salamon and Elliott, 2001, Weimer and Vining, 1999). Research on the tools of government action has focused on classifying the array of instruments available to address government and market failures (Salamon and Elliott, 2001, Weimer and Vining, 1992, Feiock and Stream, 2001). In particular, there has been considerable interest in the comparisons of private markets and market-based approaches to public bureaucracies. At the aggregate level, economic development programs combine generic policy instruments and reflect the interests of multiple constituencies (Feiock and Stream, 2001). However, specific policy choices may reveal important information about the underlying institutional framework (Rubin and Rubin, 1987).

When choosing whether to pursue community development as well as economic growth, local policymakers choose whether to promote citywide growth or to target economic growth to needy areas in order to reduce poverty and welfare dependence and reduce economic inequalities within the city. One reason for the popularity of economic development programs is that they can be targeted to specific geographical areas (Clingermayer and Feiock, 1995). Development policies may be targeted in nature or designed to benefit a locality as a whole. While many local development programs such as promotional activities or business assistance programs are not directed to specific areas based on need, targeted programs are designed to concentrate resources in particular geographic areas. Such policies may have both developmental and redistributive consequences. In implementing targeted economic development, policymakers must confront strategic choices among potential policy instruments. Development initiatives often target property characteristics as well as individual and firm behavior. In this sense, they constitute distinct types of economic development policy. Thus the targeting of development incentives has implications for how programs are evaluated.

Table 2.1 illustrates the different configurations of policy goals that can underlie economic development programs. On the vertical dimension, development programs can emphasize economic growth or can emphasize community development. On the horizontal dimension, development programs can range from primarily aggregate or citywide development to targeted development in areas of social and economic need. Where the goals of development programs fall in this typology has implications for policy evaluation. By distinguishing between both the level of impact (area- or citywide) and the anticipated policy goals (economic, such as business start-ups, job generation, or revenues; or community, such as reduced crime rates, reduced welfare dependency, reduced unemployment), the ability to more clearly link means to ends is enhanced.

Most studies have not accounted for program goals other than aggregate economic growth. Taking into account both the developmental and redistributive nature of such efforts necessitates the use of more complex evaluation methodologies. Given the mounting evidence of limited economic success, perhaps it is time for scholars to move on to methods that seek to address these questions more directly and focus on a unit of analysis that is closer to the point of impact. The following analysis compares targeted development policies that seek economic and community goals and examines their impacts at both an aggregate (city) and targeted (area) level.

In order to highlight the distinction between alternative means and ends, the empirical analysis we present examines two different types of policy

Table 2.1

Level of Development *Emphasis of Policies*	*Citywide Benefits*	*Targeted Benefits*
Economic Development	Industrial Development Bonds, reduced regulations, Economic Development Councils, Industrial Parks	Urban infill, Enterprise Zones
Community Development	Promotional activities, infrastructure/ development of physical capital, Downtown Development Authorities	Community Redevelopment Areas, Community Development Corporations

instruments that may be directed to community development as well as economic growth, and are also directed to targeted areas. The two instruments represent distinctive philosophies about how to best achieve the elimination of urban blight. Both instruments seek to target specific areas within cities that have been identified as "in need." Both also seek to rebuild neighborhoods by providing access to outside funds. But each uses a different means to do so. By comparing the impact of these two types of development instruments, we identify the consequences of both the choice of instruments by local governments and the choice of level of analysis for evaluation efforts by researchers.

Two Policy Instruments, Two Paths in the State of Florida

Economic development initiatives that seek to target certain geographic areas that are locally defined and state sanctioned should be the most logical candidates for disaggregated evaluation of multiple dimensions of development. There are two such types of initiatives within the state of Florida that have been in place for over fifteen years: state enterprise zones and community redevelopment areas. These programs, though similar in focus, rely on distinct policy instruments to promote targeted economic development. While one approach to implementation relies on market incentives, the other focuses more heavily on infrastructure development. Since Florida has had both such programs in place for a comparable length of time, it provides a unique opportunity to examine the relative impact of policy instruments representing different means toward similar ends.

Florida's Enterprise Zones

The Florida Enterprise Zone program, first passed by the state legislature in 1980, represents an economic development policy initiative based on the assumption that localities are best served when private-sector actors are offered incentives to invest in neighborhoods that have fallen into decline. To a certain extent, this approach hands the job of policy implementation over to private firms, since it is their involvement which will predict the program's success or failure. It is also a policy which assumes that employment of those on public assistance is something best leveraged at the state rather than local level. It is in this sense, perhaps, that the Enterprise Zone program differs from more traditional forms of economic development because it specifically targets employment rather than job creation as a program goal.

There have been previous attempts to gauge the success of the Enterprise Zone program (Kim, 1993; Office of the Auditor General, 1993; Tao, 1995), with less than satisfactory results. Kim (1993) followed the Auditor General's lead and used census tracts as the unit of analysis, but neither attempted to broaden their analyses to include non-participants and control for exogenous factors. Tao (1995) used a larger group of cities that controlled for preexisting levels of economic distress, but the unit of analysis was the city rather than the targeted area or zone. None of these studies demonstrated that the program was having any measurable impact on its stated goals.

In 1993 the Florida Office of the Auditor General (OAG) was commissioned to evaluate the effectiveness of the state's enterprise zone program as the program came up against a sunset deadline. Although the evaluation concluded that the program appeared to provide some benefits to residents of the designated cities (e.g., tax job credits were claimed by businesses employing 3,882 residents of enterprise zones statewide, and 773 businesses located in zones took sales tax credits that totaled $6,686,540 in FY 1990–91 statewide), the benefits were considered negligible.

When put into context, these conclusions are understandable. The 773 businesses were from a pool of 35,672 businesses located in zones statewide (roughly 2 percent of eligible businesses participated), and the employed residents represented approximately 1 percent of the eligible population (State of Florida OAG, 1993). However, the OAG recommended that the program be continued since its benefits in some of the zones appeared to be worthwhile, though in ways that were not directly measurable in monetary terms. For example, some of the more successful zones (measured in tax credits, elevated education levels, and increased hiring of residents) were those credited with greater initiative by local governments (e.g., local zone coordinators with singular duties, marketing efforts, existing institutional knowledge). However, the report acknowledged that it was impossible to gauge the relative achievements of zones with their positions had they not received programmatic benefits (the counterfactual problem).

Florida's Redevelopment Areas

Where enterprise zones rely primarily on the behavior of businesses to realize improvements at the local level, other policy instruments rely more heavily on the initiative of government. An example of one such instrument is the community redevelopment area. Redevelopment areas grew out of the 1969 Community Redevelopment Act (chap. 163, *Florida Statutes*) and represents a more traditional "invest and grow" approach toward economic development. The strategy underlying redevelopment areas is fairly simple. A local governing body (city or county commission) may pass an ordinance establishing a "redevelopment area," after which they must create a redevelopment plan. The plan outlines the way in which the local government intends to improve infrastructure in the area, thus boosting private-sector investment. Although the statutes maintain that redevelopment areas should be identified as "blighted," the local governing board has a great deal of leeway in determining which areas may be so designated. The main advantage for a local government that goes to the trouble of writing a redevelopment plan lies in the state granting permission for the local government to implement tax-increment financing. Much like the old industrial revenue bonds, no raising of local taxes is necessary. Tax increment financing allows local governments to issue bonds using the redevelopment trust fund as collateral.

Like the Enterprise Zone program, local redevelopment boards must have their plans approved by the state's Department of Community Affairs before they may take advantage of the tax-increment financing option. Thus to be implemented, both programs require state sanction and local initiative. Each of these programs requires such sanction because the tools that reputedly make the programs work are the relaxation of state laws that continue to apply to everyone else. This is where the similarities cease. Unlike the Enterprise Zone program, redevelopment areas depend primarily upon local government investment and implementation for the program to work since there is a clear causal logic between public investment and the stimulation of private activity. Thus the implementing institution is a known factor. This means that if the program is perceived to be ineffective, there will be someone to blame. The Enterprise Zone program offers no such opportunity for direct censure.

Community versus Economic Development

There are important differences in the emphasis of economic growth versus community development among these two targeted development programs. Enterprise zones seek to provide business investment within economically depressed areas of a city through tax incentives, with employment incentives offered through tax expenditure at the state level. Community redevelopment areas seek to target the expenditure of local revenues within economically depressed areas of a city. Thus one can argue that the intent for establishing a redevelopment area is more redistributive in nature than the intent for establishing an enterprise zone. Local governments have a finite budget, and though redevelopment areas allow them to augment that budget through an expanded ability to issue bonds, there is still an expectation that expenditures from the local budget will be focused on the area in question. There is no such expenditure involved at the local level with an enterprise zone.

One of the long-standing critiques of "market-oriented" approaches to development has been that they do not acknowledge the possibility that development problems result from an underlying failure of the market that requires direct government intervention. When individual pursuit of private benefits produces collective destitution, utility-maximizing behavior can be said to result in market failure. Government, acting as a representative of collective interests, may mitigate the "automatic punishing recoil of the marketplace" (Lindblom, 1982). However, market-oriented approaches to development are based, in part, on a perception of "government failure" (Stokey and Zeckhauser, 1978, Pagano and Bowman, 1995). From this perspective, government development programs divert resources from the private sector and interfere with the efficient operation of the market. Such government intervention can exacerbate the very economic development problems that local officials wish to eliminate. Which role does government play? At the local level, one may argue governments play both, evidenced by the different means employed to achieve development ends. Does one role suit local governments better than the other? This is the question that we seek to answer.

Design

In Tao and Feiock, 1999, we provided a two-stage analysis of economic development policy at the local level: first, the political, economic and demographic variables leading to adoption of either of the two policy instruments by local governments; and second, the impact of instrument adoption on economic outcomes at both the city and targeted area levels. Our findings suggested two general conclusions: cities adopting the two types of instruments demonstrated different political characteristics; and where policy adoption had little impact at the city level of analysis, there were notable findings of impact at the level of the targeted areas. Specifically, enterprise zones accounted for a substantial increase in the median household income within zones when compared to the surrounding city.

By replicating and expanding the second stage of our previous analysis, we hope to remedy some of the shortcomings exhibited by the sampling frame used in the previous analysis and to include variables that serve as better measures of the broader goals of community development as well as economic growth. In the previous study, we restricted our analysis to the cities in the state of Florida which were part of Standard Metropolitan Statistical Areas (SMSAs). This allowed us to control to some degree for factors such as population, size of government, and administrative capacity. Within these thirty-six cities, only twenty contained areas that had previously been identified as "distressed" during the Florida Department of Community Affairs' (FDCA) statewide assessment of need in 1983 (Florida Department of Community Affairs).

In this chapter, we broaden our analysis to include cities that are located outside of SMSAs, but we also restrict the analysis to only those cities containing areas that were originally identified by FDCA as economically disadvantaged. In this fashion, we hope to control for any preexisting economic disparities that may have been present across the cities in question. This also allows us to draw more general conclusions about the nature of targeted development than was possible in the previous study, since the spectrum of city types includes smaller cities in a wide variety of locations across a spectrum of political structures (for a list of the cities included in the analysis, please see appendix 2.A).

We expect that a comparison of the impact of the two programs will demonstrate different types of outcomes at different levels of impact. We expect that communities that adopt enterprise zones will see income growth at the city level, but less impact on income gaps between the targeted area and the city as a whole. On the other hand, communities that adopt redevelopment areas may see less growth at the city level, but we expect to see a reduction in the disparity between income levels in targeted areas and the surrounding cities, as well as a reduction in dependence on public assistance within areas as a proportion of the city as a whole.

The design offers a unique opportunity to compare competing "policy instruments" for the implementation of state efforts to promote urban economic development by pitting one approach toward economic development against another. This study offers an equally important opportunity to examine and extend evaluation methodologies for development policies and identify the consequences the choice of unit of analysis has for the evaluation of development programs. With these two key points in mind, we undertake: (1) an assessment of the relative effectiveness of the Enterprise Zone program and the Community Redevelopment Programs in the 1980s using cities as the unit of analysis; and (2) a similar evaluation in terms of variable definition and measures, using targeted areas within cities as the unit of analysis.

Analysis

We examined all cities originally identified by FDCA as "in need" with a 1980 population over 20,000 in the state of Florida. We limited our examination to cities over 20,000 because the Auditor General (1993) identified cities of this size as having no competition when applying for designation as enterprise zone recipients with the FDCA. Since all applicants within this population category received zone designations, we excluded them from our analysis. The remaining 32 cities contained a total of 67 areas that had been targeted for assistance. Thirty-five of these areas were designated as either community redevelopment areas (22 CRAs) or enterprise zones (13 EZs); the remaining 32 received no designation. Data for the analysis was derived from the 1980 *Characteristics of the Population: General Social and Economic Characteristics—Florida,* and the 1990 *General Population Characteristics: Florida, Social and Economic Characteristics: Florida.* Information for political structure variables was provided by the *County and City Data Book* (1982), and information for policy instruments was provided by the Florida Office of the Auditor General (1993) and the FDCA (1983). As in our previous study, the areas were measured based on census tract information. When areas did not comprise entire tracks, the analysis dropped to the block level.

City-Level Development Outcomes

Our analysis examines the relationship between adoption of the two targeted instruments at both the city and area levels of analysis. At the city level, the sample remained constant at thirty-two cities, with consistent data available for all cities in the analysis. Tables 2.2 through 2.4 present the results of the

Table 2.2 Impact of Targeted Program Adoption on Citywide Income Disparity

Dependent Variables	*Difference (1990) between Average and Median Household Income ($)*		
Independent Variables	*B*	*SE*	*Sig.*
Constant	16237.3	4321.5	.001
CRA (dummy)	–1447.4	1170.0	.228
EZ (dummy)	691.2	1174.8	.562
Change in dependent population (1980–90)	–.087	.121	(.478)
Change in minority population (1980–90)	–.136	.192	.484
Change in unemployment (1980–90)	–.040	.184	(.828)
Median Household Income ($) 1980	–.765	.310	.021
Summary Statistics	R^2	*Adj.* R^2	*F (F Sig.)*
	.275	.101	1.58 (.195)

Note. Multivariate Regression (N=32)

multivariate regression for three separate models: (1) the impact on the difference between city-level average and median household income in 1990; (2) the impact on the change in the number of households receiving AFDC between 1980 and 1990; and (3) the median property value in 1990. As in the previous study, these models included the 1980 values for each of the dependent variables as an independent predictor of change in economic performance at the city level. The results of this analysis, however, differ dramatically from those of the 1999 study.

The results reported in the tables show little evidence that development policy leads to citywide economic gain. The estimates of the first model which are reported in table 2.2 depart from those found in our earlier examination of SMSAs in 1999. We find that development programs do not prove to be a significant predictor of the relationship between average and median household income in 1990. Thus when the range of city sizes is enlarged, the ability of development policy to realize gains is greatly diminished. This would suggest that if city governments do seek to realize gains through development policies, smaller cities may be better served to seek alternative policy tools.

Table 2.3 Impact of Targeted Program Adoption on Citywide Changes in AFDC Recipiency, 1980–90

Dependent Variables	*Change in Number of AFDC Households, 1980–90*		
Independent Variables	*B*	*SE*	*Sig.*
Constant	127.1	188.0	.505
CRA (dummy)	399.3	217.3	.078
EZ (dummy)	–192.0	230.6	.413
Change in dependent population (1980–90)	.050	.022	.028
Change in minority population (1980–90)	–.008	.038	.832
Change in unemployment (1980–90)	–.029	.052	.580
Number of AFDC Households in 1980	–.037	.041	.368
Summary Statistics	*R^2.* 446	*Adj. R^2* .313	*F (F Sig.)* 3.36 (.015)

Note. Multivariate Regression (N=32)

The second model reported in table 2.3 offers only modest support for the impact of these programs. Cities that adopted CRAs witnessed, on average, an increase of almost four hundred households as recipients of AFDC between 1980 and 1990 when compared to all other cities, but this effect is only significant at a 0.10 confidence level. It also appears that there was a significant rise in the dependent population (children and the elderly) over this period, which may account for this increase in recipiency to some extent. However, the association between cities adopting CRAs and increased welfare caseloads stands in contrast to the lack of significant findings for the cities adopting EZs. Since we controlled for economic factors that may have accounted for some disparity between cities in terms of needy populations, there would be no reason to conclude that cities adopting CRAs are somehow more economically distressed than other cities in our sample.

Table 2.4 examines the impact of adoption on citywide median property value in 1990. Neither of the development instruments proved significant predictors of value, and the only variable that performed well was the 1980 median property value. Thus with the exception of the change in AFDC recipiency between 1980 and 1990, neither of the targeted instruments seems to have had significant impact on citywide economic outcomes.

Table 2.4 Impact of Targeted Program Adoption on Citywide Median Property Value in 1990

Dependent Variables	*Citywide Median Property Value in 1990 ($)*		
Independent Variables	*B*	*SE*	*Sig.*
Constant	–12563.7	7521.8	.107
CRA (dummy)	2742.9	3938.5	.493
EZ (dummy)	1601.0	3927.3	.687
Change in dependent population (1980–90)	–.304	.385	.437
Change in minority population (1980–90)	–.634	.630	.324
Change in unemployment (1980–90)	–.441	.601	.470
Median Property Value ($) 1980	1.238	.122	.000
Summary Statistics	R^2 .822	*Adj.* R^2 .780	*F (F Sig.)* 19.29(.000)

Note. Multivariate Regression (N=32)

This finding is consistent with many of the city-level analyses of targeted development programs to date (Hansen 1989; USGAO 1988; Papke 1994; Boarnet and Bogart 1996). However, given that this sample was restricted to only those cities containing areas identified as distressed, our analysis should offer a cautionary note to research that uses the city as a unit of analysis when evaluating the effects of targeted development. Since such policy instruments are meant to boost the chances of success for those areas that are disadvantaged, the effects of such incentives may often be washed out of analyses that compare the fates of cities of similar economic ilk. Improvements at the bottom of the scale for overall city performance may not keep up with improvements at the top end, thus providing little evidence of overall impact. This is where a change in the unit of analysis can prove useful.

Area-Level Development Outcomes

The area-level analysis included all areas in cities with 1980 populations of more than 20,000 that were originally identified by FDCA as economically distressed (FDCA 1983). There were 67 such areas identified within the 32 cities, and data for all 67 was available for this analysis. We used the original configurations of areas in 1983, which had been based on 1980 census tract information, as the units of analysis for both 1980 and 1990 figures. As in the city-level analysis, we were concerned with the performance of three different measures of economic and community well-being, and therefore tested three separate models for the relative influence of targeted instrument adoption. Table 2.5 examines the difference in 1990 between city and area median household income (in 1980 constant dollars). Table 2.6 examines the change in proportion of city households receiving AFDC located within areas between 1980 and 1990. Table 2.7 examines differences between city- and area-level median property value in 1990. The inclusion of three measures is a substantial improvement over the 1999 study. Again, we used 1980 values for each of the dependent variables as predictors for the 1990 conditions. The estimates from the OLS multivariate regression results are presented in tables 2.5 through 2.7.

All three of the area-level models were significant overall predictors of the outcome measures of interest, indicating a better fit for measures of rel-

Table 2.5 Impact of Targeted Programs on Income Disparity between Area and City

Dependent Variables	*Model 1 Difference (1990) between City and Area Median Household Income (1980) ($)*		
Independent Variables	*B*	*SE*	*Sig.*
Constant	–7060.1	988.9	.000
CRA (dummy)	–1222.9	1197.0	.311
EZ (dummy)	792.5	1253.9	.530
Change in area population (1980–90)	–.386	.179	.035
Change in area unemployment (1980–90)	.176	.508	.731
Difference in City and Area 1980 Median Household Income ($1980)	1.303	.156	.000
Summary Statistics	*R^2*	*Adj. R^2*	*F (F Sig.)*
	.639	.609	21.2 (.000)

Note. Multivariate Regression (N=67)

Table 2.6 Impact of Targeted Programs on Change in Proportion of AFDC Recipiency, 1980–90

Dependent Variables	*Change in Proportion of City AFDC Households within Area, 1980–90*		
Independent Variables	*B*	*SE*	*Sig.*
Constant	.0469	.019	.017
CRA (dummy)	–.0468	.023	.050
EZ (dummy)	–.0634	.025	.014
Change in area population (1980–90)	.0000	.000	.227
Change in area unemployment (1980–90)	–.00002	.000	.268
Proportion of City AFDC Recipient Households within Area (1980)	–.254	.058	.000
Summary Statistics	R^2	*Adj.* R^2	*F (F Sig.)*
	.369	.317	7.129(.000)

Note. Multivariate Regression (N=67)

ative income. There were some notable differences between the results of the area-level analysis and the city-level discussion, as well as differences from the previous study's results. In table 2.4, neither of the development policy instruments had a significant impact. The change in population within areas was the only variable of significance other than the 1980 difference between city and area median household income. Specifically, for every increase between 1980 and 1990 of 1,000 people living within an area, the income disparity between the area and the surrounding city would decrease, on average, by approximately $386 (1980 dollars). Since neither of the targeted instruments performed significantly in this model, this finding suggests that areas receiving targeted benefits were no more likely to see improvements in area income levels than areas without such targeting. This is a marked change from the findings using the SMSA as the unit of analysis (Tao and Feiock, 1999). This suggests that smaller cities (those not included in the SMSA analysis) may have been more likely to designate areas with declines in growth (loss of residents due to deteriorating infrastructure and city service conditions) as recipients of targeted policies. This certainly underscores the intent of such policies, and suggests that the intended recipients of policy benefits were correctly identified.

Table 2.7 Impact of Targeted Programs on Difference between Area and City Median Property Value in 1990

Dependent Variables	*Difference between City and Area Median Property Value, 1980–90*		
Independent Variables	*B*	*SE*	*Sig.*
Constant	–19657.9	4271.3	.000
CRA (dummy)	–6829.5	4677.3	.149
EZ (dummy)	1050.1	4905.1	.831
Change in area population (1980–90)	–.366	.706	.607
Change in area unemployment (1980–90)	1.250	2.062	.547
Difference in City and Area Median Property Value ($) 1980	1.283	.155	.000
Summary Statistics	R^2	*Adj.* R^2	*F (F Sig.)*
	.569	.533	15.824(.000)

Note. Multivariate Regression (N=67)

Table 2.6 reports strong evidence that certain development programs can reduce some symptoms of poverty in targeted areas. Both CRA and EZ programs produced significant reductions in the proportion of AFDC households concentrated in the targeted areas. Specifically, for areas designated as CRAs, the proportion of city households receiving AFDC in 1990 was 5 percent less, on average, than other areas. For areas designated as EZs, the proportion was reduced by over 6 percent, on average, when compared to non-EZs. This differs from the city-level analysis, where enterprise zones were not significant predictors of citywide reductions in welfare recipiency. When taken in conjunction with the results from table 2.2, this suggests that cities adopting CRAs may be witnessing increases in welfare roles citywide, but not within the targeted area. Thus the level of analysis changes the nature of conclusions about the effectiveness of targeted development in an area of importance to city officials.

The model estimated in table 2.7 is the only area-level analysis that does not perform as well as the city-level counterpart, though the estimate for CRAs approached statistical significance (.149). These findings suggest that targeted instruments have little impact on income and property outcomes, but do demonstrate an impact on measures of poverty (AFDC recipiency).

Discussion

The results reported in this chapter prompt several observations. First, local development programs can have impacts on community development goals such as reducing welfare dependent populations, not just on economic growth. In fact, the most significant effect that the two programs exerted was on the reduction of AFDC populations in targeted areas. Because community development goals (economic parity rather than economic growth) may often underlie the adoption of certain types of development programs, it is incumbent on evaluators to include measures of redistributive outcomes in their designs.

Second, the unit of analysis used to evaluate the effects of development can shape the conclusions drawn. The results presented here demonstrate that certain policies may be having their intended impacts on targeted areas, but their effect is lost or only partly captured in aggregate citywide analysis. This is particularly true when looking at the change in welfare recipiency. In the citywide analysis, it would appear that the cities adopting CRAs are actually attracting welfare recipients. On average, there were 400 more AFDC households in cities with CRAs than were in cities with EZs or with no policy adoption at all (see table 2.3). However, the area-level analysis presents a very different picture. Within areas, both targeted programs appeared to be reducing the proportion of AFDC households over time. Thus even though overall recipiency rates may have been rising during the 1980s, targeted areas were witnessing decreases in recipiency rates. The importance of examining the appropriate level of analysis can be further underscored with an example. Since the targeted areas for development policy tools such as these are often quite small in comparison with the city as a whole, their overall contribution to citywide conditions may be swallowed up Bradenton, for example, had a population of 43,769 in 1990. The EZ had a population of 3,572. The city expended $1,145,500 in development funds in the targeted area, where the city as a whole saw approximately $800 million in sales revenues generated that year (Manatee County Chamber of Commerce, 2002).

Finally, there may be more than one means to achieve an end. While the philosophical underpinnings of the two approaches examined here are very different, the pattern of their effects on local development were quite similar. At the city level, neither had the intended effect, but at the area level, both programs appear to have significant effects on the reduction of welfare dependency. At the same time, neither policy had any significant impact on economic variables. This has important implications for theory and practice.

Conclusion

It would appear at first blush that Machiavelli has indeed called the game correctly. However, what is perhaps most notable about these analyses is that they share similar success and similar failure. Neither policy instrument, despite their different causal logics, had an arguable impact on income distribution or on property values, both of which represent long-term measures of change in distressed communities. Thus we may conclude that community development goals do not necessarily follow from the implementation of economic development policies in spite of targeting. We might also conclude that the debate over market versus government failure is not resolved here. Since the original source of blight in these cities may be a combination of government and market factors, it is impossible to state whether targeted tools remedy a particular kind of failure. However, our final observation must be that regardless of the type of failure, such policy instruments seemed to mitigate localized problems of welfare dependency (a government initiative) but had no impact on measures, localized or aggregate, of market performance. This is the most markedly different finding from the previous 1999 study. Since this sample represented only cities that were arguably at the bottom of the economic spectrum, it appears that even if the means do not make much difference, the choice of venue does.

Neglect of distributional issues in evaluation is largely due to the separation of policy choices and outcomes in development research. Separate and distinct literatures have developed regarding development policy adoption on the one hand, and the impacts of development programs on the other. Focusing attention on both the developmental and redistributive impacts of the adoption and implementation of various economic policy instruments may provide a bridge between these literatures by extending the conceptual models from the adoption literature to the evaluation of program consequences. This is particularly important because, while policy adoption and impact generally have not been examined together, the lack of observable economic impacts found in evaluation studies are often blamed on political factors (Wolman, 1988).

The finding that both the market-based policy instrument (EZs) and the government-based policy instruments (CRAs) can be effective instruments in reducing welfare dependency in specific targeted areas suggests that policymakers have multiple means available to pursue particular ends. This may allow them to pursue their policy goals while shaping the program design to the constraints of the local political environment. There is considerable opportunity for future research to link policy adoption and impact and examine the influence of various policy instruments as means to achieve developmental or redistributive goals. Thus, cities may have the liberty to choose the policy path "less traveled by," but in the end, the choice may make little difference.

Appendix 2.A

List of Cities Included in the Sample

Bradenton
Clearwater
Coral Gables
Daytona Beach
Deerfield Beach
Fort Lauderdale
Fort Pierce
Fort Walton Beach
Gainesville
Hallandale
Hialeah
Hollywood
Homestead
Jacksonville
Key West
Lake Worth
Lakeland
Largo
Melbourne
Miami
Oakland Park
Ocala
Orlando
Pensacola
Pinellas Park
Pompano Beach
St. Petersburg
Tallahassee
Tampa
West Little River
West Palm Beach
Winter Haven

THREE

The Local Public Balance Sheet: An Alternative Evaluation Methodology for Local Economic Development

David L. Imbroscio

Introduction

The crusade for economic development endures as the central concern of local governments in the United States (Imbroscio, 1997: 5; Bowman, 1987: 8; Eisinger, 1988: 19–20; Elkin, 1987: 156). A vast amount of political and economic resources continues to be directed to achieving this goal, yet the careful and systematic evaluation of economic development policy has been largely eschewed. This neglect stems from the inherently problematic nature of the evaluative task, which confronts numerous technical, political, and normative challenges.

The character of the challenges has been perceptively elucidated in the writings of several policy analysts working in the local economic development field. Bartik and Bingham (1997), for example, discuss the inherent *technical* difficulties involved in evaluating development outcomes. Their comprehensive assessment of these difficulties impels these scholars to ask the most basic of questions: "Can economic development programs be evaluated?" In response to Bartik and Bingham's work, Giloth (1997: 282) aptly points to the *political* difficulties involved in evaluation by observing that knowledge utilization remains extremely limited in a climate where cities and states obsess over attracting major new development projects. "Bartik and Bingham's framing question," Giloth (1997: 282) suggests, "should perhaps be changed to 'Why bother evaluating economic development when no one cares?'" (also see Wolman, 1988). Reese and Fasenfest identify the difficulties arising because evaluation is inherently a *normative* undertaking. They remind us that at the heart of evaluation lies the demanding but essential task of making concrete value judgments about the appropriate goals of policy, "[h]owever much policy analysts would like to believe otherwise" (Reese and Fasenfest, 1997: 195; also see Fasenfest, Ciancanelli, and Reese, 1997).

This essay builds upon this recent work of Reese and Fasenfest—work that grapples with the normative challenges confronting the evaluation of local economic development policy. As part of their project to stress and clarify the role played by values in these evaluations, Reese and Fasenfest (1999: 3) enjoin policy evaluators to focus more attention on the: "broader goals of economic development policies, which include a greater sense of community outcomes . . . [in order to] shift the focus of evaluation from primarily market effects of economic development policies toward a social economy perspective, which encompasses the extent to which public-sector expenditures *actually bring public or community benefits*" (emphasis added). In response to the research agenda Reese and Fasenfest set out, the discussion and analysis I offer below explores a policy evaluation technique explicitly designed to assess economic development from this "social economy" framework: The "public (or community) balance sheet." Overall, through this exploration I find the technique embodies the potential to improve economic development decision-making; I thus suggest more research be devoted to strengthening its conceptual and empirical foundations.

Background and Overview

The public (or community) balance sheet concept (also known as "social cost-benefit analysis"; see Luria and Russell, 1982: 170) was developed over two decades ago, and since then has made several appearances in the alternative local economic development literature (see, e.g., Smith, 1979; Levine, 1987; Alperovitz and Faux, 1984; Luria and Russell, 1981 and 1982; Feagin and Parker, 1990; Imbroscio, 1997; Giloth, 1988). Its practitioners attribute its origin to a 1979 analysis titled *Towards a Public Balance Sheet,* written by David Smith for the National Center for Economic Alternatives (co-directed at the time by two pioneers of alternative economic thought, Gar Alperovitz and Jeff Faux). The concept's earliest applications addressed the development problems wrought by the wave of deindustrialization striking places such as Youngstown (Smith, 1979) and Detroit (Luria and Russell, 1981) during the late 1970s. Later analysts applied the concept to understand phenomena such as the real costs of economic growth on communities (Feagin and Parker, 1990: 30–32; 289–91), the critique of the corporate-center approach to central-city revitalization (Levine, 1987: 119), the economic viability of municipally owned economic enterprises (Imbroscio, 1997: 147–48), and the proper use of government-provided development subsidies (Fisher and Peters, 1998: 217).

The term itself—*public* balance sheet—places the conceptual focus of policy evaluation squarely on the issue—accentuated by Reese and Fasenfest—of the extent to which public (or community) benefits actually result from local development expenditures. So, at the most basic level, analysts use the public balance sheet concept to frame the evaluation question sharply in terms of the public vs. the private: While local economic development efforts may aid corporations and other businesses—enhancing *private* balance sheets—the call to employ a public balance sheet suggests a possible disjunction between such private benefits and those accruing to public or larger community.

For example, as Robert Giloth's (1988: 344) analysis of two prominent community economic development newsletters shows, evaluations examining "public and private balances sheets" raise serious questions about the level of public benefits generated by "mainstream development" efforts (also see Elkin, 1987; Barnekov and Rich, 1989; Squires, 1989; Krumholz, 1991). Giloth (1988: 344) points out that "[t]hese concerns about conventional development have given rise to [alternative] community economic development strategies" that produce more concrete and direct public or community-wide benefits. In a similar vein, Marc Levine concludes his comprehensive critique of Baltimore's mainstream development strategy by arguing that cities should "deploy public resources consistent with the logic of . . . the public balance sheet—an approach that calculates the *social* costs and benefits of local policies, rather than simply underwriting developers' profits in the hope that 'trickle down' will occur" (1987: 119, emphasis in original).

From the public balance sheet's general framework casting evaluation in these private vs. public terms derive two additional, more specific conceptual uses of the technique.

First, policy analysts employ the public balance sheet as an "analytical tool for scrutinizing and measuring the social costs of private-sector development" (Feagin and Parker, 1990: 289). As Feagin and Parker (1990: 290), quoting the original work of David Smith, explain: "the public balance sheet

[is] a way of tallying up . . . the 'tangible, measurable, quantifiable, costs being imposed on citizens individually and collectively by the actions of the private sector.'" These social and community costs, imposed through both the operation of private-sector enterprises and, especially, through private investment decisions, "don't show up on any firm's ledger; no accountant writes them down. They're not charged against the income the firm makes from selling its products and services." While conventional economic theory conceives of such costs as examples of "externalities," causing the market to "fail," as we will see below, public balance sheet practitioners embrace a much more expansive notion of market failure in general and externalities in particular.

Second, building in large part upon the calculation of these social costs, policy analysts utilize the public balance sheet as a tool to guide activist and positive public intervention in the market economy, that is as a guide for formulating public policies designed to stimulate local economic development. As a tool to develop policy, Alperovitz and Faux (1979: iii) explain that the public balance sheet "compares the total taxpayer and public benefits from direct intervention to maintain local employment against the total costs." Continuing, they therefore argue "it provides *a more comprehensive and rational guide* than the narrow considerations of private profit and loss that are typically used to evaluate public action" (Alperovitz and Faux, 1979: iii; emphasis added).

Each of these two conceptual uses of the public balance sheet technique is explored at length below.

Tallying up the Social Costs of Private Sector Development Decisions

The public balance sheet technique demonstrates how the actions of the private sector impose significant costs on the public (and the larger community). As noted above, conventional (i.e., neo-classical) economic theory treats these "social costs" as "externalities"—costs that stem from market processes but that will not be experienced by market actors. Instead, these costs are externalized—that is, transferred to others, usually the community at large. The presence of externalities create an instance where the competitive market will fail to maximize social welfare: "Because of the divergence between private and social (i.e., total community) returns," write Stokey and Zeckhauser

(1978: 304) in their classic statement of neo-classical theory, "uncoordinated individual actions lead to less than optimal results." Together with "public goods/bads" (essentially a variation of the externality problem, see Browning and Browning, 1983: 35–36), the need to "correct" for this "market failure" provides the basic justification in conventional economic theory for government intervention into the workings of the market economy. As such, this reasoning underlies neo-classical economics' "normative theory of the state," as Bobrow and Dryzek (1987: 33) correctly note.

Conventional economic theorists generally view the instances and scope of the externalities to be modest (Kuttner, 1997: 17).[1] Hence, in normative terms, most advocate a limited role for the public sector in society (see Stokey and Zeckhauser, 1978; Friedman, 1962). In contrast, practitioners of the public balance sheet view externalities as profound and extensive—to the point that their existence serves as a challenge to the entire underlying logic of conventional economic theory. In his original work developing the concept, Smith (1979: 5), for example, writes: "The economic rationality of the 'profit-maximizing' private corporation does not necessarily lead to 'welfare maximization' for individuals and communities, since the market does not adequately measure, and in fact explicitly ignores, the public costs and benefits of private investment decisions." Feagin and Parker's (1990) rationale for employing the public balance sheet approach builds from an even more systemic critique of conventional economic theory, as well as the capitalist economic system it justifies. That system, they write: "of necessity must transfer many internal costs to outsiders. In reality, the social costs of privately controlled industrial and real estate development are *not* 'external' to modern capitalism, but are as a rule an integral part of its everyday routine operation" (1990: 290).

The public balance sheet approach conceives of these pervasive and substantial costs imposed on the public (or community) by private controllers of capital as resulting from both the decisions of private actors *to invest* and their decisions not to invest (i.e., to *disinvest*). Each scenario is discussed in the following sections.

Costs of Private Disinvestment

The original conception of the public balance sheet technique grew from an analysis of a case of massive capital disinvestment—namely, when the Lykes Corporation, a New Orleans shipping conglomerate, abruptly closed the

Campbell Works steel mill (part of its Youngstown Sheet and Tube subsidiary). "With little more warning than proceeds a tornado," wrote Alperovitz and Faux (1979: I), "more than 4,000 jobs in the Ohio steel town were suddenly gone," to be followed by an estimated 3,600 additional jobs in grocery stores, shops, banks, and other businesses suffering the ripple effects of the shutdown. This decision, made by the private corporation,[2] imposed massive costs on public taxpayers, who had to "bear costs of $60–70 million in adjustment assistance, unemployment compensation, revenue reduction, and increased government expenditures" (Alperovitz and Faux, 1979: iii). From the point of view of Lykes, however, these costs had no bearing from an economic standpoint because such costs "do not show up on [its private] balance sheet" (Alperovitz and Faux, 1979: iii). The bill could simply be transferred (externalized) to public taxpayers (also see Jakle and Wilson, 1992: 78–79; Lustig, 1985: 133).

Public balance sheet practitioners hold that private actions to disinvest capital burden the public and the larger community with a plethora of liabilities—"externalities" usually not even acknowledged to exist in conventional economic analysis. Physical, social, individual, fiscal, and political costs are all traced to these private decisions; some of the more salient of which are described below.

One of the most exorbitant expenses foisted upon the public at large by private disinvestment—a cost frequently highlighted by practitioners of the public balance sheet approach—results from the "throwing away" of established communities (Williamson, Imbroscio, and Alperovitz 2000; Ricker, 1998). Trillions of dollars of sunk investments in physical infrastructure—including roads and other transportation systems, housing, schools, hospitals, public utilities, as well as a host of industrial facilities (plants and equipment)—are left abandoned or vastly underutilized when disinvestment occurs and people and businesses, left with greatly diminished economic prospects, are forced to leave town. In his recent book on metropolitan disparities, Orfield (1998: 171) alludes to the economic irrationality of this process when he ardently declares: "We cannot afford to throw away . . . cities, and we must not accept anyone's doing so."

The public balance sheet similarly can take an accounting of the costly destruction of the social infrastructure—that is "social capital"—of places that occurs when private disinvestment causes widespread unemployment and/or transiency, disrupting established patterns of human interaction (see

Jakle and Wilson, 1992; Dudley, 1994; *New York Times*, 1996; Castro, 1998). This social capital—"features of social organization, such as networks, norms, and trust, traditions of civic involvement and social solidarity"—is increasingly seen as crucial for facilitating the widespread cooperation among individuals necessary for overcoming collective action problems (Putnam, 1993b: 36–37). Because it appears to help facilitate collective actions, a high level of social capital in a community "seems to be a precondition for economic development, as well as for effective government" (Putnam, 1993b: 37; also see Putnam, 1993a: chap. 6). The general public hence incurs significant costs when private decisions cause a level of community disinvestment that depletes its stock social capital.

Widespread disinvestment also imposes costs on individual human beings and their families. The unemployment and forced mobility caused by this disinvestment increase levels of anxiety and stress among individuals and lead to a decline in personal self-esteem (or feelings of self-worth)—conditions that, in turn, often cause a deterioration in physical and psychological health. To some extent, heightened incidences of alcoholism, child and spousal abuse and neglect, and the increased stress on family structures result as well (see Moore, 1996; Wilson, 1987; Bluestone and Harrison, 1987).

The Youngstown case described above points to the massive public fiscal costs that can stem from private disinvestment decisions. Most notably, such decisions can directly result in the need for increased government transfer payments (unemployment compensation, public assistance, etc.), the increased demand for other government services, and the decrease in public tax revenue. More systemically, the current political-economic context—marked as it is by the widespread disinvestment (actual or prospective) brought about by the heightened mobility of capital—imposes generalized fiscal costs on the broader public. Such a system allows mobile corporations to extract overly generous locational subsidies by pitting competing places against one another, creating a situation not unlike an "arms race" with its prisoners' dilemma game logic (Imbroscio, 1997: 148). In their pursuit of capital investment, players in the game (competing local jurisdictions, e.g., states and cities) "rationally" oversupply inducements to attract mobile businesses, worsening the fiscal condition of all jurisdictions (see Levy, 1992; Peretz, 1986; Wolman, 1988). Moreover, Jones and Bachelor (1986: 203) point to an additional public fiscal burden incurred under these conditions: the so-called corporate surplus. The source of this burden is the asymmetry of information in the bargaining process that exists between the private and public sectors, where "[t]he businessman knows just what incentives will be necessary in order to affect a decision in regard to location, but the city official does not." This asymmetry allows mobile corporations to extract "an amount over what would be strictly necessary to affect the decision about location"—that is, a corporate surplus—at the general public's expense.

Finally, there are political costs. Standing on the shoulders of venerable political thinkers such as John Stuart Mill and Alexis de Tocqueville, Elkin (1999) shows why local government is the only forum where large numbers of people can learn the art of effective, public-spirited citizenship—a learning process that occurs when citizens are able to consider (and deliberate over) what is truly in the public (as opposed to individual) interests. Yet, the politics in localities plagued by substantial private disinvestment are, Elkin (1999: 57) writes, "much more likely to teach futility than what is at stake in giving concrete meaning to the public interest. Given this state of affairs, the citizens of such communities will simply be left out of local politics as a school of citizenship—or they will be assigned, as it were, to the wrong school. But a nontrivial number of citizens live in such localities, so the loss to a public-spirited citizenry is significant." Without a public-spirited citizenry, Elkin demonstrates, a republican regime built on popular sovereignty is imperiled by an excessive degree of " narrowness of concern on the part of citizens" (1999: 56).

Costs of Private Investment

Public balance sheet advocates point out that, just as costs are imposed on the public (or community) from private decisions to withdraw capital, the decisions of private actors to invest also can prove burdensome to the public or the wider community. Smith recognized this phenomenon in his original analysis of plant closings and corporate mobility. He wrote:

> There are [also] very real costs imposed on communities at the receiving end of corporate relocations. . . . Physical infrastructure, schools and social services must all be financed out of local operating and capital budgets. In addition, there can be serious impacts on local real estate markets as newcomers bid up the prices of available housing. Once again, *corporate investment decisions impose a range of costs on the public that do not show up on the corporate balance sheet.* (Smith, 1979: 4; emphasis added)

In short, those established communities "thrown-away" because of disinvestment need to be rebuilt somewhere—specifically, in places where private investors choose to move their capital. This replication (and duplication) comes at a substantial resource cost to communities receiving the investment and, by extension, the society as a whole.

Likewise, in their analysis of urban land development, using the public balance sheet approach, Feagin and Parker (1990: 289) point to the costs imposed on the public and the wider community from private investment: "The social costs . . . of . . . modern real estate capitalism take a variety of forms: the shortage of affordable rental housing, large numbers of people displaced by developments without suitable housing alternatives, chronic racial segregation, enhanced traffic congestion, air and water pollution, constrained choices for consumers because of developer decisions . . . [about] housing, and taxpayer burdens from tax subsidies for developers." Once again, costs are imposed on "the citizenry and their communities" by the private decisions of "developers, bankers, and other investors," who have no need to factor these additional expenses into their consideration of profit and loss (Feagin and Parker, 1990: 289).

Scholarship in the urban political economy field also has extensively documented this dynamic (though to date researchers have not widely employed the public balance sheet technique to frame their studies or elucidate their findings). This body of research finds its clearest manifestation in the many powerful critiques of Paul Peterson's (1981) argument that development policies unambiguously promote the well-being of cities (Stone, 1987; Swanstrom, 1988; Logan and Molotch, 1987). While economic growth brings benefits to local places such as increased employment and tax revenue, it comes at a price, urban political economists contend. Increases in tax revenue may be overwhelmed by larger increases in the demand for public services and the costs of additional infrastructure and expanded job opportunities may largely go to residents of other jurisdictions or new migrants to the area (Barnekov and Rich, 1989; Friedland, 1983; Molotch, 1976). Summing up this point, John Logan and Harvey Molotch (1987: 85) write: "for many places and times, growth is at best a mixed blessing." The public balance sheet seemingly could make a useful contribution to this research by providing urban political economists with an analytic framework to calculate and accentuate these public and community costs. In this way, the technique could allow for a more balanced assessment of the pro-growth policies favored by the "growth machine" interests (Molotch, 1976) that currently exercise hegemony over the local development agenda.

Another relatively new and lively body of research examining the social costs of private-sector development has been provoked by the ubiquitous phenomenon of urban sprawl. Once again, consistent with the public balance sheet perspective, researchers find that private decisions of investors (and the development patterns that result) impose burdensome costs on the public (and the larger community)—costs not factored into investors' private economic calculations (Persky and Wiewel, 1999: 140–42).

In a comprehensive review of the effects of sprawl (and economic segregation it exacerbates) Swanstrom (2000) identifies and explicates these myriad costs. This pattern of urban development, he explains: lessens the employment opportunities for poor residents of central cities, harms the overall economic vibrancy of the metropolitan region, drives up the cost of government services in both central cities and suburbs, increases the central city tax burden, negatively impacts the physical and psychological health of city dwellers and suburbanites alike, burdens the poor in central cities with additional consumer costs while fueling overconsumption (and the assumption of burdensome debt) in the suburbs, and exacerbates both central city and suburban crime rates (Swanstrom, 2000). To this list we can add environmental costs such as additional air and water pollution, the loss of greenspace and agricultural output, and the damage to ecosystems (Benfield, Raimi, and Chen, 1999; also see Ewing, 1997).

Engaging in the exercise of surveying these extensive public/community costs of sprawl leads Swanstrom to reflect upon the misguided way such costs are conceptualized by conventional economic analysis. Consistent with the public balance sheet's critique of this mode of analysis, he expresses a similar dissatisfaction with it: "To speak of these spatial effects as 'externalities,'" in the limited way that conventional economists' conceive of that term, "wrongly implies that they are marginal. . . . In fact, they are ubiquitous, complexly intertwined, and difficult to change" (Swanstrom, 2000: 78–79).

In this burgeoning literature on the costs of sprawl, it is again the case that researchers have yet to draw extensively upon the public balance sheet technique to frame their studies. Although currently overlooked by these researchers, the technique seemingly could make a useful contribution to this body of research, too, again by clearly calculating and accentuating the public and community costs imposed by private decision makers.

Policy Implications: Holding Private Actors Accountable

The public balance sheet focuses the attention of the evaluation of local development policy on the significant costs private decisions impose ("externalize") on the public sector (and the community as a whole). For practitioners of this approach, the policy implication logically derived from this insight is that, since it is the decisions of private actors that engender these costs, private actors should be held accountable for them (Smith, 1979; Feagin and Parker, 1990).

At the broadest level, public balance sheet advocates suggest the present system, which allows private actors largely to evade responsibility, is normatively undesirable from a political perspective and empirically unsustainable from an economic perspective. Smith (1979: 4), for example, quotes the insight of Peter Bearse, who proclaims—with poignancy—that: "A philosophy of government which says that the function of government is simply to pick up the dirty linen of private enterprise without affecting incentives to dirty the linen would bankrupt government and corrupt the political process." In more specific terms, these practitioners prescribe policies designed to hold private actors accountable by either preventing behaviors that externalize significant costs or by requiring payment of compensation.

At first glance, these general policy prescriptions seem roughly congruous with conventional economic analysis, which espouses the use of government authority to correct for negative externalities by proscribing the offending conduct or levying a tax or fee on it (Browning and Browning, 1983; Stokey and Zeckhauser, 1978). But once again, where the public balance sheet diverges from the analytical perspective of conventional economics is in its expansive conceptualization of the range and scope of what is considered to be an externality problem warranting corrective action.

Some externality problems fit the conventional model well. For example, when private production facilities pollute the air or water, this model prescribes environmental policies that either prevent the firm from polluting or that charge the firm a fee calibrated to the amount of the effluents it emits into the environment (see Browning and Browning, 1983: 38–40; Stokey and Zeckhauser, 1978: 311–14). Likewise, to take an example from economic development policy, the externalities generated by excessive investment (and the intensification of land use it causes) commonly leads rapidly growing communities to either employ zoning powers to constrain new development or to levy impact fees (exactions) on developers (fees based on the idea private land development imposes additional physical costs for roads, sewers, schools, etc., costs that should be borne by the private developers, rather than pubic taxpayers).

In contrast, conceptualizing externalities more expansively—as the public balance sheet concept does—inspires a range of more innovative (and socially transformative) policy prescriptions.

Take the impact fees (exactions) example. Traditional exactions simply require developers to provide "themselves" with the infrastructure needed to serve their new projects, "with amenities . . . accru[ing] to the property supplying them" and "local governments . . . merely [acting] as conduits for payments . . . [rather than] fulfilling broader public policy goals with the funds" (Garber, 1989: 16). Later, however, the understanding of the range and scope of the costs private investment externalizes onto the community was broadened, leading to the implementation of newer, more innovative (and redistributive) forms of exactions. Garber (1989: 16) recounts this evolution; "By the 1960s," she writes, "The *effects* of the ultimate use of land began to be treated as fair game by local governments, although those effects were often physically [i.e., geographically] removed from the development site. In short, exactions were redefined to include the obligation incurred when property transactions create social, economic or environmental costs to the larger community" (emphasis in original). Such an understanding of the external costs of property development, Garber (1990: 9–10) observes, opened the door for "a greatly expanded repertoire of methods for collecting social debts inherent in land use."

Notable among this repertoire are "linkage" or "linkage development" policies (Garber, 1990: 8–9; Garber, 1989: 16–17; also see Smith, 1989; Herrero, 1991). Such policies usually impose a fee (or exaction) on private investors in exchange for granting them the right to develop a city's prime (usually downtown) real estate by drawing a "link" between that development and the exacerbation of the city's social, economic, and environmental problems. To compensate the larger community, cities obligate developers to contribute to a special fund targeted to address pressing community needs for child care, job training, public transportation, and, most importantly, affordable housing (Levine, 1989: 30).[3] It is unsurprising that several analyses of urban problems—including the works of Feagin and Parker (1990: 291), Giloth (1988: 344) and Levine (1987: 119)—invoke the public balance sheet concept as the rationale for the adoption of linkage policies.

A Vermont law requiring that an "economic impact statement" be conducted to evaluate large development projects provides another example where a more expansive understanding of the external costs imposed by private investment leads to innovative policy. Based on the "economic impact statement" required by this law, a citizen review commission rejected Wal-Mart's attempt to open a large store in state. When the commission examined the full range of economic effects applying the "type of full-cost accounting" used by these impact statements (an accounting method not unlike a public balance sheet), it concluded that this prospective investment "would cost the community $3 for every $1 in benefits it created, as a result of its adverse [external] impact on local businesses and infrastructure" (Morris, 1998: 15).

Cases involving private capital *dis*investment provide further examples of how the public balance sheet's expansive conceptualization of externalities inspires innovative and socially transformative policy ideas.

Conventional economists rarely conceive of disinvestment as an externality problem for which private investors should be held accountable. They instead see disinvestment as part of the normal operation of well-functioning (rather than failing) market processes, as private actors reallocate capital in their efforts to secure the highest possible (risk-adjusted) returns (see Berliner, 1999: 238–39). In contrast, public balance sheet practitioners trace extensive external costs to disinvestment (such as the physical, social, individual, fiscal, and political costs described above), and the process of actually coming to terms with the extent of these costs wholly transforms their (and others') understanding of the parameters and dimensions of appropriate policy prescriptions.

This is exactly what happened to a federal judge presiding over legal action to prevent the shutdown of steel mills in Youngstown. Assessing the catastrophic social consequences of this private disinvestment drew the judge to a radically new and innovative understanding of private property law, one that suggested the possible existence of what Lynd (1987a: 927) calls a "community property right." The judge stated that:

> it seems to me that a property right has risen from this lengthy, long established relationship between United States Steel, the steel industry as an institution, the community in Youngstown, the people in Mahoning County and the Mahoning Valley in having given and devoted their lives to this industry. . . . I think the law can recognize the property right to the

> extent that U.S. Steel cannot leave that Mahoning Valley and the Youngstown area in a state of waste, that it cannot completely abandon its obligation to the community, because certain vested rights have arisen out of this long relationship and institution. (quoted in Lynd, 1987a: 940)

In the end, the judge could not find the legal basis for this new community property right, and ruled in favor of the company (Lynd, 1987a: 940). Vesting communities with rights over private property as a means of holding private actors accountable for the external costs they impose via disinvestment thus remained, as Lynd (1987a: 941) notes, "visionary, without apparent lodgment in existing law." Nevertheless, it remains clear how the public balance sheet's expansive conceptualization of these externalities can catalyze a transformation in both legal doctrine and the policy prescriptions enabled by doctrinal standards.

The same phenomenon provoked a metamorphosis in thinking about the proper uses of local government's eminent domain power, the power to take private property without the owner's consent upon paying just compensation if a public purpose is served. Traditionally, eminent domain has been employed to facilitate the process of land assembly to encourage private development or enhance public infrastructure. Increasingly, in the face of heightened capital mobility, local communities began to see this power in a more transformative light, understanding that it potentially could be used innovatively as protection against the worst pangs of corporate flight (Lynd, 1987: 941–45; Eisinger, 1988: 321–28; Portz, 1990: chap. 5; Imbroscio, 1993: 178). In the 1980s, many communities (including Oakland, California; New Bedford, Massachusetts; and Pittsburgh, Pennsylvania) attempted (or considered) using this power to condemn (acquire) the business facilities of enterprises seeking to relocate or discontinue operations in their cities. Most interesting for our purpose is that the basis for this action lay in the understanding that disinvestment imposed far ranging externalities on communities. It therefore was argued by communities that the effort to mitigate these costs (by preserving otherwise lost jobs) constituted a clear *public purpose,* hence opening the door for the legitimate use of eminent domain. Even though these efforts ultimately proved unsuccessful—being either disallowed by the courts or not fully followed through on by the communities themselves,[4] we nonetheless again see how the expansive conceptualization of externalities spawns innovation in the formulation of local development policy.

Guide to Activist and Positive Public Intervention

The public balance sheet has been used to draw attention to the social costs of private development—an essentially passive and negative exercise merely tallying costs and exacting accountability. It also can play a more activist and explicit role in policymaking—promoting the emphatic use of positive government to accomplish desirable collective ends. Specifically, this second conceptual use of the public balance sheet—ultimately rooted in the same basic logic as the first—is as a tool to guide public intervention into the market economy designed to stimulate economic development in communities.

The key postulate underlying the public balance sheet's policy prescriptions for economic development is that policymakers err when they assume a particular form of economic behavior is desirable or undesirable based solely on the actions of traditional market actors. Paralleling the disinvestment/investment dynamic framing the discussion above, development policy should not deem economic activities to be inefficient simply because market actors have shunned them due to the ostensible limited potential of these activities to generate private profits. Alternatively, when private actors do invest, this action should not automatically and unquestionably indicate that this behavior results in an efficient use of societal resources.

Public balance sheet practitioners adduce many reasons for not blindly accepting this so-called judgment of the market as their guide for prescribing economic development policies.

Market Failure

First and foremost, as elaborated upon above, the market may be "failing" in any number of ways, especially by not taking into consideration the range of positive and negative externalities impacting the public (or the larger community). Insofar as the market is failing, its judgments will not reflect the maximization of social welfare; therefore it logically follows that such judgments should not be the sole basis for policy prescriptions (Smith, 1979).

Plural Values

In the case of the disinvestment by private actors, the economic activities in question still might be judged profitable by market criteria, just not profitable enough for large corporations demanding annual returns topping 20 percent (see Morris, 1982: 38–39; Osborne and Gaebler, 1992: 216; Lynd,

1987b). In contrast, as Alperovitz and Faux (1984: 149) note: "When the public sector—either a government or a collection of people connected by their geographic community—is seen as an investor in its own right, perception of profits can change dramatically." Relatively low profit levels might be acceptable to a local polity in order to enhance other values it deems desirable—e.g., economic stability, equality, community, etc.—that is, other values beyond simply the achievement of maximum economy efficiency. Recognizing this plurality of values, the public balance sheet allows for the design of economic development policies that better reflect the normative ideals of democratic decision-making.

Socially Constructed Markets

Third, the workings of market processes are not driven exclusively by neutral, impersonal forces. As is often demonstrated, markets are, instead, socially constructed, and therefore infected with myriad other values and biases apart from strict economic rationality. Nowhere is this phenomenon more evident than in America's inner cities, where racial prejudices warp and distort economic decision-making (see Dymski, 1997: 55). For example, as Adolph Reed (1988: 170) points out, "parcels of [urban] land occupied by minorities are underutilized . . . because the presence of minority populations lowers market values." Race, filtered through the conceptual lens of largely white investors, *in and of itself*, determines investment risks and land values. Two cases evince this dynamic well. Forced by the Community Reinvestment Act (CRA) to make home mortgages (and other loans) in lower-income, predominantly minority neighborhoods, lenders found that this market, redlined as too risky for decades, was—in reality—profitable (see Imbroscio, 1997: 110–11). Likewise, for years private investors missed opportunities to invest profitably in retail ventures based in inner cities, and only now is market "rationality" beginning to conform with economic reality (as, in the words of a recent news headline, "More Retailers are [now] Sold on Cities," Fletcher, 1999: E1).

Miscalculations

Finally, market actors may simply make miscalculations about the economic viability of certain investments, causing an overinvestment in unprofitable ventures and an underinvestment in profitable ones. The multibillion-dollar losses racked up by the savings-and-loan industry in 1980s stand as a monument to the former (Kuttner, 1997: 22); the results of a program to use federal job training funds to conduct feasibility studies of industrial plants slated for shutdown offers a glimpse of the latter. These studies showed that, upon close scrutiny, many firms turned out to be economically viable after all—an indication of how many plants regularly closed by their corporate owners might be instead saved or refurbished (Williamson, Imbroscio, and Alperovitz, 2002).

Policy Implications: Intervening More Rationally

Having rejected the "judgment of market" as a flawed guide for economic development policy, the public balance sheet approach instead examines the full range of taxpayer and public benefits generated by a policy in comparison to total societal costs. As noted above, Alperovitz and Faux (1979: iii) stress that the technique therefore "provides a more comprehensive and rational guide" for public intervention because it does not simply focus on "the narrow considerations of private profit and loss." While the private profit criterion remains an important factor in this guide—without which policies could lead to gross inefficiencies—the public balance sheet situates this criterion within a broader analytical framework (Smith, 1979: 18–19; Luria and Russell, 1981: 29).

Policy prescriptions flowing from this perspective again vary in a general sense according to whether the economic development issue at hand involves private-sector disinvestment or investment. In the case of private disinvestment, the public balance sheet becomes a tool to evaluate if *public resources should be committed* to sustain and/or buttress some economic activity eschewed by the private sector. In cases where the private sector desires to invest, this tool evaluates if *such investment should be encouraged or discouraged* based on, for example, whether it tends to strengthen or weaken the local economy.

Most of the public balance sheet work to date has focused on the appropriate public policy response to private disinvestment, especially in the form of plant closures (Alperovitz and Faux, 1984; Luria and Russell, 1981; Smith, 1979). Alperovitz and Faux (1984: 147–48), for example, explain how an effort to reopen and modernize the recently closed Campbell Works steel mill in Youngstown (under the ownership of a new, locally based corporation) justifiably could have been granted a public subsidy of several hundred million dollars. When evaluated according to the accounting framework of the public balance sheet, the massive level of government expenditures/revenue losses averted, added together with the expected generation of moderate private returns, combined to make the planned reopening effort a potentially worthy outlet for public investment. Luria and Russell (1981) used the public balance sheet framework in a similar way to justify public subsidy for their plan to "rationally reindustrialize" Detroit. The following excerpt from their analysis expresses the logic of their policy prescriptions (remembering of course that the dollar figures are from 1980):

> Imagine a Detroit enterprise that employs 250 workers earning $15,000 each year, of whom two-thirds own homes and half live in Detroit. The enterprise, let us say, is losing $500,000 per year. Assuming that closing the facility makes private accounting sense to its owners, let us ask whether closing the facility is also rational for the total society. On the negative side, operating the plant costs society $500,000, the private loss. On the positive side, keeping the enterprise open garners the society about $172,000 in property taxes, $57,000 in worker-paid city income taxes, $138,000 in state income taxes, and $487,000 in federal income taxes. It also saves $920,000 in unemployment insurance (a one-time cost), welfare, and food stamps transfer payments. Adding these social benefits, one gets about $1,770,000 in year one and $850,000 each year thereafter. Netting out the annual $500,000 loss, over a decade society is better off to the tune of $4.4 million by keeping the plant open. (Luria and Russell, 1981: 31)

The public balance sheet also can be utilized to formulate appropriate economic development policy in cases where private actors seek to invest in a local economy. In these cases, as noted above, the technique examines the full range of public and community benefits compared to total societal costs in order to determine whether this investment should be encouraged or discouraged. Rather than simply letting the market judge the issue, the public balance sheet therefore evaluates private investment according to a broader set of criteria, especially its tendency to strengthen or weaken the local economy.

This type of evaluation was a central objective of an economic development initiative launched in the city of St. Paul, Minnesota in the 1980s (see Imbroscio, 1997: chap. 3). The St. Paul initiative, which sought to create a more "self-reliant city" by building a "homegrown economy," evaluated new business development "not only for the services or products . . . [these businesses] offer but for the way they affect the local economy" (Office of Mayor, St. Paul, 1983: 12). Of particular importance for this evaluation was the understanding, gleaned from the seminal work of Jane Jacobs (1969; 1984), of the crucial role played by import substitution in strengthening local economies. A key economic development official explained the approach this way: To the "extent we had businesses in St. Paul that would essentially be importing things into the city and exporting capital out, this was a net loss to St. Paul." The goal of the city's development policy under this initiative, he added, "was to reverse this situation . . . by understanding that certain kinds of businesses were good [on this score] and others were not" and encouraging the development of former, while discouraging the latter (as quoted in Imbroscio, 1997: 79).

Hence, in cases involving both market disinvestment and investment, the public balance sheet practitioners see the technique as able to guide economic development officials to intervene more rationally by considering whether this intervention generates greater public/community benefits compared to total societal costs (rather than relying solely on market-based criteria and judgments). Yet, upon careful examination, it is not altogether clear what the public balance sheet would add here to the current practice of mainstream development policy. Consider cases where public resources need to be committed to sustain economic activities otherwise shunned by the private sector. Public subsidization, of one form or another, almost always finds its justification in the claim that these subsidies generate greater benefits for the public and broader community in relation to overall costs, e.g., tax incentives for business attraction and infrastructure expenditures for items such as sport stadiums, convention centers, etc. Therefore, scholars (such as Levine, 1987, and Feagin and Parker, 1990) who implore local development officials to utilize public balance sheets to guide policy formulation seem simply to advocate what these officials claim they already do.

Nevertheless, it appears that the widespread embrace of the public balance sheet as a policymaking tool would effect two significant modifications in current practice.

First, local development policy might more intensely accentuate the benefits accruing to the public (and community) at large. Reviewing various approaches to development policy, Fisher and Peters (1998: 217) explain how policy guided by the public balance sheet would reflect this emphasis: "Others take a public balance sheet approach. . . . A cost-benefit analysis of economic development programs should be conducted, . . . weighing the public benefits against the public costs. Public funds should be used, according to these advocates, only for projects or firms that satisfy public-interest performance standards regarding labor practices, workplace safety, environmental record, wage levels, or the provisions of health insurance." For many critics of local economic policy, this change would inject a much-needed corrective to the biases plaguing current practice. As Barnekov and Rich (1989) demonstrate, *in actuality* the use of public subsidies often fails to provide substantial public/community benefits compared to the benefits garnered by private actors, despite the claims of local development officials to the contrary. They point out, for example, that "local economic development programs designed to use public funds to leverage private investment frequently result in reverse leverage—that is, private enterprise often leverages public funds to accomplish its own development objectives" (1989: 216).

Second, local development policymaking might be less constrained by the ideological blinders currently delimiting appropriate modes of public intervention into the market system. For example, though the current practice of development policy clearly views massive public subsidy as a legitimate role for public policy—witness the billions spent by states and cities on tax incentives and infrastructure expenditures—the expenditure of public funds goes almost exclusively to support privatistic forms of local development, where "priority . . . [is] given to the needs of the private sector, and public resources must be focused on the creation and enhancement of private investment opportunities" (Barnekov and Rich, 1989: 213). By placing the accent on the *public,* the public balance sheet potentially moves local development policymaking away from this strict orthodoxy of privatism and toward imaginative and innovative development policies more publicly oriented in nature.

In fact, if the public benefits outweighed total societal costs, the public balance sheet might even warrant the most radical of public interventions into the market economy: local public ownership of productive assets. Rather than justifying "lemon socialism," where the public costs exceed public benefits, this technique would only prescribe the creation of public enterprises producing the opposite result. Many states and cities are currently pursuing public ownership in various forms as a local development strategy, owning and/or operating enterprises in realms of commerce such as electric power, telecommunications, banking and insurance, venture capital provision, real estate, commercial and retail services, professional sports, recreation, and a variety of ecological areas (Imbroscio, 1995; Williamson, Imbroscio, and Alperovitz, 2002). Even mainstream thinkers such as Osborne and Gaebler (1992) now understand the value of casting off the shackles of privatism in order to fashion innovative development solutions involving local public ownership. As part of their "reinventing government" agenda, Osborne and Gaebler point out that: "In reality, there are several good reasons why government [by engaging in public enterprise] *should* sometimes compete with the private sector" (Osborne and Gaebler, 1992: 216). Insofar as the public balance sheet gains wider use as a policymaking tool for local economic development, the climate for creative policy formulation along these lines would seem to be improved.

Challenges, Responses, and Agenda for Future Research

We have seen thus far that the public balance sheet can be employed both as a tool for tallying the social costs of private development decisions and as a guide for public intervention. Whether it *ought* to be employed is another matter. Clearly, the technique faces serious challenges—challenges that public balance sheet partisans need to confront head on. I conclude by reviewing some of the most salient of these challenges and suggesting some possible avenues of response. This exercise, in turn, points to an agenda for future research.

A key objection of conventional economists to the widespread use of public balance sheets would be that the technique encourages the propping up of firms unable to attract sufficient productive economic resources (land, labor, and capital) through the private market, thus creating barriers to the dynamic movement of these resources out of declining industries and technologies to those industries and technologies on the rise. Under these conditions economic processes would be too static, resulting in large losses in economic efficiency.

This issue raises a legitimate concern, one that even ardent supporters of public balance sheet technique recognize (Alperovitz and Faux, 1984: 150). It can be addressed on two levels, however.

First, recall that the technique still factors investment returns (e.g., private profitably) into its accounting framework (albeit as one of many ledger entries). Hence, if investment returns were extremely poor in a given enterprise due to anemic demand for its product, the public balance sheet most likely would not prescribe that public resources be committed to it. Take for example the scenario described by Luria and Russell (1981: 31) excerpted above. If the enterprise they discuss were likely to lose $1,000,000 annually rather than $500,000, public intervention into market processes would not be deemed rational, as total societal returns from this intervention would be negative.

Nonetheless, conventional economists no doubt would continue to question the public balance sheet logic of subsidizing firms not sanctioned by the market (after all, Luria and Russell's hypothetical enterprise is losing $500,000 a year), as this action still inhibits market dynamism by obstructing the flow of productive resources (especially capital) into more efficient uses. Therefore, their objection must be addressed on a second, more profound level.

Namely, it needs to be understood that, while the economic *dynamism* of marketplace clearly yields efficiency gains for society, such gains also result from the economic *stability* of communities (Williamson, Imbroscio, and Alperovitz, 2002: chap. 1)—something likely to be enhanced if public balance sheets were in widespread use. We saw above, for example, how the community economic *in*stability engendered by capital mobility and disinvestment results in the inefficient "throwing away" of physical infrastructure and the erosion of social capital, among other significant costs. We also saw how this same economic instability imposed on communities by the phenomenon of urban sprawl leads to myriad inefficiencies for both cities and suburbs alike. So, if market dynamism and community stability *both* produce efficiencies for society, it remains an open question which force is more powerful and, more precisely, what the appropriate trade-off should be between them.

Unfortunately, there currently exists a paucity in the extant knowledge needed to answer this question. This paucity is due in large part to the methodological biases built into the neo-classical paradigm that imperiously reigns over the modern study of economics. Rather than approaching research questions in a "value-free" manner, as conventional economists usually claim, this paradigm intensely focuses on documenting—in both conceptual and empirical terms—the virtues of market dynamism, while practically ignoring the virtues of community stability.

Pointing to our lack of useable knowledge regarding the relative efficiencies of dynamism and stability raises another more general challenge facing the public balance sheet. Like all attempts to make decision-making more comprehensive and rational, the technique demands a considerable amount of information. In the case of the public balance sheet, it is necessary to understand with accuracy the effects of private-sector disinvestment and investment on communities. Much of this information is not currently available, however. Once again, this lacuna stems in part from the biases built into the discipline of economics. In addition, much of the required data is highly intangible in nature, such as the human, social, or political costs imposed on communities by private disinvestment decisions. This intangibility poses obvious operationalization and measurement problems.

The most befitting response to this challenge is simply to accept it as a call, not to abandon the effort to develop a workable public balance sheet evaluation methodology, but rather as a challenge to frame and execute a reconstituted agenda for future economic development research. Unlike much of the work currently conducted in the field, this agenda affords researchers an opportunity to conduct socially valuable studies that can have a real practical impact on the quality of public decision-making and local community life.

In specific terms, the effort to develop a public balance sheet methodology revolves around three central questions that frame the basic issues for future research:

- In conceptual terms, what are the full range of social and public costs and benefits for communities generated by private-sector disinvestment and investment?
- In empirical terms, how can these costs and benefits be numerically estimated? (including intangibles such as the value of: social capital, the physical and psychological well-being of human beings, or a healthy local polity).
- Based on this conceptual and empirical research, what are some appropriate economic development policy responses that flow from the use of the public balance sheet? What are the political, technical, fiscal, and legal barriers confronting these policies? How can these barriers be overcome?

One promising start on the path to answer these questions can be found in the recent work on urban sprawl. This research conceptualizes sprawl's social and public costs and benefits broadly, and has begun to develop solid empirical estimates of these costs and benefits, while at the same time formulating corrective policy responses (see, e.g., Swanstrom, 2000; Ewing, 1997; Persky and Wiewel, 1999).[5] Further research in this vein can contribute significantly to the development of a public balance sheet methodology by reaching beyond the study of urban sprawl, and exploring the social and public costs and benefits for communities generated by a wider range of economic and spatial processes of the contemporary American political economy.

Notes

This chapter was written during my appointment as a Senior Research Associate at the National Center for Economic and Security Alternatives (NCESA) in Washington, D.C. I thank the Center's president, Gar Alperovitz, for providing the research and staff support that greatly aided my work on this project. For providing comment, suggestions, and encouragement on earlier drafts, I gratefully acknowledge Bob Beauregard, Laura Reese, Todd Swanstrom, and Robyne Turner, as well as my NCESA colleagues Alex Campbell, Preston Quesenberry, and Kristin Rusch.

1. As Buss and Yancer (1999: 34) point out, cost-benefit analysis (CBA), conventional economics' key policymaking tool, rarely includes an assessment of the externalities arising from economic development policies in part because "[t]hese spillover effects" are "assume[d] . . . [to be] minimal."

2. As Lynd (1987a: 926–27) explains in his penetrating study of both Youngstown and Pittsburgh, the massive capital disinvestment occurring during this period in these cities caused the traditional distinction between the public and the private to become contested: "The traumatic collapse of the steel industries in those communities, with the social distress that followed, led to the appearance of new ideas. Local residents began to articulate and explore the . . . [idea] that *private decisions with catastrophic social consequences are really public decisions*" (emphasis added).

3. Linkage policies in San Francisco and Boston date to the early 1980s; by the early 1990s, at least 15 cities had implemented linkage policies, including Seattle (WA), Santa Monica (CA), Cambridge (MA), Cherry Hill (NJ), Hartford (CT), and Palo Alto (CA) (Herrero, 1991: 4–7).

4. As Eisinger (1988: 325) notes, however, the legality of these efforts was never fully and conclusively tested through litigation.

5. Another potentially useful body of research to guide the future development of the public balance sheet, especially on the conceptual side, is the work of "rebel [ecological] economists" to measure the environmental costs of development (see Passell, 1990).

FOUR

A Review of Alternative Economic Base Study Methods for Community Economic Development

Jordan S. Yin

The practice of community economic development has expanded rapidly in recent years and an increasing number of public, private, and nonprofit organizations are working to revitalize urban neighborhoods and communities. Although the field has established practices for evaluating development initiatives on a project basis—such as feasibility studies or financial pro forma—the field lacks a comprehensive framework informing development planning and evaluation. Unlike city- or regional-level economic development planning, the practice of community economic development lacks a general descriptive method for understanding the economic structure of its communities. If community economic development is to be viewed as a process of structural change rather than a simple matter of aggregate growth or decline, then there is a need for descriptive economic base study methods based on an understanding of the economic structure of distressed neighborhoods.

A review of efforts to understand and describe the economic base of urban neighborhoods over the last three decades of the community economic development movement indicates that there have been few attempts at this sort of analysis, as it has been generally overlooked due to a variety of conceptual and methodological challenges. However, a number of existing analyses illustrate innovative methods that contrast with traditional economic base study methods by incorporating analyses of the neighborhood social economy, as well as community-level factors that affect income distribution and wealth accumulation. These studies describe the neighborhood economic base through "balance of payments" and "transaction matrix" methods that emphasize inflows and outflows of community income, as well as linkages within the community economy. Alternative economic base study methods provide an important set of tools for planning and evaluating community economic development programs by focusing attention on the structural strengths and weaknesses of community economies.

Understanding the Economic Base of Urban Neighborhoods

The traditional economic base study has long been an essential component of the economic development toolkit. The typical economic base study applied at the city- or regional-level employs an "export base" model of development where manufacturing industries produce goods for export that in turn support service industries. This economic base provides income to the local population which then expends a portion of this income locally (Tiebout 1962; Krikelas 1992). An economic base study typically accounts for output and/or employment levels found in manufacturing- and service-sector industries, and sometimes accounts for interindustry transactions representing the chain of inputs necessary to turn raw goods into finished products.

However, for community economic development efforts addressing neighborhood-scale territories with distressed economies, the traditional economic base study model presents an incomplete framework. Beginning in the late 1960s, one line of investigation began to examine how the economic structure of the so-called ghetto economy differed from that of more prosperous areas. A comprehensive review of the literature of the day is given by Harrison (1974) who characterizes these distressed economies as having three elements in common: irregular sources of income due to high unemployment and dependence on transfer (welfare), informal, and criminal payments; too few stores and services to meet local consumer demand; and low levels of local business and housing ownership. A number of studies documented specific elements of the economic structure of poor urban neighborhoods. For example, Harrison and Vietorisz (1970) and Aldrich (1973) conducted labor market studies indicating that a the key causes of underemployment were poor education, lack of transportation and the tendency of non-resident business owners to not hire local residents in both commercial and industrial occupations. A study of consumer spending in Cleveland's Hough neighborhood contracted by the U.S. Office of Economic Opportunity's Special Impact Program, Oakland and his colleagues (1971) determined that local residents spent only 38 cents per dollar within the neighborhood and because many of the neighborhood's stores and services employed or were owned by non-residents, consumer spending in Hough had a spin-off impact of only 3 cents for every dollar spent within the neighborhood.

As various elements of the urban neighborhood economy came to be understood, the emphasis on an overall descriptive framework turned to examining how community income was obtained and how it flowed through the neighborhood, rather than the measurement of a traditional manufacturing base or interindustry transactions (Fusfeld 1973; Browne 1971; Davis 1972; Fusfeld and Bates 1984). Fusfeld (1973) delivers a representative treatment in which household income inflows from earned wages, transfer payments, and business income cycle through local business enterprises and informal activities, but also leaves the community territory through outflows of payments, including purchases by residents outside of their neighborhood, resident spending at non–locally owned businesses, rent paid to absentee landlords, taxes, loan repayments, savings and investments with commercial banks, and payments to organized crime (including gambling and narcotics). As a result of these inflow and outflow patterns, Davis (1972) observes: " the structure of the ghetto generates an outflow of money and labor resources, leaving a very narrow economic base for the development of the ghetto domestic sector" (43).

A complementary perspective on community economics based on "economic democracy" emerged in the mid-1970s in response to both the pressures of economic restructuring faced by traditional manufacturing communities, such as Youngstown (Smith, 1979), and by social movements pursuing municipal radicalism, such as Berkeley (Clavel, 1986). A passage by Berkeley's Community Ownership Organizing Project (1976), is representative of the genre: "[we seek] those economic and political polices which will lead the redistribution of city resources from the wealthy, those who have traditionally benefited from municipal policy, to those members of the community who have received little from city government in the past" (ii). Here, there was an open questioning of mechanisms that distributed income and allowed for community wealth accumulation. Many elements of the neighborhood economy were examined for their distributional impacts. The Institute for Local Self Reliance conducted energy cost studies to determine the outflow of community funds to private utilities in arguing for public ownership of utilities (Morris, 1982). Likewise, franchise and corporate retail stores, such as McDonald's restaurants, were examined to demonstrate how these enterprises drained income away from local communities, and community reinvestment advocates began studying bank lending practices to determine if banks lent as much to inner-city neighborhoods as the neighborhood's own deposits warranted (Morris, 1982; Gunn and Gunn, 1991). In general, both the "economy democracy" and "ghetto economic development" literature developed an understanding of how endogenous development strengthening internal community linkages could rebuild and restructure community economies.

Further efforts to conceptualize the urban neighborhood economy have emphasized "mechanisms linking economic development at the regional and the neighborhood level" (Wiewel et al., 1989, 94), suggesting that neighborhood economies are dependent on larger economic forces and, therefore, endogenous development efforts must be complemented by efforts to integrate community economies with external labor, financial and business markets (Tietz, 1989; Wiewel et al., 1989; Gottlieb, 1997; Nowak, 1997). At one extreme, Michael Porter's influential proposal to harness the competitive advantage of the inner-city likens the relationship between community and region to that of an international trade relationship. He suggests that the inner-city holds private business investment and marketing opportunities by serving traditionally under-served retail markets, increasing central city linkages to regional industries, and making use of the inner-city's traditionally underemployed labor force (Porter, 1997). Yet, an economic development perspective emphasizing exogenous relationships can benefit from a more detailed understanding of the neighborhood economy, as it is the community economic base of inflows, outflows, and linkages that determines how exogenous development relationships will benefit the local area.

Methods for Community Economic Analysis

Descriptive economic analysis has long been part of national and regional economic development planning; indeed, there are entire families of analytical methods in these fields. Yet, these generally have not been applied to community economic analysis because they do not easily "scale down" for use at the community level. However, a better understanding of the structure of urban neighborhood economies has informed a variety of innovative study methods, including "balance of payments" and "transaction matrix" approaches. Although a widespread practice of community economic accounting has yet to emerge, these examples illustrate how such studies can reveal important characteristics of community economies and suggest alternative community economic development strategies.

Balance of Payments Approaches

A balance of payments approach to describing the neighborhood economy is much like the single-entry bookkeeping one does with a personal checkbook. A community balance of payments illustrates the sources and uses of community income, with an emphasis on tracking how dollars flow in and out of the neighborhood territory. An early example using this method is Richard Schaffer's (1973) "community income accounts" study of the Brooklyn neighborhoods of Bedford-Stuyvesant and Borough Park. The study was sponsored by the Bedford-Stuyvesant Restoration Corporation, one of the nation's first community development corporations, which served a dense urban neighborhood of about 220,000 people, 80 percent of whom were African American. Bennett Harrison describes this as the "only sound set of community income accounts" at the time (1974: 8) and the study framework incorporates much of the conceptual commentary on "ghetto economic development" (Schaffer, 1973: 1–5). The study draws on a wide range of governmental data sources, as well as original survey data, in order to assemble the community accounts.

Schaffer's income flow framework identifies residents, businesses, and landlords as three basic entities through which various income flows are passed through. During Schaffer's study year, he estimates that the Bedford-Stuyvesant community received about $850 million in inflows, but more than $640 million left the community through outflows. Households accounted for $433 million in inflows, including income, transfer payments, and consumer credit; however, much of their income did not recirculate within the community economy as nearly 80 percent of household income left the community through personal tax payments, housing payments to non-local landlords and housing dis-investment, consumer spending outside of the community, and various expenditures on credit repayment, gambling and narcotics. Likewise, local businesses brought in $345 million in gross sales, two-thirds of which were "exports" to places outside of the community; however, more than $200 million of these receipts left the community as payments to outsiders.

In comparing Bedford-Stuyvesant to the slightly more affluent, but still lower middle class, Borough Park neighborhood, Schaffer found that though the two neighborhoods have a proportionally similar level of gross income that the Borough Park area retained much more of its wealth due to higher levels of local housing and business ownership. In general, this community income flow study emphasizes the importance of local expenditures and local ownership in contributing to the health of the neighborhood economy and the author further notes that "the use of such accounts can show the impact of various development programs, such as those undertaken by CDCs and Model Cities agencies" (Schaffer, 1974: 32).

Another example is the *Income and Capital Flow Study of East Oakland,* conducted by Henze, Lillow, and Kirschner (1979). The East Oakland economy is conceptualized as the product of three factors: the initial income base of the community considering wages, transfers and business profits; the effect of "leakage" away from the local economy through housing payments, commercial and retail purchasing outside of the area or at non–locally owned businesses, non-resident employment within the local area and credit payments to extra-local financial institutions; and the pattern of capital investment and disinvestment in the housing and building stock of the area (1979: 4–5). This framework contrasts with a traditional economic base study by emphasizing the role of income flows and by examining wealth accumulation mechanisms, such as local versus non-local business ownership and the role of financial institutions.

Henze and her colleagues find that the East Oakland economy is one where community income escapes quickly. The study observes that "housing expenditures in East Oakland represent one of the major leakages of the community's income and capital," estimating "an outflow of $290–335 million in rent dollars in the coming five-year period" and approximately $400 million in mortgage payments over the same period that are unlikely to be reinvested in the East Oakland community (Henze et al., 1979: 44). Household spending also has the effect of draining income away from the community. Of $450 million in annual household retail and service spending, East Oakland residents spend $300 million outside of the community and an additional $85 million leaves East Oakland by virtue of non-local business ownership (Henze et al., 1979: 1).

Based on their findings, the authors suggest that "the benefits of traditional economic development will accrue largely to residents outside of the East Oakland community. As an alternative, East Oaklanders can pursue strategies for locally-based, community-controlled economic development" (Henze et al., 1979: 5). Among specific recommendations, they suggest the conversion of rental housing to cooperative housing, the establishment of a community development corporation for commercial revitalization, and establishing an community development financial institution. The community development corporation is described as "an organization that can provide for residents' partnership in neighborhood economic development" and could facilitate cooperative ownership of retail enterprises resulting in the retention of an additional $45 million in community income per year (Henze et al., 1979: 61).

More recently, the Crossroads Resource Center has prepared "Community Income Statement and Balance Sheets" for various neighborhoods in Minneapolis and St. Paul during the 1990s (Meter, 1998). These studies have examined how income and expenditures flow through a community's households, real estate owners, businesses and nonprofit organizations, and the informal economy. In Minneapolis's Camden neighborhood, it was determined that "though more than $1.2 billion of economic activity takes place in the community, very few of these financial exchanges promote the accumulation of wealth by community members" as household expenditures on goods and services at non-local establishments, rental payments to absentee owners and mortgage payments to secondary financial institutions, and weak links between local businesses and residents drained resources away from the community (Meter, 1995: 3–5). The study recommends a number of corrective development strategies, including: resident ownership of local businesses, further clustering of locally owned firms, and resident commitment to socially responsible local spending.

An innovative aspect of these reports is that the studies were conducted with the cooperation of the various community sponsors—including local residents, community organizations, local businesses, and churches—in order "to assist in framing questions and performing research" (Meter, 1998: 2). Moreover, the study process established a participatory venue for examining the community economy, as noted by Ken Meter: "neighborhoods must perform their own accounting of local economic conditions if they are to achieve neighborhood goals. In this respect, a community is no different from a family that must balance its checkbook and review its portfolio to learn if it is gaining or losing ground" (1998: 1).

Transaction Matrix Approaches

A second methodological approach involves building a transaction matrix of the community economy, drawing on methods associated with "input-output tables" and "social accounting matrices" (Leatherman and Marcouiller, 1999). A transaction matrix documents the linkages between various elements of the neighborhood economy and shows how each "sector" of the community economy is related to the other sectors. For example, data on the household sector would show all the sources of household income (e.g., wages, investment profits, etc.) and show how that household income is expended to other sectors of the community economy (e.g., rents to landlords, consumer spending to stores, etc.). Like the balance of payments approach, this method incorporates inflows and outflows of income from the community territory, but it is a double-entry rather than single-entry accounting system since one sector's outlays also represent another sector's income within the community.

This approach has been used extensively for city- and regional-level economic development planning where input-output tables have been prepared to illustrate the relationship between the various economic sectors of a local economy, especially interindustry transactions among manufacturing and service industries. However, there is no evidence that similar efforts have ever been seriously undertaken by the community development movement, though there was a conference on input-output analysis held by the Center for Community Economic Development in 1976 (Block, 1977). In the early 1970s, the U.S. Community Services Administration sponsored an input-output study for the Kentucky Highlands CDC, a ten-county rural region. However, it received a lukewarm reception, according to Harvey Block, who performed the study: "the funding agency has apparently decided that the methodology is too sophisticated for use by CDCs. I find this decision particularly questionable in view of the fact that no planning methods having the breath of input/output are currently in use" (Block, 1977: ii).

Block offers two reasons why input-output was not likely to be applied to urban neighborhoods at the time. First, the method was not encouraged by federal evaluators due to its technical complexities. Second, Block notes that this study method was not necessarily applicable to impoverished urban areas: "input-output analysis is the articulation of a general theory of growth and development based on the interaction that occurs between production sectors. Such a theory would be applicable to a geopolitical area in which production sectors exist or which has natural resources around which production sectors could be developed. Attempts to consider inner cities in the light seem unproductive" (Block, 1977: 133).

As Block notes, regional input-output models typically involve advanced economic modeling methods, making them less accessible to community development practitioners. However, a recent example of a traditional input-output model with community economic development applications was developed by the University of Illinois' Regional Economics Applications Laboratory (REAL) in cooperation with Chicago United, a non-profit organization (REAL 1999; Okuyama et al., 1999). The study provides an "analysis of the nature and strength of existing economic interdependence between four areas in the Chicago metropolitan region, with particularly attention directed to predominantly minority areas," including south and west neighborhoods within the city of Chicago that have populations of about 180,000 and 120,000, respectively (REAL, 1999: 6). An examination of the internal linkages within neighborhoods and their relationship to other parts of the Chicago metropolitan area, indicates that linkages within the South and West Chicago communities are relatively underdeveloped. Every dollar of consumer spending by South Chicago households has a total spin-off impact of about 99 cents throughout the metropolitan area, but only 28 cents of that spin-off impact occurs with the South Chicago community; likewise, household consumer spending in the West Chicago community stimulates 85 cents in spin-off impact in the region, but only 6 cents of that occurs within the community (REAL, 1999: 24).

A simplified transaction matrix study—relying on census data, local government data and a locally administered survey—was recently produced by Michigan State University's Community and Economic Development Program. Their "Community Income and Expenditures Model" study of Southwest Detroit examined the linkages between households, local businesses, government agencies and nonprofit organizations. This effort indicated that while approximately $1.5 billion flowed through the community, only $214 million in activity was recirculated locally. In particular, the study identified weak linkages between local households and local businesses. While households received a total of $310 million in income, only $57 million was recirculated to local businesses; conversely, while local businesses generated nearly $1.2 billion in total income, only $56 million was paid out to local households and another $75 million to other local businesses. As a result of these weak community linkages and large income flows away from the community, household consumer spending in the Southwest Detroit community has a spin-off impact of only 23 cents for every dollar spent locally. Like the community economy studies in Minneapolis and St. Paul, these studies also engaged local parties in carrying out the study process (Community and Economic Development Program, 1997: 14).

The most ambitious effort to date in accounting for an urban neighborhood is Sam Cole's "community accounting matrix" for East Buffalo (Cole, 1994). This study provides a more complete social accounting of the neighborhood economy by incorporating a description of household income and expenditures, and income distribution resulting from business ownership, in addition to transaction data on industry and service sectors. Additionally, these community accounts include a demographic disaggregation of the community with information on the economic characteristics of the African American, Elderly and Female-with-Child sub-populations and, like the REAL study of Chicago, the East Buffalo study links the Eastside community to the remainder of the Buffalo metropolitan area. The study procedure is based on both an economic modeling estimation procedure, as well as some locally collected survey data.

This community accounting matrix indicates that the Eastside community economy suffers from both an underdeveloped internal structure and a dependent relationship with the metropolitan area. The study indicates that for each dollar of goods or services sold in the Eastside there is a total spin-off impact of an additional $1.15 throughout the metropolitan area, but only 6 cents of that spin-off activity remains in the Eastside (Cole, 1994: 116). Similarly, the Buffalo study indicates that an income stimulus to Eastside households would move quickly away from the community, as each additional dollar of income earned (or transferred) to households results in only 16 cents of spin-off impact within the Eastside (Cole, 1994: 117). Cole notes that this community accounting approach "has antecedents in national and regional development through the exploitation of community-level backward and forward linkages, and the 'ghetto economic development' strategies of earlier years" (Cole, 1996: 1). Based on this analysis, Cole's recommendations for a development strategy emphasize local initiative, but also acknowledge the area's need to attract extra-local resources: "neither stand-alone projects, such as new shopping plazas, nor even a 'territorial' approach, are likely to be effective in stemming the 'leaky bucket' syndrome of the last decades, unless considerable efforts are made to 'network' locally run enterprises in order to boost income gained through import substitution and export enhance strategies, adding weight to arguments for directing resources to neighborhood networks and community coalitions" (Cole, 1996: 1).

Uses of Alternative Analysis Methods for Community Economic Development Planning and Evaluation

Much as architects make blueprints or physicians take x-rays, the practice of community economic development can benefit from anatomical descriptions of the community economy. Such analyses represent a valuable tool for diagnosing challenges facing communities and can play an important role in the planning and evaluation of development initiatives. While methods of community economic analysis have been under-explored in both the academic and professional spheres over the last thirty years, a variety of recent efforts indicates that this type of study can improve planning processes, support alternative strategies and inform the role of community institutions in community economic development.

Community accounting methods can stimulate participatory planning processes for community economic development. As Meter (1998) observes of his experience in the Twin Cities: "neighborhoods typically neglect to measure their own economic assets and to set goals for strengthening their local economy. Unless they do so, especially in a competitive environment, economic and social impacts on the neighborhood are more likely to be negative" (Meter, 1999: 1). Most of the studies reviewed were prepared by academic or professional researchers; however, two examples employed community participation in the study process. Although the community economic base study methods used in the Southwest Detroit and Twin Cities studies are less complex than in the other examples, such efforts are capable of bringing important new information to the surface and engaging citizen participation in the study process makes it more likely that the study's results will be accepted and used by the community. Study methods involving more complicated techniques often carry a certain amount of technical mystique with them and may be viewed skeptically. However, such studies can be especially valuable if they are presented as a starting point for public discussion of the local economy and allow for confirmatory feedback processes (such as citizen forums or focus groups) in order to legitimate the data and spur further interest in community economic development planning. While the objective of a community economic base study is to provide an empirical portrait of the community economy, such studies also play a valuable heuristic role in focusing attention on community development as a process of structural change.

An informed understanding of the structure of the community economy can promote alternative community economic development strategies. Community economic development strategies have changed over the years and will continue to do so. Earlier development theories emphasized community self-sufficiency, while contemporary approaches stress the role of public-private partnerships and the relationship of neighborhood to region. However, efforts to develop effective community economic development strategies will benefit greatly from a sound empirical understanding of the neighborhood economy. Community economic base studies can play an important role in planning and evaluation by indicating how alternative development strategies, such as increased public or cooperative ownership of community resources, would correct structural problems within the local economy, as well as how traditional growth-oriented approaches might fail to promote sustained economic development (Byrun, 1987; Imbroscio, 1997). In essence, structural descriptions of the local economy provide a blueprint that can be used to develop strategic interventions following from the notion that increasing linkages within the local economy and greater control over inflows and outflows of resources, including regional linkages and external private investment, will contribute to the economic health of the community.

A structural description of the neighborhood economy can suggest corrective and coordinating roles for community economic institutions. In their classic study of the economic development of Harlem, Harrison and Vietorisz observed that "community economic development involves institution-building and not merely increasing per capita income" (1970: 29). Indeed, the structure of economic flows within communities cannot exist without agency; therefore, descriptive analysis of the local economy can suggest new community-level institutions—such as community development corporations, community development financial institutions, or housing land trusts and cooperatives—necessary to alter the workings of the local economy. Moreover, a general understanding of the anatomy of the local economy would allow diverse parties—including governmental agencies, private firms and investors, and community development organizations—to develop a better understand of their roles and inter-relationships with the local economy and work cooperatively toward effective development strategies.

The practice of community economic development has much to gain by incorporating an economic base study method as illustrated by the works reviewed in this chapter. By utilizing these tools for understanding the conditions of urban neighborhoods, it may be possible to create community economic development programs and policy initiatives capable of correcting the adverse structure of distressed community economies, rather than relying on contemporary efforts that often provide fleeting infusions of resources but ultimately fail to promote sustained community economic health.

Resources for Additional Information

Community Economic Development Program, Michigan State University. <http:www.msu.edu/user/cua/projects/CIEM percent20Project.htm>.

Crossroads Resource Center. P.O. Box 7423. Minneapolis, MN 55407. (612) 869–8664.

Institute for Local Self-Reliance. Washington, DC. <http://www.ilsr.org>.

Regional Economics Applications Laboratory, University of Illinois. <http://www.uiuc.edu/unit/real>.

FIVE

Can Evaluation for Empowerment Be Applied to Economic Development in Empowerment Zones?

Margaret Dewar

In 1994, President Clinton and Congress created a program that would constitute an important part of Clinton's urban policy, the Empowerment Zones and Enterprise Communities program. The aim of the Empowerment Zones and Enterprise Communities is to "empower American communities and their residents to create jobs and opportunity, take effective action to solve difficult and pressing economic, human, community and physical development challenges of today, and to build for tomorrow."[1] Two major goals repeated often are "creating economic opportunity" and "empowering residents and communities."[2]

The empowerment goal poses dilemmas for evaluation of the Empowerment Zones and Enterprise Communities. The usual style of assessment of outcomes at arm's length essentially means that evaluators do not buy in to the goal of empowerment, and the funding of evaluations diverts resources from efforts to achieve that goal. However, conducting evaluation in ways that are consistent with empowering residents and communities may not constitute objective enough evaluation to be useful for understanding the program results and for recommending program redirection. This may be a particular problem with assessing whether the Empowerment Zones and Enterprise Communities create economic opportunity because even when new businesses start, businesses expand, or residents get jobs, these activities may just displace other activities that would have occurred without the program and therefore bring about no new economic opportunity.[3]

This chapter considers styles of evaluation and types of evaluation that have different potential for advancing the EZ/EC empowerment goal.

"Style" refers to the degree of sharing of participation and control in the research. "Type" refers to the kinds of effects that the evaluation examines. Six evaluations are placed in the matrix of evaluation styles and types. The results show that one evaluation conforms to principles of empowerment to a much greater extent than others. Finally, the chapter points to issues to consider in designing an evaluation of EZ/EC programs to contribute to empowerment while assessing the effects on creating economic opportunity.

Styles and Types of Evaluation

Scholars writing about participatory styles of research have distinguished among four levels of participation in research by people who are usually "respondents" or "subjects." These range from participation only as objects of study to leadership in direction, design, and implementation of the research. In *contractual* research, people are brought into research projects by contract to take part in experiments, surveys, and interviews; they have no role in determining the design or nature of the research. In evaluation of the effects of the Empowerment Zone, a survey of a sample of residents to determine their experiences in the work force, their connection with Empowerment Zone programs, and their perceptions of their changing opportunities is this type of research. In *consultative* research, the researchers ask people their views about issues related to the research before making interventions. A researcher doing this style of work would lead focus groups to learn about residents' experiences in economic opportunity before constructing questionnaires for a survey of residents, for example. In *collaborative* research, researchers and local people work together on projects designed, initiated, and managed by researchers. For instance, the researcher hires and trains local people as interviewers and data entry staff for a survey of residents and has a committee of residents to comment on the questionnaire and to give reactions to findings. In *collegial* research, the researchers and local people work together as colleagues with different skills to offer, "in a process of mutual learning where local people have control over the process."[4] The subject—evaluating whether the Empowerment Zone is creating economic opportunity, for instance—may be set before the research project begins, but all other aspects of the project are decided upon in a process where local people and the researchers have equal control or where residents determine the design and direction of the evaluation.

Participatory research that is collegial has an empowering effect on participants, scholars of participatory research argue; "local people are involved in a process through which they are empowered to take charge of the research process and to organize to implement potential solutions or take action on concerns."[5] "Empowerment evaluation," building on principles of participatory research, teaches people to conduct their own evaluations and seeks to foster self-determination.[6]

These different styles of participation can be applied to different types of evaluations. In this paper, these types are distinguished as *process* or *formative* evaluation; *outcome, impact,* or *summative* evaluation; and *efficiency* evaluation or measurement of net effects, also frequently called *summative* evaluation. Process or formative evaluation looks at program implementation, monitors program operations, and often provides data to improve program administration. A formative evaluation of the Empowerment Zones would look at which programs are operating and have expended funds and at the extent of meetings involving community participation, for example. Summative evaluation assesses the utility of a program in achieving its goals. Outcome and impact evaluations look at the extent to which a program causes change in the ways desired. An Empowerment Zone evaluation could look, for instance, at the numbers of Zone businesses that use the wage tax credits or the number of Zone residents employed in Zone businesses. Impact or outcome evaluation also assesses whether the changes in outcome measures are due to Zone program activities, at whether, for instance, businesses hired more residents of the Empowerment Zone *because* of Zone programs. Efficiency evaluation assesses whether the program is the best way or better than specific alternatives for achieving the desired goals.[7]

Evaluations of the Empowerment Zones

With one exception, the designs for evaluations of the Empowerment Zones and Enterprise Communities disregard the empowerment goal and therefore run the risk of contradicting or interfering with the program's empowerment aims. As shown below, the evaluations nearly always leave the people who are supposed to be empowered—the residents of the Zones—out of the decision-making. Several evaluators have tried to find ways to evaluate in a more empowering style, but they have not yet succeeded in doing so. The following are analyses of the evaluations based on written documentation of evaluation design and on interviews with participants in the processes.

Federal Government Evaluations

Price Waterhouse/Richard Nathan Two-Year Assessment

The Department of Housing and Urban Development contracted with Price Waterhouse and with Richard Nathan of the Nelson A. Rockefeller Institute to assess the administration and management of the urban Empowerment Zones and Enterprise Communities in their first two years of operation. The evaluation did not consider outcomes. The research used a "field network" approach. The central evaluation office laid out the common approach to answering the same set of analytical questions. Field researchers in the specific locations collected the information and did the analysis. The central office then compiled the assessments into a report that cut across the sample of jurisdictions. The assessment analyzed all the urban Empowerment Zones and a sample of the Enterprise Communities designated in the first round of funding in late 1994. The major issues they considered initially were: how effectively the communities are carrying out their strategic plans, to what extent the communities are meeting their performance measures, how the communities can improve their performance, and how successful techniques and processes can be used by other communities. Central staff controlled decisions about the research, though the field researchers had considerable autonomy in deciding how they would collect the information to answer the major research questions. The subjects of the research—administrators, local officials, and Zone residents—had no role in determining the direction of the research except as interviewees.[8]

Abt Associates Interim Outcomes Assessment

HUD contracted with Abt Associates and Avis Vidal of the Urban Institute to conduct an "interim impact assessment" to assess EZ/EC progress toward community transformation over the first five years of operations, to assess program effectiveness at the five-year point, and to provide feedback to HUD for making improvements in the EZ/EC programs. The evaluation design is a mix of the field network approach and the "theory of change" approach. Consistent with the field network style, central office staff charge field researchers at the sites with collecting data and answers to a set of questions that are the same across all sites. In the "theory of change" part of the evaluation, the field researchers work with local "stakeholders" to "describe the strategies and pathways by which the EZ/EC Program will achieve the community transformation envisioned in each site."[9] The implicit and explicit "theories" about how change is to occur are articulated in detail, and the action steps needed are laid out. The local researchers work with the local stakeholders to establish milestones, interim outcomes, and long-term outcomes that relate to the theories about necessary steps for achieving the outcomes.[10] In the theory of change approach, local participants in the implementation have a role in the evaluation. Their views about how change can occur become the framework for the evaluation. However, the types of stakeholders expected as participants are the executive director of the EZ, the chair of the advisory committee of the EZ, the director of the city department of community development, the director of the city redevelopment authority, and the chair of the city council. Residents of the Zones have no role unless they also fill these elite positions.[11]

University of Tennessee Rural EZ/EC Learning Initiative

The U.S. Department of Agriculture and the Ford Foundation contracted with the University of Tennessee and John Gaventa to carry out a monitoring and outcome evaluation through a "learning initiative" over the first years of the rural EZ/EC experience. The goal of the evaluation was to teach local people—those whom the EZ efforts are supposed to affect—to evaluate and improve programs. The evaluation process itself was intended to empower residents by giving them evaluation skills and by giving them the experience of using their skills to bring about change in programs that affect them. Field researchers did a case study of each site and provided some standard information requested by the U.S. Department of Agriculture, in the style of the field network approach. After the case study, however, the field researcher acted as a resource to volunteer teams of citizens. The volunteers went through ten sessions of training in evaluation. They picked a goal of the EZ or EC, developed indicators and measurements of progress toward the goal, selected one indicator to study, gathered information, and informed decision makers about how to change programs to make them more successful. The people involved in this process were the residents of the EZ or EC, not the political leaders of the city or the administrators of programs. According to a trainer for the program and to numerous residents who participated, the people who participated felt that they had been "empowered," stating that the experience has changed forever the way they think and act. The trainer for the program stated that this evaluation was about "whose reality counts, and who counts reality."[12]

Other Evaluations

City University of New York Assessment of Community Organizations' Participation and Community Capacity-Building

A team of CUNY researchers visited the six urban Empowerment Zones and conducted interviews to determine whether the EZ meetings brought together groups not previously working together, whether the EZ process reached out to other community organizations or residents, if the EZ process facilitated creation of new community-based organizations (CBOs) and community development corporations (CDCs), if EZ projects created lasting ties between CBOs and other organizations, and the depth of CDC and CBO participation and the extent to which they represented their communities. The analysis assessed the connection between CBO participation and the development of ongoing community capacity.[13] Program administrators, Empowerment Zone staff, CBO leaders, and residents of the Zones had no role in determining the direction and character of the research.

University of Illinois at Chicago/DePaul University National Empowerment Zone Action Research Project

Faculty, staff, and students monitor the developments in the six urban Empowerment Zones with particular attention to issues of citizen participation and empowerment. They conduct focus groups and interviews with residents, organization leaders, and government officials who are actors in the Empowerment Zone implementation. The evaluators aim to tell the Empowerment Zone story in the words of those involved and to create an opportunity for course corrections as the implementation proceeds. They hope also to evaluate effects of economic development efforts on residents and communities in the Empowerment Zones. They publish a newsletter to disseminate information among those working on Empowerment Zone plans and implementation.[14] Although the project collects and circulates information with the aim of informing many people about what the Zones are doing and though the project staff hope to support citizen participation, their work has not involved Zone residents in a participatory evaluation process. The evaluation staff retains control of the decisions about the evaluation.

Detroit Evaluation in the Detroit Empowerment Zone Strategic Plan

During the preparation of the plan for the Detroit Empowerment Zone,[15] an evaluation consultant volunteered her time to work with each planning team to elicit benchmarks and measures that the planning teams thought could be used for evaluation. The evaluator drafted an overall evaluation plan that became part of the strategic plan. Over the next four years, the evaluator, her colleagues from other evaluation firms, and faculty from the state's three public research universities developed and refined the design of an evaluation. Information would be collected from program records, residents, EZ administrators, and others, and information would be provided to help improve programs, but actors in the EZ, whether administrators, elected officials, or residents had no explicitly planned role in determining the direction of the work. Although the administrators and elected officials would influence the evaluation's direction because they were the clients and would decide about funding the evaluation, residents would not have a role except as respondents. An EZ staff person pointed out to the evaluation group that the evaluation could be a major vehicle for advancing the empowerment of residents and challenged the group to structure the evaluation to accomplish this. The group grappled with this issue but did not find ways to incorporate empowering processes because most had never worked in that style and because involving residents as partners would have considerably increased the cost and reduced the scope of the evaluation.[16]

Figure 5.1 places the current Empowerment Zone evaluations in a matrix that shows where they lie in the degree of residents' participation by type of evaluation. Most evaluations have been concerned with monitoring though some are now assessing outcomes. None have analyzed whether this approach to achieving the goals is better than other approaches. While several evaluations have solicited or will solicit the views of EZ actors, usually elites, only one, the University of Tennessee evaluation, ceded control of the evaluation to residents who held no leadership positions and had no prior expertise or involvement. Only the University of Tennessee evaluation had an explicit, primary goal of empowering residents as the evaluation occurred.

The University of Tennessee evaluation, however, raises questions about whether it provides a model for others for evaluating Empowerment Zones. First, can the learning initiative's approach produce an overall assessment of

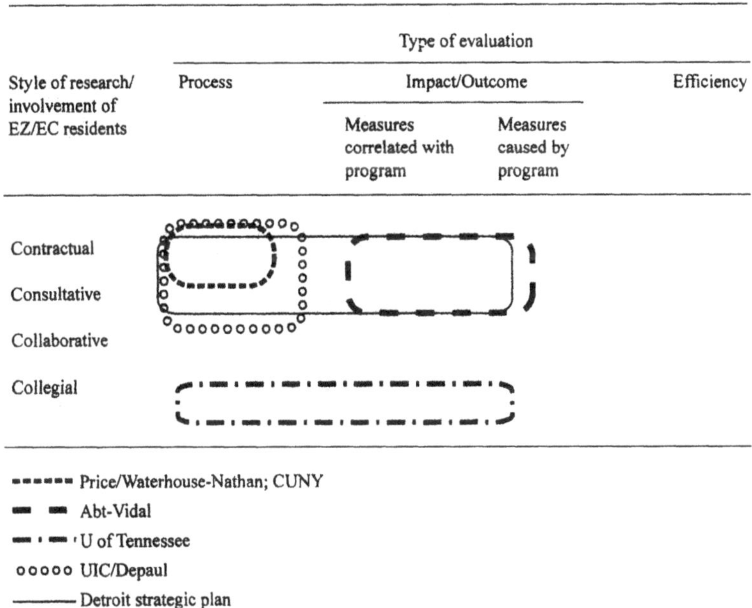

Figure 5.1 Empowerment Zone evaluations by style and type of evaluation

outcomes that is helpful to policymakers interested in results and program reforms or to administrators in other cities who want to run their own programs in better ways? Consistent with the usual style of participatory research, the purpose of the research is action; in contrast, the purpose of conventional research is understanding, perhaps leading to action.[17] If no overall understanding of results comes out of the work, action probably will be local action, as it has been thus far, not the strengthening of the program at the federal level or in other cities. The learning initiatives written evaluation includes conclusions about the overall operation of the federal program and recommendations for improvement. The recommendations come from experience with implementation rather than from measurement of outcomes. The evaluation also includes overall estimates of effects, such as numbers of jobs created, but these numbers do not come out of the participatory evaluation process.[18]

Second, is the learning initiative approach so time-consuming and expensive that it cannot provide the extent of coverage of results of programs that an evaluation might require? The learning initiative operated in only ten sites leading to assessments of only one intervention in each site in two years.

Third, the University of Tennessee evaluators describe it as an empowering mechanism rather than as an evaluation tool. However, as an empowering approach, is it cost effective? Are other ways of bringing about empowerment less expensive? The learning initiative reports effects on the participants' empowerment.[19] However, few enough people participated that the effects of their empowerment may be small and imperceptible at the scale of community change. Furthermore, the learning initiative reported change in a short period; citizen evaluators' actions after a longer time, say five years, may be more significant indicators of whether empowerment occurred in a lasting way.

Fourth, did the University of Tennessee Learning Initiative tackle the question of whether the EZ/EC effort was creating economic opportunity in ways that would lead to convincing conclusions about these effects? Four of the ten Learning Teams in rural Empowerment Zones and Enterprise Communities identified job creation or other aspects of economic development as goals they would consider in their evaluations. However, the indicators they chose to use did not appear to account for displacement of workers by new employees who bring subsidies with them and did not consider the opportunity cost of activities that did not occur because the EZ/EC activities displaced them. The evaluation appeared to suffer from the pitfall that besets much economic development planning: the assumption that widely held views about how to create economic opportunity are correct when they often are wrong.

What Would an Empowering Evaluation of Economic Development Results Look Like?

Is an evaluation possible that assesses the EZ/EC goal of creating economic opportunity in a way that can have effects on national policy and program implementation elsewhere at the same time that the evaluation is consistent with the empowerment goals of Empowerment Zones and Enterprise Communities? If evaluations are to support the programs that they evaluate, then the answer has to be yes. The following are general principles that could contribute to doing an evaluation that is consistent with empowerment and that does derive general findings. These are drawn from the practice of community-based planning, community-based research, theory-of-change evaluation, and empowerment evaluation and reflect the author's experience in trying to implement these principles in an evaluation of the Detroit Empowerment Zone's creation of economic opportunity.[20] The author's evaluation achieved a collaborative style of evaluation, not a collegial one.

1. *Begin with commitment to a partnership with EZ/EC residents.* This is a dramatic departure from the usual way that evaluation and research occur; university researchers and professional evaluators normally control the subject and the design of the work and implement the study. Further, instead of consulting with elites, this approach would require granting the residents of the Zones controlling roles in the evaluation. This approach begins with the belief that evaluators and community residents bring different knowledge and expertise, equally valuable, to the endeavor of evaluation. The residents bring the knowledge of the local situation and of their personal experiences, both of which the EZ/EC programs are supposed to affect. The evaluators bring knowledge about what evaluations of similar programs have found, how to make an evaluation's findings convincing, what techniques exist for evaluation, and how economic opportunity is believed to be created. The evaluator is a facilitator of residents' participation but also has opinions and input. A difference between this approach and the approach of the University of Tennessee is that the outside "researcher" is an equal partner in the work, not primarily a facilitator. The difficulty is that the researcher's more extensive academic background may lead community residents to defer to the researcher's views when they should not. Another difference is that the evaluation begins with the broad subject decided: does the Empowerment Zone create economic opportunity? The problem with this approach is that the decision about the subject of the evaluation is key to assuring that the evaluation deals with issues that are important to residents and to keeping residents involved in the project. Although residents often think of economic opportunity as important, they do not necessarily consider it the most important issue to evaluate, and they have much greater investment in other issues.

2. *Ask EZ/EC residents to define "creating economic opportunity."* Start by asking residents what "creating economic opportunity" means.[21] The definition has not been articulated clearly in the EZ/EC legislative history,[22] and numerous contradictions exist. For instance, does creating economic opportunity mean that new jobs exist in the Empowerment Zone whether or not EZ residents get them? Or does it mean that EZ residents have better jobs, experience less unemployment, and earn more income? For another example, has economic opportunity been created if EZ residents get jobs, no matter what the jobs are? Or does it mean that they get "good" jobs that pay enough to lift a household out of poverty, provide medical insurance, and

offer opportunities for training and advancement? And has economic opportunity been created if EZ residents who get good jobs move to neighborhoods outside the Empowerment Zones? Instead of the usual practice in evaluation of laying out what the program designers' and implementers' goals and definitions are, use residents' views of what constitutes economic opportunity for them, the intended target group.

3. *Articulate the connection between EZ/EC programs and incentives and the residents' definition of economic opportunity.* In a modified theory-of-change approach,[23] residents and their research partners should detail how the Empowerment Zone programs and incentives can create economic opportunity. For each EZ program or for a subset of the programs and incentives, ask what are the assumptions about the way economic opportunity is created that form the basis for this program or incentive. Specify what has to be true for the program or incentive to create economic opportunity. Then examine each assumption or necessary precondition to consider whether the assumption is true or the precondition exists. The evaluator/facilitator brings to the group of residents the existing research and knowledge about these assumptions and preconditions. This process is "conceptual" evaluation, a consideration of whether programs and incentives are designed in ways that can conceivably create economic opportunity. This type of evaluation identifies specific information to collect to assess whether key assumptions are true and therefore reduces the scale of data collection. It immediately leads to some recommendations for changes in the way that programs are designed and implemented.[24]

4. Based on the gaps in information identified through the conceptual evaluation, *collect specific types of information that can determine whether EZ programs and incentives are creating economic opportunity, as the residents have defined it.* Because of the process in #3 above, the range of information needed is narrower than usual in an evaluation where evaluators define outcome measures. The connection with the program activities is also explicit; this differs from evaluation that involves collection of data on outcome measures, such as change in tax base or change in local employment, for instance, which cannot be linked directly to programs and incentives. Residents should decide how the information should be collected.

5. *Develop specific recommendations for program changes that could improve the Empowerment Zone's effects on economic opportunity.* The recommendations should come from residents' conclusions based on analysis of data from #4.

6. *Plan and implement the political process of bringing the recommendations to Empowerment Zone decision makers in the local area and in Washington, D.C.* Residents and the evaluator work together to find ways to get recommendations into the policy process and to bring about change. Unlike the style of usual evaluations where the work is completed when reports are done, this step is critical for assuring that residents' work has a positive effect on EZ programs and an "empowering" influence on EZ residents themselves.

This kind of evaluation has several strengths. First, the process can leave residents who participate with new knowledge, a framework for doing quick conceptual evaluations on numerous topics. Second, residents carry out an exercise that produces implications for improving programs and can lead to change. This is the kind of process that the University of Tennessee Learning Initiative found led to increased individual and community capacity for bringing about positive change. Further, this kind of evaluation can assess the effects of the Empowerment Zones on economic opportunity and can add to more general understanding about how initiatives like the Empowerment Zones work because of the link with knowledge about other programs through the traditional evaluator, acting as a partner in the project.

This approach to evaluation also faces numerous challenges and unanswered questions, which were underscored by an effort to implement such an effort in Detroit. Beginning in 1998 the author undertook a study of how employers in the Empowerment Zone were responding to the programs and incentives that were supposed to lead to the creation of economic opportunity for Zone residents.[25] First, can the work on the project adhere to a schedule so that findings and reports due for a grant or contract can be produced? Scholars who engage in participatory research report their difficulties in assessing how long collegial decision-making and implementing take. In the Detroit evaluation, the author needed to produce reports that aided community-based partners to achieve their goals in the project and needed to meet the deadlines of the sponsoring agent who did not value the reports for the community-based organizations.[26] Second, how can the work of the evaluation be predictable enough to ensure that findings do address the initial subject of the research, the evaluation of the effects of the Empowerment Zone on economic opportunity? If most aspects of the project are decided in a collegial process, the broader group may want to decide the topic of the work as well. Can the evaluator from outside the community set boundaries on the domain of the decision-making without harming the atmosphere of collaboration? The University of Tennessee Learning Initiative specified only that the project concerned the work of the Empowerment Zone or Enterprise Community. In the case of the Detroit evaluation, the project was committed to evaluate the effects on economic opportunity of the Empowerment Zone, but the information collected could also address many other community concerns about economic development. The reporting of the findings for community partners virtually ignored the Empowerment Zone issue because it was no longer of interest.[27] Third, such evaluations normally require funding, and funders usually want to know specifics about a project before they decide to sponsor it. Can the community concern for an evaluation remain stable enough over the period of seeking funding for the evaluation to have a constituency once funding is in place? In the author's evaluation of the Detroit Empowerment Zone, representatives from community-based organizations supported an evaluation of the economic development effects of the Zone; by the time the funds were available to do the work, most people had lost faith that the Empowerment Zone would have any positive effects, and other issues were much more important. Because this is such a common phenomenon, many community-based or participatory-action researchers focus their own writing and research on methods and techniques in the process of such evaluation, issues that do not change as the topics of evaluation shift.[28]

How can participants deal with the issues related to their positions or structural locations in "multiplex communities"[29] so as not to allow the differences in their identities to emerge in difficult power dynamics that disrupt the work? In a project where university faculty and students and community residents aim to participate as equal partners, differences in age, education, income, race, gender, and other positions exist; and participants respond to these. These differences need to be examined explicitly and addressed thoughtfully in order for the work on the principal agenda to progress.

Finally, who should be involved in an evaluation of the Empowerment Zone in order to ensure that the process does involve the people whom the Empowerment Zone programs intend to affect? Who count as the Zone "residents" for this purpose? The University of Tennessee Learning Initiative staff involved people who lived in the Empowerment Zone or Enterprise Community but had no other roles in the planning, implementation, or management of the EZ or EC. Residents who participated became important actors in the implementation of the EZ or EC later on, however. In some cities, the EZ/EC board members and staff are predominately residents. However, because of their elite positions and their vested interests in supporting the EZ programs, involving them in the evaluation process does not constitute participation from the individuals the EZ and EC are supposed to affect. How can a participatory evaluation gain the commitment to participate from people who have not led the EZ or EC efforts?

Conclusion

"Empowering" evaluations of Empowerment Zones are rare, and the one good example has not demonstrated that the participatory process can produce findings that are general enough to influence policy outside specific local situations; indeed, the goal of the learning initiative is local action to improve conditions for people who have little power. This chapter lays out initial guidelines for a style of evaluation that could have empowerment effects and that could produce general findings about whether the Empowerment Zones are creating economic opportunity. This kind of evaluation differs from most evaluations in numerous ways: residents, *not* evaluators or elites, control the evaluation, the evaluation begins with a conceptual phase that specifies the assumptions in the connection between programs and the goal of creating economic opportunity, collection of data is narrowed to needs identified in the conceptual phase, the evaluation is linked to a political process of getting recommendations for change adopted.

Notes

Partial funding for this research came from the National Center for the Revitalization of Central Cities, University of New Orleans.

1. *Federal Register* 1994, 2700.
2. For example, U.S. Department of Housing and Urban Development, 1995; Clinton, 1995.
3. For example, see Bartik, 1991; Anderson and Wassmer, 2000; Fisher and Peters, 1998.
4. Cornwall and Jewkes, 1995: 1669.
5. Ibid., 1671.
6. See Fetterman, 1994; Fetterman, Kaftarian, and Wandersman, 1996; Eng and Parker, 1994.
7. Rossi and Freeman, 1985; Brintnall, n.d.; Israel et al., 1995; Public Policy Associates, 1997.

8. Nelson A. Rockefeller Institute of Government, 1997; David J. Wright, project manager, Empowerment Zone/Enterprise Community Initiative, Nelson A. Rockefeller Institute of Government, State University of New York, Albany, NY, phone conversation with author, Sept. 1997; Nathan, 1982; Richard DeLeon, John Stuart Hall, and Robin Boyle, field researchers for the EZ/EC Initiative, discussions with the author, Oct. 1996, Aug. 1997.

9. Abt Associates, 1997, 6; Roundtable on theory of change evaluation and Empowerment Zones, conference of the Association of Collegiate Schools of Planning, Pasadena, CA, fall 1998.

10. Abt Associates, 1997; Sharon Milligan and Claudia Coulton, "Implementing a Theories of Change Evaluation in the Cleveland Community Building Initiative," as condensed by James P. Connell, Center for Urban Poverty and Social Change, Mandel School of Applied Social Sciences, Case Western Reserve University, June 1996; James P. Connell, "Making State and Local Partnerships Work for Children and Families: How States Can Use a Theories of Change Approach to Catalyze, Support and Evaluate Comprehensive Community Initiatives," prepared for the Roundtable for Comprehensive Services for Children and Families, July 1996; Carol Hirschon Weiss, 1995.

11. Abt Associates, 1997: 4.

12. Shanna Ratner, trainer for learning teams, Yellowood Associates, VT, phone conversation with the author, Sept. 1997; Cruz Torres, local facilitator/researcher, Department of Sociology, University of Texas Panamerican, discussions at the meetings of the COPC Evaluation Working Group, Wilmington, DE, Oct. 1996; Cruz Torres, abstract submitted to Michael Lieber for the COPC Conference on Evaluation, Oct. 1996; Michael D. Lieber, "COPC Conference on Evaluation," Oct. 1997, 32–35; "Findings and Recommendations of the Community Partnership Center EZ/EC Learning Initiative," vol. 1, Community Partnership Center, University of Tennessee, Knoxville, Feb. 1998. The author enrolled in a training program to learn about this style of evaluation, the Community Learning Teams Workshop, University of Tennessee, Knoxville, Mar. 1998.

13. Marilyn Gittell, Janice Bockmeyer, Robert Lindsay, and Kathe Newman, "The Urban Empowerment Zones: Community Organizations and Community Capacity Building," Howard Samuels State Management and Policy Center, Graduate School and University Center, City University of New York, May 1996; Janice L. Bockmeyer, 1996; Marilyn Gittell et al., 1998.

14. "National Empowerment Zone Action Research Project," pamphlet describing the project, Great Cities Institute, University of Illinois at Chicago; *EZ Exchange: The National Empowerment Zone Quarterly*, Great Cities Institute, University of Illinois at Chicago, various issues from vols. 1, 2; National Empowerment Zone Action Research Project, Great Cities Institute, University of Illinois at Chicago, draft reports, 1996–97; Michael Bennett, presentation at the meetings of the Great Lakes Economic Development Group, Chicago, Oct. 1996; Cedric Herring et al., 1998; Jenkins and Bennett, 1999.

15. The author was part of this evaluation planning process, and the dilemmas in finding ways to evaluate programs while being consistent with the empowerment goal were the instigation for this paper. In 1998, the Detroit Empowerment Zone Development Corporation selected another team to do the evaluation, so the evaluation described here ended.

16. "Jumpstarting the Motor City," strategic plan for the Detroit Empowerment Zone, submitted to the Department of Housing and Urban Development, June 1994, Sec. 6 and App. C; June Thomas, Margaret Dewar, and Diane Brown, concept paper for assessment of goal achievement, submitted to the Detroit Empowerment Zone Development Corporation, June 1996; meetings and discussions of the informal Empowerment Zone Evaluation Collaborative, Detroit, Aug. 1996–Dec. 1998.

17. Cornwall and Jewkes, 1995: 1669.

18. "Findings and Recommendations of the Community Partnership Center EZ/EC Learning Initiative."

19. Ibid.

20. Dewar and Isaac, 1998; Fetterman et al., 1996; Connell et al., 1995; Israel et al., 1998; Dewar, 2003.

21. This was the recommendation of Shanna Ratner, trainer for the University of Tennessee Learning Initiative.

22. For instance, see U.S. Congress, House of Representatives, May, June 1993; U.S. Congress, Senate, June 1993; U.S. Congress, House of Representatives, Mar. 1994; U.S. Congress, House of Representatives, Feb. 1994.

23. This is a model I have used in teaching economic development planning students how to evaluate proposed or existing programs when they cannot collect new data. The students have produced dozens of excellent evaluations.

24. An example of conceptual evaluation is Immergluck and Hilton, "Breaking Down Barriers: Prospects and Policies for Linking Jobs and Residents in the Chicago Empowerment Zone," Woodstock Institute, Chicago, Nov. 1996.

25. Dewar, 2003.

26. Gutierrez and Alvarez, 1997.

27. For example, Deshazo, et al., "Opportunities for Growth in the Grinnell/City Airport Industrial District: Analysis of Workforce and Selected Industrial Sectors," Detroit Community Partnership Center, Urban and Regional Planning Program, University of Michigan, May 2000; Argumedo, et al., 2000.

28. Research presentations at the faculty seminar on participatory research, Center for Community Service and Learning, University of Michigan, 1998–99.

29. Rosaldo, 1993.

SIX

Evaluating the Welfare Outcomes of Local Economic Development Programs: A Job-Chains Approach

Joseph Persky, Daniel Felsenstein, and Virginia Carlson

Introduction

Local employment generation is an issue high on the public policy agenda. Invariably, cities and states will compete with each other to lure businesses to their jurisdictions. However, considerable uncertainty still surrounds the evaluation of welfare benefits from local job creation and retention. Cities and states have engaged in expensive programs of subsidizing business with only a very imperfect understanding of the social value of those programs. When evaluation has been done at all, it has most often taken the form of simple impact analysis—an adding up of new payrolls and taxes (Reese and Fasenfest, 1997). But even assuming the new jobs can be traced to the public subsidies involved, standard impact assessments can hardly answer the most telling criticisms of local economic development efforts, that they bring jobs to those who don't need them: to high-skilled workers who already hold jobs and to those who have little claim on the local community: in-migrants from elsewhere in the country. In this view, project benefits don't trickle down to those local residents most in need. The job-chains approach developed in this paper provides an analytic framework for carrying out program evaluations based on the principles of welfare economics. In doing so it allows a natural empirical assessment of the trickle down question.

This chapter focuses on strengthening the theoretical understanding and empirical evaluation of local job creation with special emphasis on the welfare of low- and medium-skilled workers. Central to our approach is a "chain" model of local labor markets characterized by unemployment. When a worker moves into new job A, the previously held employment (job B) now becomes available to others. One worker's move up the job ladder potentially opens opportunities all down the ladder, even to the bottom rung if the local chain is not broken. Employment generation therefore triggers a set of chain reactions (termed here "job chains") in the labor market. At each completed step up a chain, workers move closer to their fully employed status. Workers can make employment gains either in jobs newly generated by the subsidized program or as a result of vacancies opened by job chains.

We know a rise in local personal income does not translate dollar for dollar into a rise in the economic welfare of the local population (Leatherman and Marcouiller, 1999). Rather the principles of welfare economics tell us that for each affected resident a comparison must be made between their well-being with and without the program. From a job-chain perspective both those obtaining new jobs and all those moving into vacancies opened by job chains must be included in the analysis. Estimating the incremental gains to each participant in local job chains becomes the central issue in determining the true welfare benefits of job creation and, hence, in evaluating local economic development programs.

At a broader level, the job-chains approach also offers a platform for the process of "hysteresis" proposed by Bartik (1991). Hysteresis in Bartik's sense occurs when a high demand situation allows workers to move up to higher level positions and in the process enhance their stocks of human capital. Augmenting the short-run job-chains approach with a theory of human capital accumulation at various job skill levels would allow an extension of the model into the long run.

The rest of this chapter is divided into five parts. The following section offers a brief review of relevant literature and lays out our theoretical intuitions concerning job chains in local labor markets. That is followed by preliminary empirical findings on the value of job moves to workers. Next, we put forward an ambitious research agenda and methodology in order to establish job chains on an empirical footing parallel to that achieved by local input-output analysis. A hypothetical example is then presented that illustrates the method for measuring welfare outcomes. Finally, we offer our still-tentative conclusions and suggestions for future work.

Job Chains and Trickle-Down Effects

A theory of job chains in local labor markets grows naturally out of the new Keynesian economics with its rediscovery and "legitimization" of involuntary unemployment and relatively rigid wage structures (Davidson, 1990; Mankiw and Romer, 1991). The information and agency costs inherent in labor markets (whether generated by searching, monitoring, motivating, or coordinating) leave some involuntarily unemployed and many considerably underemployed. A local labor market in such a new Keynesian world necessarily generates job chains. Of course, even in a new Keynesian world, relatively large demand or supply shocks will eventually alter wage structures. However, since our primary interest is the evaluation of economic development projects in a metropolitan context, the modest size of these projects relative to the labor markets on which they impact, suggest that resulting changes in wage structure will be of slight consequence. The major effects at the project level will follow from movements along job chains.

A theory of local job chains must then go on to explain the different labor market circumstances under which they form, the impacts of in-migrants on their length and the likelihood of their completion within a local labor market. Particular focus will be placed on the likely differential impacts of chains formed in different occupational classes, geographic areas (high growth and low growth) and in different industrial sectors.

The notions of "chain" and "trickle down" effects have been utilized as an analytical framework in various areas in the social science literature over the years. In the regional development literature for example, "trickle down" was always considered the antidote to the tendencies toward self-entrenching growth and uneven regional development (Siebert, 1969; Martin and Sunley, 1998). Work in economics however, has consistently shown a weakening in the trickle-down effect over time such that the benefits of job creation do not permeate to those most in need due to social and economic barriers (Danziger and Gottschalk, 1986). Rather than "trickling down," some even claim that the relationship between economic growth and low income reduction is beginning to "fizzle out" (Zyblock and Lin, 1997).

The trickle-down construct has also been used in the evaluation of training programs (Hamermesh, 1971; Johnson and Thomas, 1984), in the study of large scale organizations (White, 1970a) and in the empirical study of the housing market (Lansing et al., 1969). In the area of urban studies and regional science, housing market analyses have been particularly prolific in adopting the "trickle down" metaphor. Much of this work has involved simple mapping of vacancy chains in the housing market and counts of moves per chain as new housing is added at the top end of the market (Watson, 1974). Other work has used the chain analogy in models of residential segregation in the housing market (Huff and Waldorf, 1988).

Another approach has been to model moves through the chain as a Markov process. This has been done for example in the study of moves of clergy among pastorates in national churches in the US (White, 1970a) and for analyzing moves in the housing market (White, 1970b). In this literature, the length of an individual chain is the sum of all the moves triggered by the initial vacancy. If disruptive events (e.g., in-migrants, new entrants, or job destruction) are equally likely at every rung of the ladder, chains will have a longer expected length if initiated at the top. The actual length of chains, of course, is an empirical matter.

In the area of labor market analysis, a Markov approach has been used for looking at inter-regional migration (Mackinnon and Rogerson, 1980). However at the *local* labor market level, while there is much interest in matching vacancies with unemployment (Holzer, 1989; Gorter and van Ours, 1994), this work does not adopt a job-chain perspective. In the main, it is concerned with looking at how demand shifts and business cycle vagaries affect labor market equilibrium.

One study that has recognized the "trickle down" effects arising from employment creation is Webster (1979). However, aside from the simple charting of the chains arising from a particular employment program in northeast Alberta Canada, Webster does not go very far is developing a general model of chain dynamics in the local labor market.

In general, research on local economic development has overlooked the job-chain implications arising from local efforts to stimulate employment. Chain analysis and related linear systems have often been criticized for their mechanical character and lack of a theoretical base. However, the time is particularly ripe for reconsidering the local job-chain approach. The emergence of new Keynesian economics provides a set of theoretical tools consistent with relatively stable labor market structures. A job-chain approach to evaluating local economic development programs fits naturally on such a base.

The current literature on economic development evaluation is characterized by a broad gulf dividing studies that meticulously count 100 percent of the wages of every new job as a net gain and those which basically deny the existence of any possible gain. On the one hand, the impact analyses count job and wage creation as output measures of success and expend great efforts in accurately counting jobs generated by a proposed (or ex-post, a completed) project. Markley and McNamara (1995) for example, in analyzing the economic impacts of a business incubator go to great efforts in calculating the wages and personal incomes earned by these employees and estimating a cost per job created as a measure of efficiency. Welfare gains in these studies are equated to the increases in personal income generated by new direct, indirect, and induced jobs.

This common approach to impact assessment greatly overstates outcomes. This is because it invariably fails to recognize that many workers at new subsidized facilities would have found alternative employment in the community or outside. The welfare gain to the individual worker from a new job will not in general be equal to that worker's wage. Rather it will be a much smaller amount, equal to the difference between wages on the new job and the worker's wage in his or her next best alternative. In the extreme case of smooth and perfectly functioning labor markets, these alternative wages will be close to the wage level on a new job. Indeed, this is why, in a fully employed market, wages are not only a private cost to the business but a social cost as well. In a fully employed labor market, wages indicate the value of alternative production given up when a worker shifts to a new enterprise. In such a world, simply counting additional employment may not teach us very much about the efficacy of economic development programs (Courant, 1994).

At the other end of the literature spectrum, researchers who are cognizant of the need to include opportunity costs often equate them with "reservation wages": the minimum wage acceptable for entering into employment. Empirical estimates of reservation wages of unemployed job seekers are generally quite high. Jones (1989) claims a figure of 90 percent of wages actually achieved. (For a considerably lower figure, but still far more than zero, see Sridhar, 1996.) These high reservation wages suggest that the actual welfare gains of new local employment are likely to be modest if not negligible even when unemployed workers are targeted. Since most subsidized jobs are likely to be filled by employed workers, the gains may be considered negligible.

It would seem that we are left with all or nothing. On the one hand impact studies credit new jobs with all the wages they generate, while researchers emphasizing opportunity costs give those jobs little if any weight. This chapter suggests that a realistic way out of this "all or nothing" dichotomy lies in recognizing that in real-world labor markets, new job formation begins a chain reaction that will affect many workers in addition to those who actually obtain the newly created jobs. In a less than fully employed economy, a tightening in the labor market allows underemployed workers all along the line to move up. A full analysis of the local welfare effects of new jobs requires considering these chains seriously.

A job-chain mechanism recognizes that workers move up the job ladders connected to new jobs. The movement from link to link in the chain (vacancy to vacancy in the labor market) has a spatial expression. From a local development perspective, a chain ends in two ways. The first is when it is truncated by an outsider, for example an in-migrant, a local new entrant or a previously unemployed local resident filling a vacancy. The second way is when a link disappears altogether, via job destruction. In these instances no new vacancy or link is simultaneously being created—that is, there is no replacement. Some chains are likely to involve many moves (links) while others are likely to be disturbed after one job switch. The important issue is that from a local economic development viewpoint, all chain development outside the local economy is irrelevant. Understanding this process of chain formation in the labor market therefore becomes a central issue to the evaluation of local economic development policy.

Preliminary Estimate

Our application of the job-chain approach to local labor market analysis effectively bridges the gulf between impact analysis and reservation wage theories. The worker who gains a newly created job may improve his or her condition only marginally, but in turn other workers find their position improved over their expectations as they move up a job ladder. Admittedly, the sum of all these gains is likely to fall short of the total new local wages identified as benefits by impact analysis. As so often is the case, the answer lies somewhere in between.

In our recent work, we have made a preliminary estimate of job-chain length and welfare gains from job creation. The key simplification is to assign opportunity costs in the evaluation of local economic development programs on the basis of an average job chain (Persky et al., 1997; Felsenstein and

Persky, 1999). Our first estimate assigns an opportunity cost for average jobs at approximately 50 percent of their earnings. This means that in evaluating economic development programs, about half of new income earned in an average new job is credited to the program generating it.

This estimate (Persky and Felsenstein, 1999) starts with the observation that for every 100 new jobs in a community we expect the long run in-migration response to be about 80 percent or 80 net new in-migrant workers (Bartik, 1993), that is, m/dj = in-migrants/net job change = 0.8. However, for any 100 gross job openings, either new jobs or links in a job chain, we only expect the in-migrant share to be 13.3 percent, i.e. m/v = in-migrants/gross job vacancies = 0.133. This latter figure is derived from the ratio of annual migration to employment (m/j) for metropolitan areas in the US (PUMS 1993) and the proportion of permanent job openings from total employment (v/j) of around 15 percent (based on rough calculations using US Bureau of Labor Statistics quit rates). These parameters imply that on average a job chain will have six links since $(m/dj)/(m/v) = (v/dj)$ (*i.e.* gross vacancies /net job change) = 0.8/0.133 = 6.[1]

On each link we assume that the worker (whether an in-migrant or not) has a reservation wage equal to 88 percent of his or her new wage[2]. Then the welfare gain associated with an average new job will just be the sum of the increments (relative to the initial wage) at each of the six average links: 12 percent + 10.56 percent + 9.19 percent + 8.18 percent + 7.20 percent + 6.34 percent = 53.47 percent. (It should be noted that this calculation refers to the welfare gain of the average job chain. The average gain of all chains will be slightly less because longer chains will add less welfare than shorter ones subtract. Using a geometric series extended to infinity results in a more conservative estimate of about 45 percent).

Research Agenda

We see these estimates as only a starting point for useful theoretical and empirical research on job chains. More specifically, we put forward the following set of hypotheses for testing. These relate to the expected welfare outcomes arising from economic development programs. In particular, we stress the welfare gains likely to be attained from low- and medium-skilled jobs relative to high-skilled jobs. While this list is hardly meant to be definitive, it is suggestive of the range of possibilities.

Hypotheses

The first hypothesis relates to the *size of the economic development program and the number of jobs created.* This hypothesis simply advances the relevance of the job-chain approach. We suggest that the number of people significantly affected by the initial stimulus of an economic development program, is much greater than the total number of new jobs created by the program itself. This is because of the ripple-through effect generated by the job-chain mechanism. This should not be confused with the standard employment multiplier, which measures direct and indirect employment generated by an initial (demand-side) stimulus. Rather, we are referring to the job chains in the local economy that are set in motion through the creation of a new place of employment and their cumulative welfare impact. Job chains are stimulated by both direct and induced new jobs.

The second proposition relates to the *distribution of the benefits of new job creation.* A job-chain approach suggests that during periods of growth, individuals' welfare gains will be more the result of progression along a job chain than of income increases in situ. This hypothesis posits job-chain stimulation as a major vehicle for effecting change in local welfare. This approach is grounded in the logic of opportunity cost theory applied to job chains. It also implies that the supply characteristics of labor are not the sole determinant of income growth.

A further hypothesis examines the *relative welfare increases attributable to new low and moderate skill jobs.* Our claim is that they are likely to generate a larger welfare increase per dollar of wages than high skill jobs. Chains set in motion by new skilled jobs are potentially longer. If they can be largely completed within a local labor market they promise considerable welfare gains through "trickle down." However, high-skilled markets are also less local. Mobility rates are higher. Skilled workers are participants in truly national markets. Hence job chains are more likely to be disrupted by in-migration at high skill links than at low skill ones. In addition, skilled jobs requiring extensive credentials may not draw extensively on job ladders. On net, we expect new low- and moderate-skilled jobs to provide more local welfare gains per dollar of wages. In effect, this hypothesis asserts that "trickle down" fails on both efficiency grounds and distributional grounds. While this is clearly an empirical question requiring serious investigation, work by Appold (1998) on the formation of local labor markets for high-skill engineers, seems to offer some support for these contentions.

Finally, we posit a relationship between *the length of the job chain generated and the growth pattern of the metropolitan area.* Faster growing areas will have shorter chains than slower growing areas. Rapidly growing areas attract more in-migrants and higher in-migration rates will shorten chains. In fast growth regions such as Silicon Valley, local labor market dynamics are based more on "matching" workers to positions than on "pooling" existing labor. The result is much greater reliance on in-migrants and worker mobility to enable this growth (Appold, 1998). This makes for shorter chains based substantially on in-migrants. In the formative years of Silicon Valley for example, only 38 percent of engineering openings were filled by locals (Appold, 1998). These shorter chains will generally create lower welfare gains per dollar of new wages. Notice this hypothesis is not tautological, since in-migration might increase only slowly with growth and hence job chains might actually lengthen.

Methodology

In order to test the above propositions, we are currently attempting to measure the major parameters of chain formation. To achieve this, we use an indirect method based on the construction of simulated job chains from longitudinal labor force survey data. For each type of job vacancy we identify the origins of hired workers (movers from other jobs, first-time job entrants to the labor market, unemployed labor reentering the labor market and so on). To make this task manageable, we identify a series of occupational-industry groupings to represent rungs on the job ladder.

On this basis, a national matrix of origin probabilities can be constructed. The inter-rung probabilities can be represented as a square (origin-destination) matrix (Q) with elements q_{ij} which show the chance that a job vacancy of a j-type position is taken by a worker currently in an i-type position. Two such matrices are estimated, one for high unemployment years and the other for low unemployment years. These matrices will allow us to approximate the net consequences (under high and low unemployment conditions) of job creation of each type.

Converting this national table to a local one is quite similar to the problem of using a national input-output table as the basis of estimating a regional one (Treyz, 1993). In particular, in-migrants to the local labor market play a role parallel to purchases of inputs from outside the region in the case of input-output tables. For each occupational group i, we are attempting to estimate the probability of drawing a local resident r_i as opposed to an in-migrant.[3] The elements in the local inter-occupational matrix now become $r_i q_{ij}$, each showing the chance that a job vacancy of a j-type position is taken by a *local* worker currently in an i-type position. In taking this approach to in-migration, we implicitly assume that, even in an underemployed economy, there are relatively strict limits on the ability and willingness of firms to draw down the ladder to fill higher level vacancies. We also intend to explore differences in these in-migration proportions across areas.

We then combine the probability of moving from job to job with chain "localness." A simple Leontieff-type inversion of the locally modified origin-destination matrix $(I\text{-}RQ)^{-1}$, will yield a multiplier-type matrix of m_{ij}'s which show the gross number of local i-type vacancies generated by a j type vacancy. Summing down the columns of this matrix gives us the total number of links or vacancies per chain, triggered-off by jobs of each rung. Thus $\sum_i m_{ij}$ gives the total number of expected vacancies associated with a newly created j-type job. In this way, we combine the (known) probabilities of moving between different jobs with the residual probability of in-migrants or new entrants truncating the chain. Together they yield estimates of chain lengths for each type of new job.

A rough approach to empirically estimating average chain length (i.e., expected number of links or vacancies triggered off by a new job) has been presented above. Here as there, the key to measuring the length of chains is estimating the probability of a chain being truncated by an in-migrant, unemployed worker or new entrant. But here these probabilities can vary with the type of job. Hence, we have to pay particular attention to the probabilities of moves between jobs as vacancies shift from one rung to another. Estimating these probabilities and chain lengths directly addresses the first hypothesis posited above relating to the trickle-down dynamics of employment creation. But knowing the nature of the various job chains also sets the stage for measuring differential welfare effects across chains.

Once the length and local spatial configuration of the different job chains are determined, the next logical step is simply to measure the (average) increment in local welfare arising from moving up the job chain. This can be achieved if we have good wage data. In particular, for each type of vacancy, i, we suggest $\sum_j r_i q_{ij}(w_i\text{-}w_j)$ as the expected wage gain of the locally employed winner of this vacancy. These wage differences should be estimated from a sample of actual job changers, and not from group averages. (Notice the above expression also requires an estimate of the average gain of those changing jobs within the same occupational group, $w'_i - w_i$.) For in migrants, unemployed or entrants who might take this vacancy we need an estimate of their expected reservation wage, w^*. Putting these elements together then suggests an overall expected gain of adding a j- type job is just given by:

$$(1)\ \Sigma_i m_{ij} (\Sigma_j q_{ji} (w_i - w_j) + p_i (w_i - w^*)).$$

Estimates of these welfare gains across job classes address the question of chain-generated welfare increases relative to those resulting from income increases without progression up a chain (Hypothesis 2). They also relate directly to the welfare increases per dollar of wages for low- and medium-skilled jobs relative to high skill jobs (Hypothesis 3). While equation (1), above, refers to a typical region or metropolitan area, a further extension would be the empirical comparison of welfare effects across fast and slow growth areas. This would allow us to explore chain length and welfare growth in areas experiencing different mobility and growth patterns and would provide a test of Hypothesis 4 that faster growing metropolitan areas have shorter chains than slow growth areas. The approach suggested here thus allows a natural framework for exploring hypotheses concerning differences in local unemployment rates or growth rates. These differences have direct and measurable impacts on model parameters. As such we can explore the resulting implications for job-chain lengths and welfare changes.

Worked Example

Both to clarify our methodology and to get a first sense of the likely magnitudes of key parameters, we present here a rather extensive worked example. Table 6.1 shows hypothetical, but we think plausible, "origin" probabilities for a set of six job categories or rungs. These are the $r_i\ q_{ij}$'s of the previous section. Category 1 is the highest skill level and six is the lowest. The seventh row shows the probability that a vacancy of that column type will be filled by someone not currently on the job ladder. The table is triangular from below, reflecting that voluntary job-chain movement will be up the chain or ladder, not down. The highlighted diagonals of table 6.1 show movement within each category. As an empirical matter we know that these diagonal entries will far exceed the off-diagonal ones.

Table 6.1 Hypothetical Origin Probabilities

	Destination Category					
Origin Category	*1*	*2*	*3*	*4*	*5*	*6*
1	**0.6**	0	0	0	0	0
2	0.05	**0.50**	0	0	0	
3	0	0.15	**0.550**	0	0	
4	0	0	0.15	**0.60**	0	
5	0	0	0.05	0.1	**0.7**	0
6	0	0	0	0.05	0.1	**0.8**
Off Job Ladder	0.35	0.35	0.25	0.25	0.2	0.2

Note. Each entry *ij* represents the probability of a vacancy in column *j* being filled from row *i*.

From the hypothetical case in table 6.1 we can see that the while probabilities of job creation on other rungs of the ladder decreases with skill level (entries on the diagonal increase), the greatest probability is that job creation at a given skill level will simply create more opportunities at that same level. In addition, as expected, the probability of vacancies being taken up by an individual off the job ladder (i.e., someone who leaves no replacement position when climbing the ladder, such as an in-migrant or new entrant), increases with labor skill level. The make-believe case in table 6.1 therefore shows little "trickle-down" effect at the highest skill levels with some modest gains in the medium skill categories.

The multiplier effects associated with the above probabilities are easily calculated by taking the inverse of the origin-destination matrix $(I\text{-}RQ)^{-1}$) in table 6.1. This gives us the number of jobs set in motion down the chain, when a job is created at a given skill level (table 6.2). The last row of table 6.2 gives the overall vacancy multiplier for the corresponding column. These numbers are substantially larger than one, though somewhat smaller than our "average" estimate in the preliminary calculation offered earlier. For the example, we can also see that the job multipliers are larger for the less-skilled jobs.

Under the circumstances of the example, job creation at more skilled levels is not effective in moving workers from one category to another. New jobs are filled primarily from the same level and not from people moving up job ladders. For example a new job at (high) skill level 1 sets in motion another 1.5 jobs in that same skill class and very little elsewhere. As a result, much of the welfare gain in this case can be expected to go primarily to high

Table 6.2 Hypothetical Job Chain Multipliers Associated with the Creation of a New Job at Different Skill Levels

Destination Category ?						
Origin Category?	*1*	*2*	*3*	*4*	*5*	*6*
1	2.50	0.00	0.00	0.00	0.00	0.00
2	0.25	2.00	0.00	0.00	0.00	0.00
3	0.08	0.67	2.22	0.00	0.00	0.00
4	0.03	0.25	0.83	2.50	0.00	0.00
5	0.02	0.19	0.65	0.83	3.33	0.00
6	0.02	0.16	0.53	1.04	1.67	5.00
Column Sum	2.9	3.3	4.2	4.4	5.0	5.0

Note. Each entry *ij* represents the number of local vacancies of type *i* generated by a new job of type *j*.

skill workers. In contrast, a new job at level 5 triggers off another 2.33 jobs at that level and a further 1.67 jobs at the level below. Here there is more evidence of welfare trickling down.

Conclusion

The example worked here highlights some important issues relating to the implications to be drawn when analyzing local economic development policy using this kind of approach. First, if job transitions are dominated by movement within job categories and not by movement between those categories, then trickle down effects stimulated by job creation will produce only limited benefits for low skill workers. Under the assumptions of the example, job creation is more likely to trigger-off a process of "trickle-within" than of "trickle down." If this were found to be the case on the basis of empirical data, it would point to either the existence of serious (human capital) constraints of moving from one skill level to another or alternatively, to constraints imposed by the existence of segmentation in the labor market. Insights such as these cannot be gained from aggregate analyses of welfare change.

Implications can also be drawn with respect to policy. In the hypothetical case described above, new jobs that open up are likely to be filled by workers from the skill strata in which those jobs fall. This suggests that undirected employment creation programs may not reach those most in need and suggests a case for targeting. If a new job created at a high skill level does not open up opportunities down the job chain, this would imply limitations to the use of "trickle down" as an economic development strategy.

In the absence of rigorous empirical analysis, the hypothetical example presented here must for the time being, be treated only as a "guesstimate." Nevertheless, it helps to sharpen our sense of the central issues. An obvious next step is to extend the analysis in order to estimate welfare gains in dollar terms. This would involve translating moves into actual wage gains, something that can only be done on the basis of empirical data. A further issue likely to arise when faced with real-world data relates to down-movers in the labor market. Our assumption in the above example is that the musical chairs triggered off by the creation of a new job, leads to all participants switching to jobs with higher wages than their previous job. In the event of the opposite occurring, we can either incorporate this welfare reduction into the estimate of welfare change or effectively discount it, claiming that the down-movers opportunity cost is reflected by the job into which s/he is (down) moving. While not resolved here, these issues present further challenges for operationalizing the job-chains model and presenting plausible estimations on the basis of real-world data.

Notes

1. The average number of links in a job chain is also equal to (1/(1–p)), where p is the probability of a vacancy being filled by a locally employed worker. Hence our result above implies that a vacancy has about an 83 percent chance of being filled by an existing local worker and thus creating another local vacancy, i.e. (6 = 1/(1–.83)).

2. This justification for using this proportion is based on data from the PSID (Population of Study of Income Dynamics). This is a longitudinal survey of almost 9,000 households comprising a probability sample of U.S. households. For each time period, detailed data are available on a string of socioeconomic variables relating to income and employment. Using data relating to the period 1990–91, we see that the average wage increase for people changing jobs which reduces to 13 percent when adjusting for inflation. The reservation wage literature often uses the work of Jones (1989) who estimated reservation wages as 90 percent of real wages (i.e., a welfare gain of 10 percent). Our approach here is to take the weighted average of these two proportions, which yields a reservation wage of close to 88 percent of real wage.

3. These estimates are to be based on the cross-sectional Public Use Microdata Sample of the Census.

SEVEN

Regional Economic Modeling and the Study of Distributional Issues

John C. Leatherman and David W. Marcouiller

Introduction

Regional economic problem analysis encompasses the application of a widely varying array of policy analysis tools to address informational needs of economic decision makers. The substance of these applied analytical tools represent, in large part, methods developed within the multidisciplinary field of regional science. Key questions addressed through regional economic analysis include how the economic structure of regions adapt given change in their respective components. Tracking both temporal and spatial patterns of change represent an important input into regional economic decision-making. Although much success in conceptual development and empirical application has addressed issues associated with economic growth, tools that begin to disaggregate growth into developmental contexts are just now becoming available. As discussion turns from growth to development, several additional characteristics become important. One important development criteria involves disaggregating growth into impacts among alternative income categories. In this way, we are now better able to assess the set of questions that deal with who benefits from economic growth.

Recent strong growth and low unemployment in the United States obscures the growing inequality in the distribution of income. Although academic debates continue, there does exist a growing literature that identifies increasing income disparities between income groups (Ngarambé, Goetz, and Debertin, 1998; Rowley, Redman, and Angle 1991) and among regions of the United States (Lipshutz, 1992; Levernier, Partridge, and Rickman 1995; Braun, 1991; Renkow, 1996; Fan and Casetti, 1994). Disparities in income levels among groups increases concerns related to economic segregation and the concentration of problems associated with poverty. Although the issue has received attention among academics and policy analysts, little of that concern has filtered into decision-making and policy at the local level.

The ability to address issues of income distribution through economic and fiscal policies has elements of both public and private importance. It is becoming increasingly apparent that public policies that address direct redistribution of income are largely out of favor. Recent welfare reform legislation points to the increasing emphasis on private markets to provide for individual welfare. To be sure, there remains a modicum of progressive federal and state taxation policies that attempt to shift the incidence of taxation toward higher income groups. At the time of this writing, however, it remains unclear whether political winds at the federal level will continue to erode support for progressive income tax policies with the current debate over across-the-board tax cuts.

As with many public programs and services, economic development is increasingly seen as a local responsibility. Local units of government, however, may be reluctant to enact equity policies that create perceived competitive disadvantage for economic development opportunities. Rural areas, in particular, are sensitive to these issues due to a generally more limited set of development options. Equity concerns remain largely unspoken. Furthermore, distributional issues of rural areas are further complicated by cost-of-living and rural quality-of-life measures that cloud purely economic aspects of rural development (Fournier and Rasmussen, 1986).

The current situation can be characterized as decentralized, competitive, and market-oriented with an increasingly stark disparity between income groups. The question arises whether local policy can address issues of distribution in this context. In this chapter, we argue that tacit distributional impacts result differentially by economic sector. Public and private policies can address distributional issue simply by influencing growth in targeted sectors. The issue becomes one of identifying the inherent distributional patterns associated with economic sectors and disaggregating the impacts associated with economic growth to household income classes. Regional economic accounting methods can track the flow of income from production activities to households disaggregated by income category.

The purpose of this chapter is to provide an overview of a number of techniques developed by regional scientists over the recent past that provide a better understanding of distributional issues. The techniques generally increase in complexity as they incorporate more realistic assumptions about economic relationships and temporal dimensions. Given the increasing power of computer hardware and the continuing development of estimation techniques and commercial software, it is conceivable that even the most complex modeling techniques will become accessible to local practitioners and policy makers. This will open a new realm to local policy discussion, moving community goal setting beyond the desire to maximize aggregate economic growth to incorporate more of the ideals implied by the term "development."

This chapter is presented in three sections. The first section presents a brief overview of some of the concepts used by economists who perform quantitative policy analysis. The second section provides a brief, nontechnical survey of economic modeling techniques that can be used to understand distributional issues. These techniques are generally built on the basic concept of accounting, with many variations of increasing complexity to more closely approximate economic behavior. Infused in this overview, is an example of a study that considers the distributional impacts of alternative local economic development policies. The final section discusses several issues associated with the inclusion of distributional concerns in community economic development goal setting.

Assessing Local Economic Development Policy

In policy analysis, the process begins by specifying what we are interested in knowing. In evaluating local economic development policy, we must first define what we mean by "development." For many, development equates to aggregate growth of jobs and income. Others argue to the extent there is public investment in local economic development, programs should benefit the least among us, such as jobless persons or the working poor. Still others focus on quality measures such as increasing the number of firms paying a "living wage," or those that enhance the "sustainability" of the community.

To a large degree, the type of policy analysis technique used depends on the questions asked. The questions, in turn, reflect the goals established for an economic development program. Often presumed and unspoken, the policy analysis process begins by answering a simple, yet difficult question: just what are we trying to accomplish?

Role of Economic Models in Policy Analysis

There are a number of advantages associated with using economic models for policy analysis (Dervis, de Melo, and Robinson, 1982). First, the modeling process provides a means for validating our perceptions about complex relationships in the world. Analyzing policy requires quantifying outputs and specifying the nature of the relationships that exist between economic entities. We make clear our assumptions about how the world works, including acknowledging the simplifying and limiting assumptions of our techniques.

Another benefit of economic models is the capacity to consider the indirect effects associated with policy. Many indirect effects are subtle and may be far removed from the immediate proximity of a policy. Modeling approaches can trace these indirect effects over time and across space.

Finally, economic models have the capacity to simultaneously consider multiple objectives and outcomes. Often, the conclusion to a policy debate is characterized in terms of net benefit or cost, when, in fact, the impacts are several and separate. Economic models provide an improved ability to consider the trade-offs that are often inherent in choosing a course of action.

Steps in Policy Analysis Using Economic Models

Policy analysis that incorporates economic models occurs in two steps (Sadoulet and de Janvry, 1995). The first involves building models intended to reflect economic relationships of interest. Typically, these models consist of at least three components: the economic agent of interest (households, business sectors, etc.) internal to the model (community, state, nation); the external factors that impinge on the system for which there are no internal control mechanisms (non-local taxes, tariffs, commuting patterns); and the policy instrument intended to affect the economic agent of interest (local tax breaks, income transfers, etc.).

The process of "solving" the model involves specifying some baseline condition. The baseline, or base run, is intended to reflect observed conditions in the economy. Sometimes, the process of solving the model is as simple as inserting readily available data of observable activity into the model. Other times, values must be estimated using econometric methods or solved as residuals when there are no sources for the needed information. The process of replicating what are assumed to be existing economic conditions is an essential part of the model validation process.

Another essential purpose of the base run is to establish a benchmark against which to assess the impact of the policy or event. Without the policy, there would still exist some state of affairs in the community. The impact of the policy is the incremental difference between what was assumed to exist before and what happens after the policy is implemented. The baseline might be a static snapshot of pre-policy conditions or it might include a trend line if temporal relationships are considered.

Many analysts who perform impact or policy analysis, present the "gross" impacts of a new business or activity in terms of jobs or similar measures. Failing to consider an alternative state of affairs would be to suggest that, had the new business not existed, all of the workers and their families would exit the region, the land and facilities would have no alternative use, and the investment would necessarily go elsewhere. This clearly overstates the impact of the activity, though credibly guessing the alternative state of affairs often presents very difficult challenges.

Criteria for Policy Analysis Using Economic Models

As indicated, evaluation depends on the goals the policy was intended to achieve. From the modeler's perspective, however, it may not always be possible to know the true and full intent of the policymaker. Thus there are a number of established economic concepts that are often used to quantify the "goodness" of a policy (Sadulet and de Janvry, 1995).

Efficiency-type measures are the most straightforward. Efficiency measures are typically such things as increased sales, income, or jobs. At a state level, it might be expressed as gross state product, or gross domestic product at the national level. Other potential measures of interest, however, are not so easily quantified.

Changes in the *welfare* of individuals and groups are frequently the focus of policy analysis and can be quantified in monetary terms. We would assert that individuals are better off if the price they pay for an item goes down, if the price they receive for their labor increases, or if they are willing to pay more for access to some new alternative. This is referred to as consumer surplus. While it is a simple and compelling concept, it can be very difficult to sort out when there are multiple price and income changes occurring simultaneously.

A frequently used concept intended to reflect consumer surplus is called compensating variation. This is the amount of money which, when taken away (or added) after the price or income changes in response to the policy, leaves a person at exactly the same level of satisfaction as before. The notion of compensation to accept some change is commonly used and can be quantified and aggregated across individuals.

Probably the simplest measure of individual welfare is a change in real (inflation adjusted) income. Measuring changes in welfare using real income has the advantage of simplicity and can be meaningfully aggregated. A potential difficulty using this measure is the selection of the price index used to adjust nominal into real income. Frequently used national price indices may not reflect local conditions.

There are a number of common measures intended to reflect the aggregate welfare of groups of people. Policy analysis at a state or national level might incorporate very broad aggregate measures such as trade balances or gross domestic product.

Another common aggregate welfare measure is poverty. Many believe one of the objectives of economic intervention by government should be the alleviation of poverty. The measurement of poverty itself, however, is a matter of debate. The most common way to measure poverty is to estimate the cost of the minimal quantity of goods and services needed by an individual or family compared to their actual income. What that minimal quantity is, and the variability of prices across places are the issues of debate. Sometimes alternative measures are used, such as health status or nutrition.

Measures of the inequality in the distribution of national income are frequently used as a measure of the aggregate welfare. Several measures of inequality exist. The simplest measure is the coefficient of variation, which is the ratio of the standard deviation of income to mean income.

A more complete measure of income inequality is the Gini coefficient and its graphical sibling, the Lorenz curve. The Lorenz curve maps on a graph the cumulative percentage of the population on the x-axis versus the cumulative percentage of income controlled by that proportion of the population on the y-axis. A perfectly diagonal line indicates a perfectly equal distribution of income. The further from the diagonal the actual curve is, the more unequal the distribution of income.

A convenient way of quantitatively expressing the degree of existing inequality is the Gini coefficient, which is a measure of the area between the Lorenz curve and the diagonal line divided by the area of the triangle under the diagonal line. A Gini coefficient of zero would indicate perfect equality in the distribution of income, while a coefficient of one indicates perfect inequality.

Many of these concepts related to individual and aggregate welfare are incorporated into the quantitative models capable of dealing with distributional concerns. Often, they are used to help specify the relationships between the economic agents being modeled. Certainly, they are useful in discussing the outcomes of the policy analysis.

Among the class of models introduced in the next section are those that build a set of economic accounts that represent regional economic activity. These accounts highlight the relationships among economic sectors, the social institutions that mediate economic relationships, and households. The accounts can be disaggregated in a fashion that highlights impacts to specific groups and sectors. In so doing, they shed light on the distributional consequences of economic policies and activities.

Regional Models to Assess Income Distribution

There are a variety of methods used for policy analysis that are capable of quantifying individual and aggregate welfare. Hedonic pricing methods are used to measure willingness-to-pay for many public and private goods and services (Rosen, 1974). Benefit-cost analysis is also frequently used for social decision-making, quantifying both positive and negative values associated with alternatives (Boardman et al., 1996). The branch of quantitative analysis techniques dealt with here is generally termed regional economic modeling. Regional models generally build on a set of economic accounts and add variations to enhance the realism of the system.

Determining the distributional characteristics of economic development policies requires identifying the relationship between productive activities and household income. Regional modeling techniques can identify these relationships. The class of models dealt with here begins by specifying a series of economic accounts that chart various transactions. The realism of these models increases as the accounting becomes more comprehensive, as assumptions regarding the relationships between the entities being modeled are allowed to vary, and as temporal dimensions are incorporated.

In this section, we'll proceed with a discussion of how regional economic accounts are constructed and how increasingly sophisticated adaptations enhance the realism of these models. We'll point out how these models explicitly and implicitly provide insight into distributional issues.

Input-Output Analysis

A major branch of regional quantitative analysis that opens possibilities for understanding distributional relationships begins with input-output analysis (Miller and Blair, 1985; Hewings, 1985; Miller, 1998). Input-output (I-O) analysis is a system of accounting for the economic flows in a region at a point in time. The I-O system is fundamentally concerned with the economic flows between regional industries in the process of production. Each industry is conceived as both a producer and as a consumer of goods and services. Industries produce goods and services through the use of factor inputs (labor, capital, land). The transactions between regional industries are specified in monetary units and organized to show how each industry purchases factor inputs and sells goods and services to every other. The flow of goods and services between industries is termed "interindustry transactions."

In addition to interindustry transactions, the I-O accounting system shows the sources of demand for an industry's production output. This is termed final demand, and generally consists of regional household consumption, private capital investment, government demand, and exports to demand outside the region. Interindustry transactions plus final demand provide an estimate of total regional industrial output. The structure of a simplified I-O account is shown in table 7.1.

An I-O table with three production sectors and two sources of final demand is presented in table 7.2 to illustrate how the accounts reflect the structure of the local economy. On the production side, I-O accounts also track inputs into the production of goods and services. In addition to the interindustry transactions, production inputs generally include value added and imported components of production. Value added includes the costs of labor, government taxes, interest payments on capital, land rental payments, profits, and adjustments to inventories. Alternatively, value added can be thought of as payments to the factors of production: land, labor, and capital plus indirect business taxes.

Information is organized into a transactions table that simultaneously shows production and consumption relationships in the region (nation, state, or sub-state area) during a period of time (typically one year). The elements

Table 7.1 Simplified Schematic of Input-Output Transactions

Processing Sectors	*Ag.* *Mfg.* *Service*	*Households*	*Exports*	*Output*
Agriculture Manufacturing Services	Interindustry Transactions	Household Demand	Exports	Total Industry Output
Households	Value Added			
Imports	Imports			
Total Inputs	Total Industry Inputs			

of the transactions table can be thought of as a series of "T accounts" used in financial accounting. In a T account, debits (expenses) are recorded on the left side while credits (revenue) are recorded on the right. The matrix format used in I-O modeling incorporates the same information in a more compact form. Each cell of the matrix simultaneously represents both the debits and the credits depending on the direction from which it is read. The debits of the T account are read in the columns of the transactions table, and the credits are read across the rows.

Industries are arrayed along both the top and lefthand side of the table. Also shown at the top of the table are categories of final demand. Along the left side are the transposed industries plus value added and imports to production. Reading across the top of the table, industries are viewed as purchasing sectors, and the same industries read down the side are selling sectors. Reading a column in total shows an aggregate production function for each sector. This production function is important for the purpose of using input-output analysis to estimate the impacts of economic change.

Table 7.2 Input-Output Transactions

	Purchasing Sectors			*Final Demand*		
Processing Sectors	*Ag.*	*Mfg.*	*Services*	*HH*	*Exports*	*Output*
Agriculture	4	8	2	4	12	30
Manufacturing	7	15	6	2	20	50
Services	6	5	4	8	2	25
Households	8	10	10			
Imports	5	12	3			
Total Inputs	30	50	25			

The predictive power of the accounting system is realized through a number of straightforward transformations. The first transformation involves converting all of the dollar figures in the table to a per dollar basis. That is, all of the table entries in the production-sector columns are divided by the column total. Now it becomes possible to see what proportion of the total each of the entries identified along the rows contributes to producing one dollar of output by the production sector listed at the top.

Once converted, the resulting direct requirements table provides a "production recipe" by reading down a column for each of the sectors listed at the top. If demand for output from any of the production sectors increases, it becomes possible to estimate how demand for the backward-linked industries will also change.

We know, however, that the economic interactions between the agents shown in the table are much more complex. As demand for the backward-linked industries increases, these industries also must increase their purchases of inputs. Similarly, households earn income of various types from the production activities. They, too, increase their purchases for household goods. All of this activity can be captured in a total requirements table. It can be easily constructed using matrix algebra.

Constructing the total requirements table generates economic multipliers of various types that can be used to project or estimate the impact of an event or policy to such things as the level of local economic activity, income generation or jobs.

Limiting Assumptions of Input-Output Analysis

Conventional I-O accounting embodies several important assumptions about production in the economy (Miller and Blair, 1985). The first is the

Table 7.3 Direct Requirements Matrix

	Purchasing Sectors		
Processing Sectors	*Ag.*	*Mfg.*	*Services*
Agriculture	.13	.16	.08
Manufacturing	.23	.30	.24
Services	.20	.10	.16
Households	.27	.20	.40
Imports	.17	.24	.12
Total Inputs	1.00	1.00	1.00

Table 7.4 Direct and Indirect Requirements Matrix

	Purchasing Sectors		
Processing Sectors	*Ag.*	*Mfg.*	*Services*
Agriculture	1.28	.32	.21
Manufacturing	.55	1.64	.52
Services	.37	.27	1.30
Total Inputs	2.20	2.23	2.03

assumption of a fixed production function. This is to say that production is a linear process where changing output creates no economies or diseconomies of scale. This also suggests that the technology of production is uniform across all similar sectors, with no variation in proportion or substitution in the use of factor inputs. Of course, both of these assumptions are unrealistic in that internal economies of scale are achieved in many firms and industries, and serve as an important source of enhanced productivity. Similarly, factor substitution is basic to competitive markets.

The second important assumption is that of fixed prices. Prices are fixed in the year of the analysis and remain invariant despite changing technology, consumption demand, factor migration, etc. This makes I-O analysis static and fixed to the conditions existing in the year of the analysis. This, too, is unrealistic in that the price of factor inputs has important effects on consumption patterns, production technologies, and firm competitiveness.

Similarly, the assumption of fixed technologies between firms and over time is unrealistic. In some economic sectors, for example, trade and certain consumer services, the assumption is less problematic. However, technology is rapidly changing in many manufacturing processes and professional services.

Finally, input-output is typically reflective of a demand-driven system. This is to say that the only sources of change to the system are exogenously induced changes in demand. There are assumed to be no supply constraints in any material or factor inputs—that is, supply is perfectly elastic. All of these assumptions point to the static nature of the analysis and the need to interpret analyses cautiously. In general, I-O accounting systems provide valuable insight into the structure of regional economic relationships. As a predictive tool, I-O is best used to estimate the impacts associated with smaller changes and in a short-term framework.

Input-Output Applications to Distributional Issues

The input-output framework has been used to model regional socioeconomic characteristics. The principle means has been through the disaggregation of value added and consumption accounts (Rose and Miernyk, 1989; Batey and Rose, 1990). Disaggregation indirectly addresses income distribution by separately accounting for the impacts of policies or change on population subgroups. Batey (1985) demonstrated ten extended I-O modeling procedures to represent household income classes, employment and unemployment in a static framework. Sharma and Saxena (1998) examined industry-labor linkages to project the employment impacts associated with trade liberalization. Several studies have estimated variable expenditure patterns and tax and transfer policies associated with labor migration in response to an economic shock (Miernyk et al., 1967; Batey and Madden, 1988; Batey and Weeks, 1989).

A second general extension of socioeconomic I-O analysis has been to incorporate occupational and labor market information (Richardson, 1985; Rose and Miernyk, 1989). The creation of an industry by occupation matrix embodies the same fixed proportion assumptions as the technical coefficients. By pre-multiplying the matrix by a vector of output change, it becomes possible to determine how an exogenous change will impact occupational opportunities (Rose and Miernyk, 1989). The creation of national occupation by industry matrices will likely lead to increased consideration of these effects (Li, Rose, and Eduardo, 1999; Rose, Stevens, and Davis, 1988).

Yet another method of using I-O techniques to assess distributional impacts is to compare regional input-output tables at two points in time. The observed changes can be analyzed to determine the fundamental sources driving that change, many of which have distributional implications. Siegel, Alwang, and Johnson (1995) demonstrated a method whereby regional structural change could be attributed to individual sources, such as changing labor to output or capital to output relationships. The technique, called structural decomposition, can be used to determine how changes are likely to affect sectoral employment, household income by income group, capital versus labor income growth, or other economic characteristics with distributional implications. Franke (1999) used similar techniques to show how changing technology in the economy influences distributional patterns.

Directly addressing income distribution, Miyazawa (1976; Hewings et al., 1999) disaggregated value added and consumption coefficients by household income class. Miyazawa's "interrelational income distribution multipliers" permits estimates of the impact that the direct change in income of one household income class will have on another income class. Recently, Rose and Li (1999) utilized interrelational multipliers to demonstrate how federal income transfers to low income households actually benefit high income households in the long run through the combination of consumer behavior, tax policy and production technology. Other applications of this approach in the United States have been made at the national and state levels (Rose and Beaumont, 1988, 1989), and for small rural regions (Bernat and Johnson, 1991).

The next extension of I-O analysis to explicitly address issues of income distribution is social accounting matrix (SAM) analysis. SAMs are highly detailed and flexible accounting systems that emphasize income flows and use the household as the salient unit of analysis. Whereas I-O methodologies tend to focus on the interaction of production sectors and how economic growth occurs, SAM methods were built to focus on the interaction between economic *and social* structures and how wealth is distributed.

A SAM can include disaggregated matrices of demographic and occupational structure. In addition, a SAM incorporates critical organizational structures that determine how income (including savings and investment) flows through the economic system. Social accounts detail the linkages between production, the institutions that organize wealth, and household income classes. Thus, SAM analysis has several important advantages over input-output analysis in the study of distributional issues: it focuses on the household as the unit of analysis and it includes consideration of more income sources that are important to distributional patterns. Following is a discussion of the use of this method to assess regional income distribution.

Social Accounting Matrix Analysis

The social accounting matrix is a comprehensive and disaggregated accounting system that captures the interdependencies of the socioeconomic structures present in a region (Thorbecke, 1998). As such, it provides unparalleled insight into the structure of the economy and a means for a wide range of policy and impact analyses.

The SAM is structured similar to an I-O table, but fully accounts for the flow of regional income. Following the stylized SAM diagram in table 7.5, the production sectors make payments to the value added and import

Table 7.5 Simplified Single Region Social Accounting Matrix

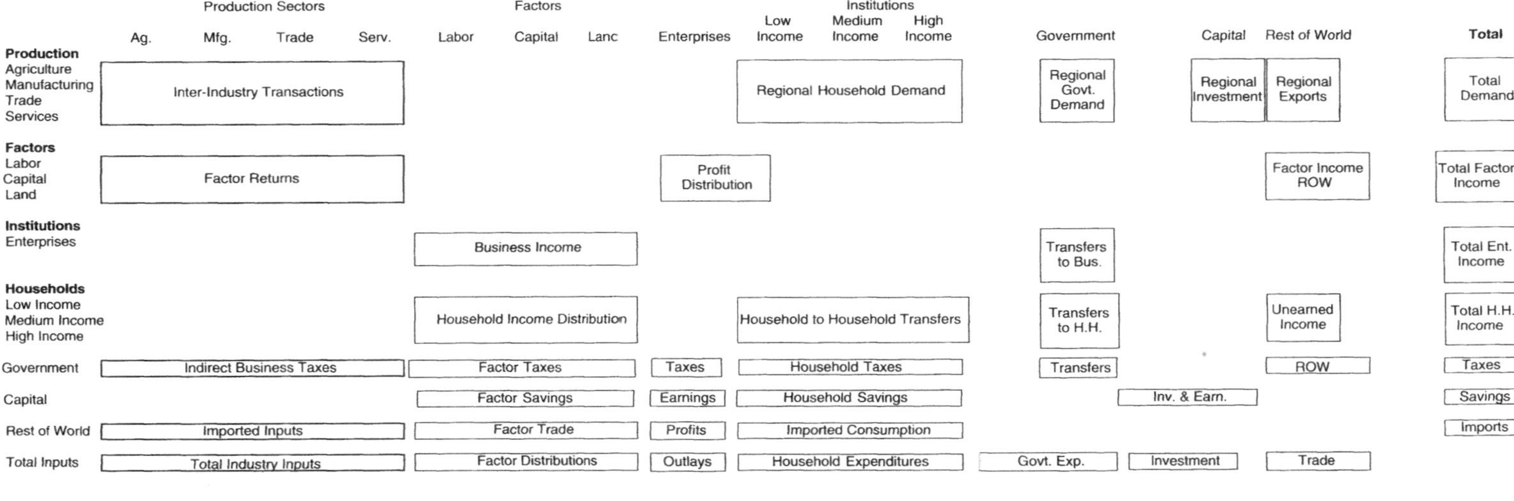

	Production Sectors				Factors				Institutions						
	Ag.	Mfg.	Trade	Serv.	Labor	Capital	Lanc	Enterprises	Low Income	Medium Income	High Income	Government	Capital	Rest of World	**Total**
Production Agriculture Manufacturing Trade Services	Inter-Industry Transactions								Regional Household Demand			Regional Govt. Demand	Regional Investment	Regional Exports	Total Demand
Factors Labor Capital Land	Factor Returns							Profit Distribution						Factor Income ROW	Total Factor Income
Institutions Enterprises					Business Income							Transfers to Bus.			Total Ent. Income
Households Low Income Medium Income High Income					Household Income Distribution				Household to Household Transfers			Transfers to H.H.		Unearned Income	Total H.H. Income
Government	Indirect Business Taxes				Factor Taxes			Taxes	Household Taxes			Transfers		ROW	Taxes
Capital					Factor Savings			Earnings	Household Savings				Inv. & Earn.		Savings
Rest of World	Imported Inputs				Factor Trade			Profits	Imported Consumption						Imports
Total Inputs	Total Industry Inputs				Factor Distributions			Outlays	Household Expenditures			Govt. Exp.	Investment	Trade	

accounts. In SAM analysis, the income included in the value added account is transformed into payments to the factors of production (labor, land, and capital). The factor accounts distribute the income to institutions. Institutions typically consist of households, enterprises, and government. Institutions save and invest in a variety of capital accounts and pay taxes to the government accounts.

Regional households, government, investment, and exports continue to provide final demand for regional production. In addition, other sources of income are represented, including transfer payments to households and enterprises as well as other income from outside the region. Finally, there are several accounts that reconcile regional and non-regional trading relationships.

The strengths of the SAM system are its comprehensive accounting of income sources, such as transfer payments, unearned income, and interregional (commuting) flows. This makes a wider variety of policy analyses possible. It is also a very robust system in its capacity to capture the influence of institutional rules and structure. Finally, the capacity to disaggregate accounts makes for more sensitive policy analysis. For example, households can be disaggregated by income classes to understand the distributional consequences of policies. Its major weakness, however, is the same set of simplifying assumptions inherent in input-output systems: linear production functions, fixed prices, and no factor substitution.

Applications of Social Accounting Matrix Analysis

The first fully articulated social accounting matrices were developed for national economies, beginning in the late 1970s (Pyatt and Thorbecke, 1976). Most national studies focused on less-developed countries, guiding policies to enhance prospects for large under-class populations. The development of SAMs for sub-national regions began only recently.

Social accounting and extended input-output methodologies have been used to assess a number of policy questions. In developing countries, Lewis and Thorbecke (1992) considered the relative ability of different production sectors to generate household income, and how income groups' expenditure patterns differed. Similar analyses were conducted in Italy (Civardi and Lenti, 1988) as well as in the United States (Reinert and Roland-Holst, 1992). James and Kahn (1993) showed how progressive income distribution policies promoted increased employment growth due to the differential expenditure patterns of income classes. A large number of studies have evaluated the distributional impacts of agriculture policies and trade liberalization (Townsend and McDonald, 1998; Dorosh and Haggblade, 1993). A SAM for the United States evaluated alternative agricultural policies (Adelman and Robinson, 1986; Kilkenny, 1991). Others have used various multiplier decomposition techniques to look at poverty alleviation (Thorbecke and Jung, 1996) and the relationship between income classes (Pradhan and Sahoo, 1996).

In the subnational studies, Lewis and Thorbecke (1992) critiqued a national development policy assumption regarding the ability of the agriculture sector to lead rural development in Kenya, while Kammas and Salehi-Esfahani (1992) undertook a similar evaluation of the tourism industry in Cyprus. The study of a Mexican village considered the effects of worker migration and alternative policies targeted to landless householders (Adelman, Taylor, and Vogel, 1988), while the India village study incorporated information related to land ownership and agricultural cropping systems (Subramanian and Sadoulet 1990). Rose, Stevens, and Davis (1988) developed a method for assessing the distributional impacts of natural resource policies for sub-state regions. Applications were made to a coal mining region and in areas affected by national forest management policies.

The social accounting matrix system is very robust. Applications of the concept have proliferated in numerous permutations. Community accounting matrices have been constructed for metropolitan regions, highlighting the interaction between inner-city neighborhoods and the rest of the metro region (Cole, 1987, 1999). Cole also applied SAM principles in building cultural accounts for a country to show how the cultural division of labor affects the well-being of different household groups (Cole, 1993). The concept has also been applied to environmental policies in various forms of E-SAMs (Weale, 1991; Edwards, 1996; Marcouiller and Deller, 1996; Pireddu and Dufournaud, 1996; Xie, 2000). Intergovernmental fiscal relations have been modeled in a fiscal SAM (Kilkenny, 1999).

Application of SAM Analysis to Identify Distributional Impacts of Local Economic Development Policies

A study by Leatherman and Marcouiller (1999) considered the distributional impacts of alternative, locally initiated economic development strategies in a small rural region. Development strategies focused on expanding productive activity in four sectors typically important in resource-dependent areas:

agricultural production, agricultural processing, timber production and wood processing, and tourism development. To assess the distributional impacts of local economic development strategies, a fixed-price multiplier analysis examined the impacts of a small change in final demand to the production sectors. The production accounts of interest included agricultural production, timber production and wood products processing, nondurable goods manufacturing (almost entirely food processing after removing wood products), and trade and services (within which tourism-sensitive enterprises are located). Effects were noted between income classes and across development strategies.

An exogenous shock was introduced in the form of a $10,000 increase to production. Shocks were sequentially applied to agricultural production, agricultural processing (nondurable manufacturing), forestry production and processing, and tourism (trade and services), while holding other sectors constant.

The total change to regional production is shown in table 7.6. Impacts are shown in actual dollars and share of total impact. The strategy with the largest aggregate regional impact was timber production and processing, with total regional economic activity increasing by $17,432. The least aggregate return to regional production was associated with tourism development at $12,274. If the objective is to maximize the growth of regional economic activity, local development officials would choose a forestry development strategy as highest priority.

A typical I-O analysis would account for the growth in regional income as aggregate value added. The strength of SAM analysis is the ability to go beyond computing value added to look at the distribution of factor returns. For regional households, labor returns are the primary source of income. SAM analysis considers the intensity of labor inputs into various economic activities and charts the returns flowing to different income groups. Labor returns were further disaggregated by occupational category.

The tourism development strategy shown in table 7.7 generated the most total factor returns with $6,999, as well as the largest total return to labor at $4,592. Tourism was a relatively labor-intensive activity compared to sectors that required a higher content of intermediate purchased inputs, capital, and imported inputs. Tourism development also provided the largest total returns to capital with $2,099. This was due to locally owned investments in tourism-sensitive businesses.

Table 7.6 Impact to Kickapoo Valley, WI, Regional Output by Economic Sector of a $10,000 Demand Increase to Alternative Development Sectors, 1991

	Agricultural Production		*Agricultural Processing*		*Timber Production and Wood Processing*		*Tourism*[a]	
Production Sector	*Dollars*	*Percentage*	*Dollars*	*Percentage*	*Dollars*	*Percentage*	*Dollars*	*Percentage*
Agriculture	10,580	82.3	2,713	18.7	119	0.7	46	0.4
Forestry and wood products	3	0.0	4	0.0	12,815	73.5	3	0.0
Construction	81	0.6	32	0.2	74	0.4	70	0.6
Nondurable manufacturing	106	0.8	10,178	70.0	40	0.2	52	0.4
Durable manufacturing	10	0.1	4	0.0	10	0.1	4	0.1
Trade	547	4.3	483	3.3	551	3.2	5,549	45.2
Services	1,510	11.8	1,103	7.6	3,789	21.7	6,510	53.0
Government and schools	17	0.1	23	0.2	34	0.2	40	0.3
Total Output	12,854	100.0	14,540	100.0	17,432	100.0	12,274	100.0

[a] Tourism was assumed to include lodging, food/restaurants, gas and auto repair, and other tourism. Exogenous demand change was equally applied to trade and service sectors.

Table 7.7 Impact to Kickapoo Valley, WI, Regional Factor Returns and Occupational Structure of a $10,000 Demand Increase to Alternative Development Sectors, 1991

	Agricultural Production		*Agricultural Processing*		*Timber Production and Wood Processing*		*Tourism*	
Factors	*Dollars*	*Percentage*[a]	*Dollars*	*Percentage*	*Dollars*	*Percentage*	*Dollars*	*Percentage*
Labor	2,539	74.4	1,933	68.6	2,764	61.2	4,592	65.6
Capital	687	20.1	801	28.4	1,487	32.9	2,099	30.0
Land	189	5.5	84	3.0	265	5.9	308	4.4
Total Factor Returns	3,415	100.0	2,818	100.0	4,516	100.0	6,999	100.0
Labor—Occupations								
Management/professional	580	22.8	478	24.8	755	27.3	1,371	29.8
Technical/sales/support	401	15.8	425	22.0	558	20.2	1,902	41.4
Services	81	3.2	61	3.1	127	4.6	265	5.8
Farm/forestry/fishing	1,160	45.7	298	15.4	939	34.0	9	0.2
Production/craft/repair	317	12.5	671	34.7	385	13.9	1,045	22.8
Occupation sum	2,539	100.0	1,933	100.0	2,764	100.0	4,592	100.0

[a] Factor percentages sum to total factor returns. Occupational return percentages sum to total labor returns.

Disaggregating labor returns by occupational category provided insight into how economic change distributed benefit across the labor force. This information can be of value for those places seeking to upgrade the "quality" of their labor force by creating demand for higher-paying occupations.

The impacts to households are shown in table 7.8. Again, the tourism development strategy provided the largest return to total household income with $6,143. Tourism development also funneled the largest relative share of impact to the low- (3.7 percent) and high-income (65.1 percent) groups. This was because the tourism sector generally consisted of relatively lower-skill, labor-intensive enterprises owned by upper-income proprietors. The medium-income group received its largest relative share from agricultural production, with 35.6 percent of the total impact. These results suggest that a tourism development strategy will benefit upper- and lower-income categories relatively more.

In this study, economic growth associated with timber production and processing generated the most economic activity, whereas tourism growth generated the largest share of local income. This was due to the factor input requirements associated with different sectors. Tourism-sensitive businesses required a larger relative share of labor inputs, whereas other strategies required a larger relative share of intermediate production inputs, capital, or imported inputs.

Aggregate measures, such as total output or income, tell us little about the beneficiaries of economic growth, which may be an important consideration if the goal is to enhance the long-term viability of the community. The advantage of social accounting matrix analysis is in the detail of disaggregated accounts. This detail provides more information about who benefits (or pays) when economic change occurs. Such information can allow local officials to attach normative judgments regarding the capacity of one strategy versus another to benefit targeted socioeconomic groups.

The SAM approach disaggregates impacts to specific groups identified by household income or occupational categories. This study compared the impacts associated with sectors that are often the targets of local economic development strategies. Across all strategies, high-income households received between 61 percent and 65 percent of the earned income generated by productive activities. Medium-income households received between 31 percent and 36 percent of earned income, and low-income households received between 3 percent and 4 percent. Thus, any growth in regional activity that generates income will maintain distributional disparities,

Table 7.8 Impact to Kickapoo Valley, WI, Regional Households by Household Income Group of a $10,000 Demand Increase to Alternative Development Sectors, 1991

	Agricultural Production		*Agricultural Processing*		*Timber Production and Wood Processing*		*Tourism*	
Household Income Class	*Dollars*	*Percentage*	*Dollars*	*Percentage*	*Dollars*	*Percentage*	*Dollars*	*Percentage*
Low (less than $20,000)	94	3.0	92	3.5	145	3.3	230	3.7
Medium ($20,000–$40,000)	1,118	35.6	849	32.5	1,484	33.6	1,917	31.2
High (more than $40,000)	1,932	61.4	1,671	64.0	2,784	63.1	3,996	65.1
Total Household Income	3,144	100.0	2,612	100.0	4,413	100.0	6,143	100.0

though the differences in share will add up over time to affect the rate of improvement or decline between income classes.

High-income households own a disproportionate share of land and capital resources and account for the highest value of labor resources. Any factor returns associated with regional economic activity will disproportionately accrue to this group based on these ownership characteristics. Thus, in the absence of intervening forces, existing wealth will generate more wealth. One obvious implication for local development strategies intended to raise the relative position of those at the low end of the income distribution would be to invest in training programs to increase the value of low-income household labor resources.

Low- and high-income households received their largest relative share of income from a tourism development strategy, whereas medium-income households received their largest share from agricultural production. This was due to the combined effects of initial endowment of factors by household income classes in combination with the factor input requirements of the different economic sectors. Agricultural producers tended to be middle-income households owning land and capital inputs to agricultural production. Tourism businesses were owned by high-income proprietors who received the greatest share of returns to capital (proprietary income and other property income). Similarly, tourism businesses employed a relatively large number of lower-skilled workers, the type of labor resources owned by low-income households who received most of their earned income from wages. One of the implications associated with the promotion of a tourism development strategy would be the potential of "hollowing-out" the income distribution over time.

The analysis of occupational impacts showed the income accruing to five labor categories. This type of analysis has relevance to the extent that local development programs may seek to promote greater opportunities in better-paying occupations to attract and hold the region's human resources. Again, it becomes possible to attach normative judgments to the relative distribution of income flowing to various occupational categories.

Linear Programming Models

Input-output and social accounting matrix approaches offer insight into regional economic relationships. They incorporate a number of simplifying assumptions, however, that limit their utility in evaluating policy alternatives.

Linear programming models can extend the basic linear structure of input-output systems while introducing additional flexibility into the assumptions governing economic relationships. Linear programming approaches work well when the need is to determine how to best use scarce resources to maximize certain objectives (Isard, 1998a).

Linear programming (LP) models permit policy analysis that reveal "optimal" outcomes based on multiple objectives, taking into account the role of prices, and specifying in detail the constraints to which the system is subject. The constraints can include such considerations as levels of production, income generation and distribution, and political feasibility. Such programming models can simultaneously consider alternative perspectives in response to a policy change, including those of policymakers, regional producers, and households.

Linear programming models can be relatively simple sectoral models or very large national planning models. Whether large or small, however, they are all formulated on a simple basic structure. That is, the model will (1) maximize one or more specified objectives, (2) utilize a set of policy instruments, and (3) be subject to a series of pre-specified constraints.

The advantage the LP approach offers is that the maximization of multiple objectives implies many potential solutions to the policy problem, whereas input-output approaches typically imply only one best outcome. Secondly, the introduction of the constraints can allow much greater flexibility in specifying trade-offs and other limitations associated with the use of factor inputs and the types of production outputs. Finally, the models are considered dynamic because they can extend over a period of time.

A number of LP models have been created for use in policy analysis. One of the first was a model developed for Mexico for agriculture policy analysis (Hazell and Norton, 1986) The model contained over 2,200 equations representing supply and demand specifications for thirty-three crops, organized spatially into four major regions and twenty subregions. From a development perspective, interregional labor migration and household labor were incorporated suggesting potential impacts of agricultural policy and events to different regions with known development needs. Similar models have also been developed for Egypt, Turkey, the Philippines, Tunisia, and Malaysia. Other recent applications have addressed natural resource use (Onal et al., 1998; Cornwell and Creedy, 1997) and the multiple reasons poverty remains persistent in a developing country (Alwang and Siegel, 1999).

LP methods represent an improvement in modeling economic relationships, but also have several disadvantages (Sadoulet and de Janvry, 1995). The price feedback relationships within the model are imperfect, limiting some of the realism of analysis results. New methods of introducing nonlinear relationships into programming models, however, will help improve this problem (Isard, 1998a). The larger models are also cumbersome and data intensive. Finally, the optimization rules used to govern behavior are largely arbitrary. The weights attached to different policy objectives are largely a matter of subjective discretion.

Integrated Regional Models

There has long been interest among regional scientists in integrating methodological approaches (Isard, 1960, 1998b). From the perspective of regional modeling with distributional implications, the integration of input-output and econometric methods is most relevant. Rey (1999) recently reviewed the status of integrated econometric/input-output (EC/I-O) modeling. He indicated there were both theoretical and practical advantages associated with integrated models.

The principal theoretical motivation for integrating EC/I-O models is to compensate for the restrictive assumptions associated with using either approach in isolation. As indicated, I-O modeling assumes linear production functions, no economies of scale, and no price responsiveness. Regional EC models can incorporate more realistic behavioral assumptions. Given the extensive data and calibration requirements, however, EC models are generally highly aggregated. I-O models, on the other hand, can be built with the high degree of disaggregation. By integrating these approaches, both are improved. More realistic economic behavioral assumptions can be incorporated into policy analysis, yet the high degree of disagregation needed for understanding impacts for specific sectors and entities is maintained.

On the practical side, integration can help to improve forecast performance, create more comprehensive impact analysis capability, and reduce measurement error. Much of the improvement stems from creating a dynamic model that incorporates a temporal dimension, yet maintains intersectoral detail.

There have been many applications of integrated models that directly or indirectly inform distributional policy. Some models consider substantive aspects of a region within a broader economic context. Examples include integrated economic-environment models (West and Jackson, 1998; Briassoulis, 1986; Hafkamp and Nijkamp, 1981). A number of other modelers have incorporated demographic, social, and labor market characteristics into extended I-O frameworks. Batey and Rose (1990) develop a framework for incorporating both a labor market and household income distribution component into an extended input-output framework. The fusion of regional science methods probably represents the next frontier in quantitative policy analysis (Isard, 1998b).

Computable General Equilibrium Models

Regional computable general equilibrium (CGE) models currently represent the state-of-the-art in modeling policy and economic impact analysis. CGE models begin with a fully specified, balanced social accounting matrix that comprehensively accounts for interregional commodity and income flows (Kraybill, 1991). The accounts are imported into specialized computer programs that specify relationships between the economic entities incorporated into the model.

The advantage of this system is the capacity to specify nonlinear relationships between economic entities based on changes in relative prices associated with output, labor and other factors. Thus, as production levels change, labor and capital can be substituted. Similarly, the level of demand for production outputs vary between regional and imported commodities. The capacity to incorporate prices and nonlinear relationships into CGE models enhances policy analysis because it more accurately reflects known economic behavior. CGE models can also incorporate a temporal dimension by allowing the model to solve for one time period and recursively feed the solution into a next time period.

Most early CGE models were constructed at a national level, principally for analysis of trade and tax policies (Shoven and Whalley, 1992; de Melo, 1988; Pereira and Shoven, 1988). More recently, there have been advances in the development of regional CGE models (Partridge and Rickman, 1998). Regional CGE models have been used to analyze a wide variety of policies and events, including federal fiscal policies and tariffs (Hanson and Reintert, 1997); agricultural, environmental and natural resource policies (Schreiner et al., 1996; Bernat and Hanson, 1995; Wiese, Rose, and Schluter, 1995); and regional tax policies (Waters, Holland, and Weber, 1997; Li and Rose, 1995).

In a development context, CGE models have been constructed to assess the impacts of agricultural policies on levels of poverty (de Janvry and Subbarao, 1986; Storm 1997, 1999; Yao, Liu, and Greener, 1996). Adelman and colleagues have developed a framework for specifying CGE models for village economies to assess the effects of policies on households disaggregated by land holdings, educational levels, and other demographic characteristics that affect household prospects (Adelman, Taylor, and Vogel, 1988; Taylor, Yunez-Naude, and Dyer, 1999; Taylor, Yunez-Naude, and Hampton, 1999).

While CGE models represent a significant improvement in the capacity to incorporate additional realism into regional policy analysis models, they are also not without drawbacks (Sadoulet and de Janvry, 1995). First, in a modeling system that incorporates so many behavioral relationships and responses, it becomes difficult to disaggregate the accounts in any great detail. Most models will typically contain perhaps eight to twelve production sectors, two to four types of labor, and three to six types of households. Among the reasons for the high degree of aggregation is the paucity for data that quantifies relationships, leaving the modeler to "guesstimate" many parameter values. Secondly, in many instances there is no real need to build a complex model when a simpler model can provide sufficient, albeit somewhat more crude, information needed for policy analysis.

Discussion and Implications

Regional accounting methods can improve our understanding about how the structure of the economy contributes to income disparities. Differences in factor input requirements across production sectors yield differential returns to household income groups based on their factor ownership characteristics. Changes in regional economic structure associated with macroeconomic trends or government transfer policies will alter local distributional patterns. This review showed how local economic development policy can also influence the distribution of income.

The analysis of alternative strategies in a small rural region illustrated several points related to local economic development decision-making. The first deals with the selection of impact measures which, in turn, reflect the objectives motivating local development programs. In the absence of detailed information, most development programs seek to maximize economic output, total income, or job creation. These are easily understood and communicated objectives, and are typically deemed sufficient to justify local investment of energy and resources. The results, however, suggested that the economic sector generating the most economic activity is not necessarily the sector that will maximize local income.

The local policy arena is complicated by numerous contextual factors, and variable prospects for economic sectors. Further, the ability of local policy to substantially affect distributional patterns is limited by regional factor ownership patterns. Yet, local policy exhibits distributional characteristics. When these characteristics are known, policymakers have the option of incorporating distributional concerns into local decision-making. It is our contention that distributional patterns have important implications for local economic viability. Thus there is a need to consider how distribution can be incorporated into decision-making. Regional accounting methods offer a means to gain insight into distributional impacts of local policies.

When the objective is to maximize total economic growth, aggregate impacts are sufficient without regard to distribution. The selection of the alternative maximizing total income return would be selected. If the objective is to maximize growth within a given income class, a disaggregate actual measure will show the total monetary flow to each income class. If the differences between income classes are important, a relative distributional measure will show which alternative will have the effect of increasing or decreasing those differences.

The perspective we support assumes that gross inequality in income distribution will negatively impinge on the viability of communities, and should be reduced when feasible. The feasibility of incorporating distributional objectives depends on the "cost" inherent in alternatives. A primary consideration is that the cost in regional income growth should not be too great. What cost is too great will be determined by local conditions and the perceived importance of distributional issues to the community.

Such a policy perspective will compare all available distribution measures. In communities or situations where it is more important to reduce the gap between high and low income groups, relative measures will be weighed more heavily in decision-making. However, this felt importance for reducing the distributional gap must be considered in the context of the actual amount of aggregate growth. At times, the differences may be small, and the decisions will be relatively easy. The community may have to grapple with difficult questions related to near-term affordability of a development perspective versus the long-term viability of the community.

By bringing distributional issues to the policy arena, the local community will facilitate a development perspective to economic decision-making. By considering the distributional costs and benefits of alternatives within the context of public debate, the community is taking steps toward making rational choices about its economic future.

This review demonstrates an ability to assess the distributional characteristics of local economic sectors and the distributional biases of local economic development strategies. SAM analysis is an accessible extension of I-O analysis; it provides a comprehensive accounting of regional income flows and a greater level of detail regarding the distribution of impacts. While other techniques currently may not be as readily accessible, continued development of technique and computer software programs will one day make them available to planners and economic development practitioners.

The extent to which distributional objectives ought to be considered in local policy will vary from place to place. In some communities, growth of any type may be needed to maintain an economic base. In other communities, the desire may be to foster a higher "quality" of economic opportunity or labor force, to promote the "middle class," or to use public resources to help the least advantaged in the community. In these places, quantitative analysis techniques provide a means to help achieve a more diverse set of normative objectives.

Distributional objectives can be accomplished without explicit redistribution policies that may create local competitive disadvantage. Instead, local development officials can use the information to help focus assistance programs and prioritize development alternatives, as is currently common with industrial targeting. In this way, local policy has an opportunity to broaden the goals of local economic development beyond aggregate growth. Regional accounting methods provide another tool to help craft more integrative local development policies.

REFERENCES

Abt Associates. 1997. "Interim Outcomes Assessment: Local Research Design Development." Pt. 1, ch. 2, Cambridge, MA, August.

Adelman, I. J., and S. Robinson. 1986. "U.S. Agriculture in a General Equilibrium Framework: Analysis with a Social Accounting Matrx." *American Journal of Agricultural Economics* 68(5): 1196–207.

Adelman, I. J., E. Taylor, and S. Vogel. 1988. "Life in a Mexican Village: A SAM Perspective." *Journal of Development Studies* 25(1): 5–24.

Aldrich, H. "Employment Opportunities for Blacks in the Black Ghetto: The Role of White-Owned Businesses." *American Journal of Sociology* 78 (1973): 1403–25.

Alexander, E. R. 2000. "Rationality revisited: Planning Paradigms in a Post-Modernist Perspective." *Journal of Planning Education and Research* 19: 242–56.

Alperovitz, G., and J. Faux. 1979. Introduction to "Towards a Public Balance Sheet," by David Smith. Washington, DC National Center for Economic Alternatives.

———. 1984. *Rebuilding America*. New York: Pantheon.

Alwang, J., and P. B. Siegel. 1999. "Labor Shortages on Small Landholdings in Malawi: Implications for Policy Reforms." *World Development* 27(8): 1461–75.

Anderson, J. E., and R. W. Wassmer. 2000. "Bidding for Business: The Efficacy of Local Economic Development Incentives in a Metropolitan Area." Kalamazoo, MI: W. E. Upjohn Institute.

Appold, S. J. 1998. "Labor Market Imperfections and the Agglomeration of Firms: Evidence from the Emergent Period of the US Semiconductor Industry." *Environment and Planning A*, 30: 439–62.

Argumedo, D., et al. 2000. "Strengthening Neighborhood-Oriented Retail Districts." Detroit Community Partnership Center, Urban and Regional Planning Program, University of Michigan, March.

Barnekov, T, J, and D. Rich. 1989. "Privatism and the Limits of Local Economic Development Policy." *Urban Affairs Quarterly* 25: 212–38.

Bartik T. J. 1991. *Who Benefits from State and Local Economic Development Policies?* W. E Upjohn Institute for Employment Research, Kalamazoo, Michigan.

———. 1993. "Who Benefits from Local Job Growth; Migrants or the Original Residents?" *Regional Studies* 27(4): 297–313.

Bartik, T, J., and R. D. Bingham. 1997. "Can Economic Development Programs Be Evaluated." In *Dilemmas of Urban Economic Development,* ed. R. Bingham and R. Mier, 246–77. Thousand Oaks, CA: Sage.

Bates, T. 1997. "Response: Michael Porter's Conservative Urban Agenda Will Not Revitalize America's Inner Cities: What Will?" *Economic Development Quarterly* 11(1): 39–44.

Batey, P. W. J. 1985. "Input-Output Models for Regional Demographic-Economic Analysis: Some Structural Comparisons." *Environment and Planning A* 17(1): 73–99.

Batey, P. W. J., and M. Madden. 1988. "The Treatment of Migration in an Extended Input-Output Modelling Framework." *Ricerche Economiche* 42(1): 34–66.

Batey, P. W. J., and M. J. Weeks. 1989. "The Effects of Household Disaggregation in Extended Input-Output Models." In *Frontiers of Input-Output Analysis,* ed. R. E. Miller, K. R. Polenske, and A. Z. Rose, 119–33. New York: Oxford University Press.

Batey, P. W. J., and A. Rose. 1990. "Extended Input-Output Models: Progress and Potential." *International Regional Science Review* 13(1): 27–49.

Baum, Robert. 1987. "The Economic Effects of State and Local Business Incentives." *Land Economics* 63: 348–360.

Beaumont, E. F., and H. A. Hovey. 1985. "State, Local and Federal Economic Development Policies: New Federal Patterns, Chaos or What?" *Public Administration Review* 45: 327–32.

Beauregard, R. A. 1994. "Constituting Economic Development." In *Theories of local economic development,* ed. R. D. Bingham and R. Mier, 267–83. Newbury Park, CA: Sage.

Benfield, F. K., M. D. Raimi, and D. D. T. Chen. 1999. *Once There Were Greenfields.* Washington, DC: National Resources Defense Council.

Benus, J. M., M. Wood, and N. Grover. 1994. "A Comparative Analysis of the Washington and Massachusetts UI Self-Employment Demonstrations." Unpublished report prepared for the U.S. Department of Labor, Employment and Training Administration, Unemployment Insurance Service, Contract no. 99–8-0803–98-047–01.

Berliner, J. S. 1999. *The Economics of the Good Society.* Malden, MA: Blackwell.

Bernat, G. A., Jr., and K. Hanson. 1995. "Regional Impacts of Farm Programs: A Top-Down CGE Analysis." *Review of Regional Studies* 25(3): 331–50.

Bernat, G. A., Jr., and T. G. Johnson. 1991. "Distributional Effects of Household Linkages." *American Journal of Agricultural Economics* 73(2): 326–33.

Bingham, R. D., and J. P. Blair. 1984. *Urban Economic Development.* Urban Affairs Annual Reviews 27. Beverly Hills, CA: Sage.

Blakely, E. J. 1989. *Planning Local Economic Development: Theory and Practice.* Newbury Park, CA: Sage.

Block, A. H. 1977. *Impact Analyses and Local Area Planning: An Input/Output Study.* Cambridge, MA: Center for Community Economic Development.

Bluestone, Barry, and B. Harrison. 1987. "Jobs, Income and Health." In *Deindustrialization and Plant Closure,* ed. P. D. Staudohar and H. E. Brown. Lexington, MA: Lexington.

Boardman, A. E., D. H. Greenberg, A. R. Vining, and D. L. Weimer. 1996. *Cost-Benefit Analysis: Concepts and Practice.* Upper Saddle River, NJ: Prentice Hall.

Boarnet, M. G., and W. T Bogart,. 1996. "Enterprise Zones and Employment: Evidence from New Jersey." *Journal of Urban Economics* 40(2): 198–216.

Bobrow, D. B., and J. S. Dryzek. *Policy Analysis by Design.* Pittsburgh: University of Pittsburgh Press.

Bockmeyer, J. L. 1996. "Community Coup: CDC Activism in Detroit's Empowerment Zone." Paper prepared for the meetings of the American Political Science Association, San Francisco.

Bowman, A. O'M. 1987. *The Visible Hand.* Washington, DC: National League of Cities.

———. 1988. "Competition for Economic Development Among Southeastern Cities." *Urban Affairs Quarterly* 23: 511–27.

Braun, D. 1991. "Income Inequality and Economic Development: Geographic Divergence." *Social Science Quarterly* 72(3): 520–36.

Briassoulis, H. 1986. "Integrated Economic-Environmental Policy Modelling at the Regional and Multiregional Level." *Growth and Change* 17(1): 22–34.

Brintnall, M.. "Evaluating State Enterprise Zone Programs: Performance Monitoring and Comparative Research." American Political Science Association, unpublished paper, n.d.

Brown, D. L., and M. E. Warner. 1991. "Persistent Low-Income Nonmetropolitan Areas in the United States: Some Conceptual Challenges for Development Policy." *Policy Studies Journal* 19: 22–41.

Browne, R. 1971. "Cash Flows in a Ghetto Economy: An Introductory Essay." *Review of Black Political Economy* 2: 28–39.

Browning, E. K., and J. M. Browning. 1983. *Public Finance and the Price System.* New York: Macmillan.

Bryun, S. 1987. "Beyond the Market and the State." In *Beyond the Market and the State,* ed. S. Bruyn and J. Meehan. Philadelphia: Temple University Press.

Burchell, R. W., J. H. Carr, R. L. Florida, J. Nemeth, M. Pawlik, and F. R. Barreto. 1984. *The New Reality of Municipal Finance: The Rise and Fall of the Intergovernmental City.* New Brunswick, NJ: Center for Urban Policy Research, Rutgers University.

Buss, T. F., and L. C. Yancer. 1999. "Cost-Benefit Analysis: A Normative Perspective." *Economic Development Quarterly* 13: 29–37.

Castro, B. 1998. "Manufacturing Jobs, Local Ownership, and the Social Health of Cities—A Research Note." *Responsive Community* 8: 63–66.

Cernea, M. 1991. "Knowledge from Social Science for Development Policies and Projects." In *Putting people first: Sociological variables in rural development,* ed. M. Cernea, 1–42. Oxford: Oxford University Press.

Civardi, B. A., and R. T. Lenti. 1988. "The Distribution of Personal Income at the Sectoral Level in Italy: A SAM Model." *Journal of Policy Modeling* 10(3): 453–68.

Clarke, S. E., and G. L. Gaile.. 1992. "The Next Wave: Postfederal Local Economic Development Strategies." *Economic Development Quarterly* 6: 187–98.

———. 1998. *The Work of Cities.* Minneapolis: University of Minnesota Press.

Clavel, P. 1986. *The Progressive City.* New Brunswick, NJ: Rutgers University Press.

Clingermayer, J., and R. C. Feiock. 1990. "The Adoption of Four Economic Development Policies in Large Cities." *Policy Studies Journal* 18: 539–52.

———. 1995. "Distribution and Redistribution in Economic Development: City Council Support for Targeting of Economic Development Policy Benefits." *Journal of Politics* 57: 508–20.

———. 1998. *Institutional Constraints and Local Policy Choices: An Exploration of Local Governance.* Albany: State University of New York Press.

Clinton, W. J. 1995. "Address before a Joint Session of the Congress on the State of the Union." Jan. 25, 1994, *Public Papers of the Presidents of the United States: William J. Clinton, 1994.* Book 1. Washington, DC: GPO.

Cole, S. 1987. "Growth, Equity and Dependence in a Restructuring City Region." *International Journal of Urban and Regional Research* 11(4): 461–77.

———. 1993. "Cultural Accounting in Small Economies." *Regional Studies* 27(2): 121–36.

———. 1994. "A Community Accounting Matrix for Buffalo's East Side Neighborhood." *Economic Development Quarterly* 8: 107–26.

———. 1996. "Neighborhood Development: Bootstrapping the East Side Economy." Working paper prepared for the Center for Regional Studies, State University of New York at Buffalo.

———. 1999. "In the Spirit of Miyazawa: Multipliers and the Metropolis." In *Understanding and Interpreting Economic Structure,* ed. G. J. D. Hewings, M. Sonis, M. Madden, and Y. Kimura, 263–86. New York: Springer.

Community and Economic Development Program, Michigan State University. 1997. *Community Income and Expenditure Model: Linkages and Leakages among Businesses, Households and Nonprofit Organizations in Southwest Detroit Zip Code 48209.* Lansing, MI: Community and Economic Development Program.

Community Ownership Organizing Project. 1976. *The Cities Wealth.* Washington, DC: Conference on Alternative State and Local Policies.

Connell, J. P., A. C. Kubisch, L. B. Schorr, C. H. Weiss, eds. 1995. *New Approaches to Evaluating Community Initiatives: Concepts, Methods and Contexts.* Washington, DC: Aspen Institute.

Cornwall, A., and R. Jewkes. 1995. "What Is Participatory Research?" *Social Science and Medicine* 41(12).

Cornwall, A., and J. Creedy. 1997. "Measuring the Welfare Effects of Tax Changes Using LES: An Application to A Carbon Tax." *Empirical Economics* 22(4): 589–613.

Corporation for Enterprise Development. 1999. *Strategic Planning for Economic Development.* Washington, DC: Corporation for Enterprise Development.

Courant P. N. "How Would You Know a Good Economic Development Policy If You Tripped Over One? Hint: Don't Just Count Jobs." *National Tax Journal* 47(4): 863–81.

Danziger, S., and P. Gottschalk. 1986. "Do Rising Tides Lift all Boats? The Impact of Secular and Cyclical Changes on Poverty." *American Economic Review* 76(2):405–10

Davidson, C. 1990. *Recent Developments in the Theory of Involuntary Unemployment.* W. E. Upjohn Institute for Employment Research, Kalamazoo, Michigan.

Davis, F. G. *The Economics of Black Community Development: An Analysis and Program for Autonomous Growth and Development.* Chicago: Markham, 1972.

De Janvry, A., and K. Subbarao. 1986. *Agricultural Price Policy and Income Distribution in India.* Delhi: Oxford University Press.

de Melo, J. 1988. "Computable General Equilibrium Models for Trade Policy Analysis in Developing Countries: A Survey." *Journal of Policy Modeling* 10(4): 469–503.

Dervis, K., J. de Melo, and S. Robinson. 1982. *General Equilibrium Models for Development Policy.* Washington, DC: World Bank.

Dewar, M. E. 2003. "The Detroit Empowerment Zone's Effect on Economic Opportunity: Employers' Responses to the Zone's Programs and Incentives." Report to the National Center for the Revitalization of Central Cities, University of New Orleans, March.

Dewar, M., and C. Isaac. 1998. "Learning from Difference: The Potentially Transforming Experience of Community/University Collaboration." *Journal of Planning Education and Research* 17(4).

Dorosh, P., and S. Haggblade. 1993. "Agriculture-led Growth: Food Grains versus Export Crops in Madagascar." *Agricultural Economics* 9(2): 165–80.

Dudley, K. M. 1994. *The End of the Line: Lost Jobs, New Lives in Postindustrial America.* Chicago: University of Chicago Press.

Dymski, G. A. 1997. "Business Strategy and Access to Capital in Inner-City Revitalization." In *The Inner City: Urban Poverty and Economic Development in the Next Century,* ed. T. D. Boston and C. L. Ross. New Brunswick, NJ: Transaction.

Economic Development Administration. 2000. *Comprehensive Economic Development Strategy Guidelines.* Washington, DC: U.S. Department of Commerce.

Edwards, T. H. 1996. "A Simplified CGE Approach to Modelling the Welfare Effects of Japanese Carbon Abatement Measures." In *Economic Modelling Under the Applied General Equilibrium Approach,* ed. A. Fossati, 3–31. Aldershot, UK: Avebury.

Eisenschitz, A. 1993. "Business Involvement in Community: Counting the Spoons or Economic Renewal?" In *Community Economic Development: Policy Formation in the US and UK,* ed. D. Fasenfest, 141–56. London: Macmillan; New York: St. Martin's.

Eisinger, P. 1988. *The Rise of the Entrepreneurial State: State and Local Economic Development Policy in the United States.* Madison: University of Wisconsin Press.

Elkin, S. L. 1987. *City and Regime in the American republic.* Chicago: University of Chicago Press.

———. 1999. "Citizen and City: Locality, Public-Spiritedness, and the American Regime." In *Dilemmas of Scale in America's Federal Democracy,* ed. M. Derthick, 41–60. Cambridge: Cambridge University Press.

Eng, E., and E. Parker. 1994. "Measuring Community Competence in the Mississippi Delta: The Interface between Program Evaluation and Empowerment." *Health Education Quarterly* 21(2): 199–220

Ewing, R. 1997. "Is Los Angeles–Style Sprawl Desirable?" *Journal of the American Planning Association* 63: 107–25.

Fan, C. C., and E. Casetti. 1994. "The Spatial and Temporal Dynamics of US Regional Income Inequality, 1950–1989." *Annals of Regional Science* 28(2): 177–96.

Farr, C. 1990. "Encouraging Local Economic Development: The State of Practice." *Municipal Yearbook, 1990.* Washington DC: International City Management Association.

Fasenfest, D. 1986. "Community Politics and Urban Redevelopment: Poletown, Detroit and General Motors." *Urban Affairs Quarterly* 22(1): 101–23

———. 1993. "Cui Bono? Public Subsidies and Business Locations Strategies." In *Grand Designs: Corporate Strategies and Their Effects on Unions, Workers and Communities,* ed. C. Craypo and B. Nissen, 119–37, Ithaca, NY: Cornell University Press.

Fasenfest, D., and P. Ciancanelli. 1988. "Public Costs and Private Benefits: The Pitfalls of Capital Budgeting for Reindustrialization." *Journal of Urban Affairs* 10: 291–307.

Fasenfest, D., P. Ciancanelli, and L. A. Reese. 1997. "Value, Exchange and the Social Economy: Framework and Paradigm Shift in Urban Policy." *International Journal of Urban and Regional Research* 21(1): 7–22.

Fasenfest, D., and L. A. Reese. 2002. *Evaluation Of EDA's Planning Program.* Washington, DC: Economic Development Agency, Department of Commerce.

Feagin, J. R., and R. Parker. 1990. *Building America's Cities: The Urban Real Estate Game.* Englewood Cliffs, NJ: Prentice Hall.

Federal Register. 1994. 59:11, January 18, 2700.

Feiock, R. C., and J. Clingermayer. 1986. "Municipal Representation, Executive Power, and Economic Development Policy Adoption." *Policy Studies Journal* 15: 211–30.

———. 1992. "Development Policy Choice: Four Explanations for City Implementation of Economic Development Policies." *American Review of Public Administration* 22: 49–65.

Feiock, R. C., and C. Stream. 2001. "Environmental Protection Versus Economic Development: A False Trade-off?" *Public Administration Review* 61(3): 313–22.

Felsenstein D., and J. Persky. 1999. "When Is a Cost Really a Benefit? Local Welfare Effects and Employment Creation in the Evaluation of Economic Development Programs." *Economic Development Quarterly* 13(1): 46–54.

Fetterman, D. M. 1994. "Steps of Empowerment Evaluation: From California to Cape Town." *Evaluation and Program Planning*, 17(3): 305–13.

Fetterman, D. M., S. J. Kaftarian, and A. Wandersman, eds. 1996. *Empowerment Evaluation: Knowledge and Tools for Self-Assessment and Accountability.* Thousand Oaks, CA: Sage.

Fisher, P. S., and A. H. Peters. 1998. *Industrial Incentives: Competition among American States and Cities.* Kalamazoo, MI: W. E. Upjohn Institute.

Fleischmann, A., G. P. Green, and T. M. Kwang. 1992. "What's a City To Do? Explaining Differences in Local Economic Development Policies." *Western Political Quarterly* 45: 678–99.

Fletcher, M. A. 1999. "More Retailers Are Sold on Cities." *Washington Post,* March 5, E1, E10.

Fournier, G. M., and D. W. Rasmussen. 1986. "Real Economic Development in the South: The Implications of Regional Cost of Living Differences." *Review of Regional Studies* 16(1): 6–13.

Franke, R. 1999. "Technical Change and a Falling Wage Share If Profits Are Maintained." *Metroeconomica* 50(1): 35–53.

Friedan, B. J., and L. Sagalyn. 1989. *Downtown, Inc.* Cambridge: MIT Press.

Friedman, M. 1962. *Capitalism and Freedom.* Chicago: University of Chicago Press.

Fusfeld, D. 1973. *The Basic Economics of the Urban Racial Crisis.* New York: Holt, Rinehart and Winston.

Fusfeld, D., and T. Bates. *The Political Economy of the Urban Ghetto.* Carbondale: Southern Illinois University Press, 1984.

Garber, J. A. 1989. "The Legal Crisis of Local Land Regulations: An Evaluation. *Urban Resources* 5: 15–20, 26.

———. 1990. "Law and the Possibilities for a Just Political Economy." *Journal of Urban Affairs* 12: 1–15.

Garn, H. A., and L. C. Ledebur. 1980. "The Economic Performance and prospects of cities." In *The Prospective City*, ed. A. Solomon, 204–51. Cambridge: MIT Press.

Giloth, R. 1988. "Community Economic Development: Strategies and Practices of the 1980s." *Economic Development Quarterly* 2: 343–50.

Giloth, R. 1997. "Commentary on 'Can Economic Development Programs Be Evaluated." In *Dilemmas of Urban Economic Development*, ed. R. Bingham and R. Mier, 278–83. Thousand Oaks, CA: Sage.

Gittell, M., J. Bockmeyer, R. Lindsay, K. Newman. 1998. "Expanding Civic Opportunity: Urban Empowerment Zones." *Urban Affairs Review* 33(4): 530–58.

Goetz, E. G. 1990. "Type II Policy and Mandated Benefits in Economic Development." *Urban Affairs Quarterly* 26: 170–90.

Gorter C., and J. van Ours. 1994. "Matching Unemployment and Vacancies in Regional Labor Markets: An Empirical Analysis for the Netherlands." *Papers in Regional Science* 73(2): 153–68.

Gottlieb, P. D. 1997. "Neighborhood Development in the Metropolitan Economy: A Policy Review." *Journal of Urban Affairs* 19: 162–82.

Green, G. P., A. Fleischmann, and T. M. Kwang. 1996. "The Effectiveness of Local Economic Development Policies in the 1980s." *Social Science Quarterly* 77: 609–25.

Guest, A. 2000. "The Mediate Community: The Nature of Local and Extralocal Ties within the Metropolis." *Urban Affairs Quarterly* 35(5): 603–27.

Gunn, C., and H. Gunn. 1991. *Reclaiming Capital: Democratic Initiatives and Community Development.* Ithaca, NY: Cornell University Press.

Gunnell, J. G. 1968. "Social Science and Political Reality: The Problem of Explanation." *Social Research* 35: 187–200.

Gutierrez, L., and A. Alvarez. 1997. Presentation at the faculty seminar on participatory research, University of Michigan, Ann Arbor, November.

Hafkamp, W., and P. Nijkamp. 1981. "Multiobjective Modeling for Economic Environmental Policies." *Environment and Planning A* 13(1): 7–18.

Hamermesh, D. S. 1971. *Economic Aspects of Manpower Training Programs: Theory and Policy.* Lexington, MA: D.C. Heath.

Hansen, S. B. 1989. "Targeting in Economic Development: Comparative State Perspectives." *Publius* 19(2): 47–62.

Hanson, K. A., and K. A. Reinert. 1997. "The Distributional Effects of the U.S. Textile and Apparel Protection." *International Economic Journal* 11(3): 1–11.

Harrison, B. 1974. "Ghetto Economic Development: A Survey." *Journal of Economic Literature* 12: 1–37.

Harrison, B., and T. Vietorisz. 1970. *The Economic Development of Harlem.* New York: Praeger.

Harrison, B., and A. K. Glasmeier. 1997. "Response: Why Business Alone Won't Redevelop the Inner City: A Friendly Critique of Michael Porter's Approach to Urban Revitalization." *Economic Development Quarterly* 11(1): 28–38.

Hazell, P., and R. Norton. 1986. *Mathematical Programming for Economic Analysis in Agriculture.* New York: Macmillan.

Henze, L., E. Kirschner, and L. Lillow. 1979. *An Income and Capital Flow Study of East Oakland, California.* Oakland, CA: Community Economics.

Herrero, T. 1991. "Housing Linkage: Will It Play a Role in the 1990s?" *Journal of Urban Affairs* 13: 1–19.

Herrick, B., and C. P. Kindleberger. 1983. *Economic Development.* New York: McGraw-Hill.

Herring, C., M. Bennett, D. Gills, and N. T. Jenkins. *Empowerment in Chicago: Grassroots Participation in Economic Development and Poverty Alleviation.* Chicago: Great Cities Institute, 1998.

Hewings, G. J. D. 1985. *Regional Input-Output Analysis.* Beverly Hills, CA: Sage.

Hewings, G. J. D., M. Sonis, M. Madden, and Y. Kimura. 1999. "Introduction." In *Understanding and Interpreting Economic Structure,* ed. G. J. D. Hewings, M. Sonis, M. Madden, and Y. Kimura, 1–12. New York: Springer.

Hill, C. 2000. "Measuring Success in the Redevelopment of Former Military Bases: Evidence from a Case Study of the Truman Annex in Key West, Florida." *Economic Development Quarterly* 14 (August): 265–75.

Holzer H. J. 1989. *Unemployment, Vacancies and Local Labor Markets,* W. E. Upjohn Institute for Employment Research, Kalamazoo, MI.

Holzer, H. J., R. N. Block, M. Cheatham, and J. H. Knott. 1993. "Are Training Subsidies for Firms Effective? The Michigan Experience." *Industrial and Labor Relations Review* 46 (July): 625–36.

Huff, J. O., and B, Waldorf. 1988. "A Predictive Model of Residential Mobility and Residential Segregation." *Papers of the Regional Science Association* 65: 59–77.

Imbroscio, D. L. 1993. "Overcoming the Economic Dependence of Urban America." *Journal of Urban Affairs* 15: 173–90.

———. 1995. "Nontraditional Public Enterprise as Local Economic Development Policy." *Policy Studies Journal* 23: 218–30.

———. 1997. *Reconstructing City Politics: Alternative Economic Development and Urban Regimes.* Thousand Oaks, CA: Sage, 1997.

Isard, W. 1960. *Methods of Regional Analysis: An Introduction to Regional Science.* New York: Wiley.

——— 1998a. "Programming and Industrial and Urban Complex Analysis." In W. Isard, I. J. Azis, M. P. Drennan, R. E. Miller, S. Saltzman, and E. Throbecke, *Methods of Interregional and Regional Analysis,* 211–41. Aldershot, UK: Ashgate.

———. 1998b. "New Channels of Synthesis: The Fusion of Regional Science Methods." In W. Isard, I. J. Azis, M. P. Drennan, R. E. Miller, S. Saltzman, and E. Throbecke, *Methods of Interregional and Regional Analysis,* 419–63. Aldershot, UK: Ashgate.

Israel, B. A., K. M. Cummings, M. B. Dignan, C. A. Heaney, Daniel P. Perales, Bruce G. Simons-Morton, and Marc A. Zimmerman. 1995. "Evaluation of Health Education Programs: Current Assessment and Future Directions." *Health Education Quarterly* 22(3): 364–89.

Israel, B. A., A. J. Schulz, E. A. Parker, and A. B. Becker. 1998. "Review of Community-Based Research: Assessing Partnership Approaches to Improve Public Health." *Annual Review of Public Health* 19: 173–202.

Jacobs, J. 1969. *The Economy of Cities.* New York: Random House.

———. 1984. *Cities and the Wealth of Nations: Principles of Economic Life.* New York: Random House.

Jakle, J. A., and D. Wilson. 1992. *Derelict Landscapes.* Savage, MD: Rowman and Littlefield.

James, J., and H. A. Khan. 1993. "The Employment Effects of an Income Redistribution in Developing Countries." *World Development* 21(5): 817–27.

Jenkins, N. Temaner, and M. I. J. Bennett. 1999. "Toward an Empowerment Zone Evaluation." *Economic Development Quarterly* 13(1): 23–28.

Johnson P. S., and R. B. Thomas. 1984. "Government Policies Towards Business Formation: An Economic Appraisal of a Training Scheme." *Scottish Journal of Political Economy* 31: 131–46.

Jones, B., and L. Bachelor. 1986. *The Sustaining Hand.* Lawrence: University Press of Kansas.

Jones, S. 1989. "Reservation Wages and the Cost of Unemployment." *Economica* 56: 225–46.

Just, R., Hueth, D., and A. Schmitz. 1982. *Applied Welfare Economics and Public Policy.* Englewood Cliffs, NJ: Prentice-Hall.

Kammas, M., and H. Salehi-Esfahani. 1992. "Tourism and Export-led Growth: The Case of Cyprus, 1976–1988." *Journal of Developing Areas* 26(4): 489–506.

Kilkenny, M. 1991. "A SAM for Farm Policy Analysis." In *Proceedings: IMPLAN.* May 20–22, 91–104. Western Rural Development Center. Corvallis: Oregon State University.

———. 1999. "Interregional Fiscal Accounting." *Growth and Change* 30(4): 567–89.

Kim, H. 1993. "The Florida Enterprise Zone Program." Tallahassee, Florida State University, Department of Urban and Regional Planning. Ph.D. dissertation.

Kirby, A. 1985. "Nine Fallacies of Local Economic Change." *Urban Affairs Quarterly* 21: 207–20.

Knott, J. H., and G. J. Miller. 1987. *Reforming Bureaucracy: The Politics of Institutional Choice*. Englewood Cliffs, NJ: Prentice-Hall.

Kraybill, D. S. 1993. "Computable General Equilibrium Analysis at the Regional Level." In *Microcomputer-Based Input-Output Modeling: Applications to Economic Development*, ed. D. M. Otto and T. G. Johnson, 198–215. Boulder, CO: Westview Press.

Krikelas, A. C. 1992. "Why Regions Grow: A Review of Research on the Economic Base Model." *Economic Review of the Federal Reserve Bank of Atlanta* 77(4): 16–29.

Krumholz, N. 1991. "Equity and Local Economic Development." *Economic Development Quarterly* 5: 291–300.

Kuttner, R.. 1997. *Everything for Sale: The Virtues and Limits of Markets.* New York: Knopf.

Ladd, H. F., and Yinger, J. 1989. *America's Ailing Cities Fiscal Health and the Design of Urban Policy.* Baltimore: Johns Hopkins University Press.

Lansing J. B., C. W. Clifton, and J. N. Morgan. 1969. *New Homes and Poor People; A Study of Chains of Moves.* Ann Arbor: Institute for Social Research, University of Michigan.

Leatherman, J. C., and D. W. Marcouiller. 1999. "Moving Beyond the Modeling of Regional Economic Growth: A Study of How Income Is Distributed to Rural Households." *Economic Development Quarterly* 13(1): 38–45.

Levernier, W., M. D. Partridge, and D. S. Rickman. 1995. "Variation in U.S. State Income Inequality: 1960–1990." *International Regional Science Review* 18(3): 355–76.

Levine, M. V. 1987. "Downtown Redevelopment as an Urban Growth Strategy: A Critical Appraisal of the Baltimore Renaissance." *Journal of Urban Affairs* 9: 103–23.

———. 1988. "Economic Development in States and Cities: Toward Democratic and Strategic Planning in State and Local Government." In Marc Levine et al., *The State and Democracy*, 111–46. New York: Routledge.

———. 1989. "The Politics of Partnership: Urban Redevelopment since 1945." In *Unequal Partnerships: The Political Economy of Urban Redevelopment in Postwar America*, ed. G. D. Squires, 12–34. New Brunswick, NJ: Rutgers University Press.

Levy, J. M. 1992. "The US Experience with Local Economic Development." *Environment and Planning C: Government and Policy* 10: 51–60.

Lewis, B. D., and E. Thorbecke. 1992. "District-Level Economic Linkages in Kenya: Evidence Based on a Small Regional Social Accounting Matrix." *World Development* 20(6): 881–97.

Li, P. C., and A. Rose. 1995. "Global Warming Policy and the Pennsylvania Economy: A Computable General Equilibrium Analysis." *Economic Systems Research* 7(2): 151–71.

Li, P. C., Rose, A., and B. Eduardo. 1999. "Construction of an Input-Output Income Distribution Matrix for the U.S." In *Understanding and Interpreting Economic Structure,* ed. G. J. D. Hewings, M. Sonis, M. Madden, and Y. Kimura, 191–213. New York: Springer.

Lieber, M. D. 1997. "COPC Conference on Evaluation: Transcript of Conference Discussions." Department of Anthropology, University of Illinois at Chicago, October, 32–35.

Lindblom, C. E. 1982. "Markets as Prison." *Journal of Politics* 44: 324–36.

Lipshitz, G. 1992. "Divergence versus Convergence in Regional Development." *Journal of Planning Literature* 7(2): 123–38.

Loftman, P. 1995. "The Politics of Evaluation Research: A case Study of Birmingham's Prestige Projects." Paper presented at the annual meeting of the Urban Affairs Association, Portland, Oregon.

Logan, J. R., and H. Molotch. 1987. *Urban Fortunes.* Berkeley: University of California Press.

Luria, D., and J. Russell. 1981. *Rational Reindustrialization: An Economic Development Agenda for Detroit.* Detroit: Widgetripper Press.

———. 1982. "Rebuilding Detroit: A Rational Reindustrialization Strategy." *Socialist Review* 12: 163–83.

Lustig, R. J. 1985. "The Politics of Shutdown: Community, Property, Corporatism." *Journal of Economic Issues* 19: 123–51.

Lynd, S. 1987a. "The Genesis of the Idea of a Community Right to Industrial Property in Youngstown and Pittsburgh, 1977–1987." *Journal of American History* 74: 926–58.

———. 1987b. "Towards a Not-For-Profit Economy: Public Development Authorities for Acquisition and Use of Industrial Property." *Harvard Civil Rights-Civil Liberties Law Review* 22: 13–41.

———. 1989. "The Genesis of the Idea of a Community Right to Industrial Property in Youngstown and Pittsburgh, 1977–1987." *Changing Work* (spring): 14–19.

Machiavelli, N. 1964. *The Prince and Other Works.* Trans. Allan H. Gilbert. New York: Hendricks House.

MacKinnon, R., and P. Rogerson. 1980. "Vacancy Chains, Information and Inter-Regional Migration." *Environment and Planning A* 12: 649–58.

Manatee County Chamber of Commerce. 2002. "Business and Economic Development" Bradenton, FL: Manatee County Chamber of Commerce.

Mankiw, N. G. and D. Romer, eds. 1991. *New Keynesian Economics.* Vol. 2. Cambridge: MIT Press.

Marcouiller, D. W., and S. C. Deller. 1996. "Natural Resource Stocks, Flows, and Regional Economic Change: Seeing the Forest and the Trees." *Journal of Regional Analysis and Policy* 26(2): 95–116.

Markely D., and K. McNamara. 1995. "Economic and Fiscal Impacts of a Business Incubator." *Economic Development Quarterly* 9(1): 273–78.

Markusen, A. R. 1987. *Regions: The Economics and Politics of Territory.* Totowa, NJ: Rowman and Littlefield.

Martin, R., and S. P. 1998. "Slow Convergence? The New Endogenous Growth Theory and Regional Development." *Economic Geography* 74(3): 201–27.

McGuire, M. 2000. "Collaborative Policy Making and Administration: The Operational Demands of Local Economic Development." *Economic Development Quarterly* 14: 276–91.

Meter, K. 1995. *Camden Community Income Statement and Balance Sheet.* Minneapolis: Crossroads Resource Center.

———. 1998. "Neighborhood Balance Sheets Assess Local Economies." Chicago: Working paper prepared for the American Planning Association, 1998 Casey Symposium on Indicators, October 29–30. <http://www.planning.org>

Mier, R., and R. D. Bingham. 1994. "Metaphors of Economic Development." In *Theories of Local Economic Development,* ed. R. D. Bingham and R. Mier, 284–304. Newbury Park, CA: Sage.

Miernyk, W. H., E. R. Bonner, J. H. Chapman, Jr., and K. L. Shellhammer. 1967. *Impact of the Space Program on a Local Economy.* Morgantown: West Virginia University Library.

Miller, R. E. 1998. "Regional and Interregional Input-Output Analysis." In W. Isard, I. J. Azis, M. P. Drennan, R. E. Miller, S. Saltzman, and E. Throbecke. *Methods of Interregional and Regional Analysis,* 41–133. Aldershot, UK: Ashgate.

Miller, R. E., and P. D. Blair. 1985. *Input-Output Analysis: Foundations and Extensions.* Englewood Cliffs, NJ: Prentice-Hall.

Mintrom, M., and L. Ramsey. 1995. "State Policy Signaling and Firm-Level Employment Decisions." Paper presented at the Annual Meeting of the American Political Science Association, Chicago, September 1.

Miyazawa, K. 1976. *Input-Output and the Structure of Income Distribution.* New York: Springer-Verlag.

Molotch, H. 1976. "The City as a Growth Machine." *American Journal of Sociology* 82: 309–32.

———. 1982. *The New City-States.* Washington, DC: Institute for Local Self-Reliance.

Moore, T. S. 1996. *The Disposable Work Force: Worker Displacement and Employment Instability in America.* New York: Aldine de Gruyter.

Morris, D. 1998. "Defending Community in an Age of Globalization." *Canadian Dimension* 32(3): 15–19.

Nathan, R. P. 1982. "The Methodology for Field Network Evaluation Studies." In *Studying Implementation: Methodological and Administrative Issues,* ed. W. Williams. Chatham, NJ: Chatham House.

Nelson A. Rockefeller Institute of Government. 1997. "Building a Community Plan for Strategic Change: Findings from the First Round Assessment of the Empowerment Zone/Enterprise Community Initiative." State University of New York, Albany.

New York Times. 1996. *The Downsizing of America.* New York: Times Books.

Ngarambé, O., S. J. Goetz, and D. L. Debertin. 1998. "Regional Economic Growth and Income Distribution: County-level Evidence from the U.S. South." *Journal of Agricultural and Applied Economics* 30(2): 325–37.

North, D. C. 1990. *Institutions, Institutional Change, and Economic Performance.* Cambridge: Cambridge University Press.

Nowak, J. 1997. "Neighborhood Initiative and the Regional Economy." *Economic Development Quarterly* 11: 3–10.

Nunn, S. 1994. "Regulating Local Tax Abatement Policies: Arguments and Alternative Policies for Urban Planners and Administrators." *Policy Studies Journal* 22: 574–88.

Oakland, W. H., F. T. Sparrow, and H. L. Stettler. 1971. "Ghetto Multipliers: A Case Study of Hough." *Journal of Regional Science* 11: 337–45.

Office of Mayor, Saint Paul. 1983. *Saint Paul's Homegrown Economy Project: A New Economic Policy and Program for a Self-Reliant City.* Saint Paul, MN: City of Saint Paul.

Okuyama, Y., M. Sonis, and G. J. D. Hewings. 1999. "Creating and Expanding Trade Partnerships Within the Chicago Metropolitan Area: Applications Using a Miyazawa Accounting system." Urbana: Technical series working paper prepared for the Regional Economics Applications Laboratory, University of Illinois at Urbana-Champaign.

Onal, H., K. A. Algozin, M. Isik, and R. H. Hornbaker. 1998. "Economically Efficient Watershed Management with Environmental Impact and Income Distribution Goals." *Journal of Environmental Management* 53(3): 241–53.

Orfield, M.. 1998. *Metropolitics.* Washington, DC: Brookings.

Osborne, D., and T. Gaebler. 1992. *Reinventing Government.* New York: Addison-Wesley.

Pagano, M., and A. O'M Bowman. 1995. *Cityscapes and Capital: The Politics of Urban Development.* Baltimore: Johns Hopkins University Press.

Papke, L. 1994. "Tax Policy and Urban Development: Evidence from the Indiana Enterprise Zone Program." *Journal of Public Economics* 54(1): 37–49.

Partridge, M. D., and D. S. Rickman. 1998. "Regional Computable General Equilibrium Modeling: A Survey and Critical Assessment." *International Regional Science Review* 21(3): 205–48.

Passell, P. 1990. "Rebel Economists Add Ecological Costs to Price of Progress." *New York Times,* November, 27. C1; C13.

Pereira, A. M., and J. Shoven. 1988. "Survey of Dynamic Computational General Equilibrium Models for Tax Policy Evaluation." *Journal of Policy Modeling* 10(4): 401–36.

Peretz, P. 1986. "The Market for Incentives: Where Angels Fear to Tread." *Policy Studies Journal* 5: 624–33.

Persky, J. J,, D. Felsenstein, and W. Wiewel. 1997. "How Do We Know That 'But-For the Incentives' the Development Would Not Have Occurred?" In *Dilemmas of Urban Economic Development,* ed. R. D. Bingham and R. Mier, 28–45. Thousand Oaks, CA: Sage.

Persky, J. J., and W. Wiewel. 1999. "Economic Development and Metropolitan Sprawl: Changing Who Pays and Who Benefits." In *The End of Welfare?* ed. Max B. Sawicky, 127–56. Armonk, NY: M. E. Sharpe.

Peterson, P. 1981. *City Limits.* Chicago: University of Chicago Press.

Pireddu, G., and C. M. Dufournaud. 1996. "Eco-taxes in an Italian CGE Model: Double Dividend Effects and the Distribution of Tax Burdens." In *Economic Modelling under the Applied General Equilibrium Approach,* ed. A. Fossati, 47–76. Aldershot, UK: Avebury.

Porter, M. 1997. "New Strategies for Inner-City Economic Development." *Economic Development Quarterly* 11(1): 11–27.

Portz, J. 1990. *The Politics of Plant Closings.* Lawrence: University Press of Kansas.

Pradhan, B. K., and A. Sahoo. 1996. "Social Accounting Matrix and Its Multipliers for India." *Margin* 28(2): 153–69.

Public Policy Associates. 1997. "Performance Measures." MJC Ren Zone Benchmarking Project, August 6.

Putnam, R. D. 1993a. *Making Democracy Work.* Princeton, NJ: Princeton University Press.

———. 1993b. "The Prosperous Community: Social Capital and Public Life." *American Prospect* 13 (spring).

Pyatt, G., and E. Thorbecke. 1976. *Planning Techniques for a Better Future.* Geneva: International Labour Office.

Pyatt, G., and J. I. Round, eds. 1985. *Social Accounting Matrices: A Basis for Planning.* Washington, DC: World Bank.

REAL (Regional Economics Applications Laboratory, University of Illinois at Urbana-Champaign). *Creating and Expanding Trade Partnerships in the Chicago Region: Economic Interaction within the Chicago Metropolitan Region.* Urbana,

IL: Final report prepared for Chicago United and the MacArthur Foundation, 1999. <http://www.uiuc.edu/unit/real/tradechi.pdf>.

Reed, A., Jr. 1988. "The Liberal Technocrat." *Nation,* February 6, 167–70.

Reese, L. A. 1991. "Municipal Fiscal Health and Tax Abatement Policy." *Economic Development Quarterly* 5: 23–32.

———. 1992. "Local Economic Development in Michigan: A Reliance on the Supply-Side." *Economic Development Quarterly* 6: 383–93.

———. 1998. "Sharing the Benefits of Economic Development: What Cities Utilize Type II Policies?" *Urban Affairs Review* 33: 686–711.

Reese, L. A., and D. Fasenfest. 1996. "More of the Same: A Research Note on Local Economic Development Policies Over Time." *Economic Development Quarterly* 10: 280–89.

———. 1997. "What Works Best? Values and the Evaluation of Local Economic Development Policy." *Economic Development Quarterly* 11(3): 195–207.

———. 1999. "Critical Perspectives on Local Development Policy Evaluation." *Economic Development Quarterly* (February): 3–65.

Reese, L. A., Rosenfeld, R. A., and D. Fasenfest. 2002. "The State of Local Economic Development Policy." *2002 Municipal Year Book.* Washington DC: ICMA.

Rein, M. 1976. *Social Science and Public Policy.* New York: Penguin.

Reinert, K. A., and D. W. Roland-Holst. 1992. "A Detailed Social Accounting Matrix for the USA, 1988." *Economic Systems Research* 4(2): 173–87.

Renkow, M. 1996. "Income Non-convergence and Rural-Urban Earnings Differentials: Evidence from North Carolina." *Southern Economic Journal* 62(4): 1017–28.

Rey, S. J. 1999. "Integrated Regional Econometric and Input-Output Modeling." Unpublished manuscript. Department of Geography. San Diego State University.

Richardson, H. W. 1985. "Input-Output and Economic Base Multipliers: Looking Backward and Forward." *Journal of Regional Science* 25(4): 607–61.

Ricker, T. 1998. "Estimating the Capital Costs of Community Destabilization." Washington, DC: National Center for Economic and Security Alternatives.

Rolnick, A. 1992. "Is State and Local Economic Development Policy a Zero-Sum Game?" Paper given at The State and Local Economic Development Strategy Summit, Hubert H. Humphrey Institute of Public Affairs, University of Minnesota, Minneapolis, December 4–5.

Rosaldo, R. 1993. *Culture and Truth: The Remaking of Social Analysis.* Boston: Beacon.

Rose, A., and P. Beaumont. 1988. "Interrelational Income-Distribution Multipliers for the West Virginia Economy." *Journal of Regional Science* 28(4): 461–75.

———. 1989. "Interrelational Income Distribution Multipliers for the U.S. Economy." In *Frontiers of Input-Output Analysis,* ed. R. E. Miller, K. Polenske, and A. Z. Rose, 34–47. New York: Oxford University Press.

Rose, A., and P. C. Li. 1999. "Interrelational Multipliers for the US Economy: An Application to Welfare Reform." In *Understanding and Interpreting Economic Structure,* ed. G. J. D. Hewings, M. Sonis, M. Madden, and Y. Kimura, 347–64. New York: Springer.

Rose, A., and W. Miernyk. 1989. "Input-Output Analysis: The First Fifty Years." *Economic Systems Research* 1(2): 229–71.

Rose, A., B. Stevens, and G. Davis. 1988. *Natural Resource Policy and Income Distribution.* Baltimore: Johns Hopkins University Press.

Rosen, H. S. 1985. *Public Finance.* Homewood, IL: Richard D. Irwin, Inc.

Ross, D. P., and Usher, P. J. 1986. *From the Roots Up: Economic Development as If Community Mattered.* Croton-on-Hudson, NY: Bootstrap Press.

Rossi, P. H., and H. E. Freeman. 1985. *Evaluation: A Systematic Approach.* Beverly Hills, CA: Sage.

Rowley, T. D., J. M. Redman, and J. Angle. 1991. "The Rapid Rise in State Per Capita Income Inequality in the 1980s: Sources and Prospects." Economic Research Service. Staff Report AGES 9104. Washington, DC: U.S. Department of Agriculture.

Rubin, B. M., and C. K. Zorn. 1985. "Sensible State and Local Economic Development." *Public Administration Review* 45: 333–40.

Rubin, H. J, and I. Rubin. 1987. "Economic Development Incentives: The Poor Pay More." *Urban Affairs Quarterly* 22: 32–62.

Rubin, H. J. 1989. "Symbolism and Economic Development Work: Perceptions of Urban Economic Development Practitioners." *American Review of Public Administration* 19: 233–48.

Sadoulet, E., and A. de Janvry. 1995. *Quantitative Development Policy Analysis.* Baltimore: Johns Hopkins University Press.

Salamon, L. M., and O. V. Elliott. 2001. *The Tools of Government: A Guide to the New Governance.* New York: Oxford University Press.

Schaffer, R. L. 1973. *Income Flows in Urban Poverty Areas: A Comparison of the Community Income Accounts of Bedford-Stuyvesant and Borough Park.* New York: Lexington.

Schneider, M., P. Teske, and M. Mintrom. 1995. *Public Entrepreneurs: Agents for Change in American Government.* Princeton, NJ: Princeton University Press.

Schneider, M. 1989. *The Competitive City.* Pittsburgh: University of Pittsburgh Press.

Schreiner, D. F., H. S. Lee, Y. K. Koh, and R. Budiyanti. 1996. "Rural Development: Toward an Integrative Policy Framework." *Journal of Regional Analysis and Policy* 26(2): 53–72.

Sharma, S. P., and K. K. Saxena. 1998. "Structural Reforms and Their Impact on Employment Generation in India: An Input-Output Approach." *Indian Journal of Labour Economics* 41(2): 303–16.

Sharp, E. B., and D. Elkins. 1991. "The Politics of Economic Development Policy." *Economic Development Quarterly* 5: 126–39.

Shoven, J. B., and J. Whalley. 1992. *Applying General Equilibrium.* Cambridge: Cambridge University Press.

Siebert H. 1969. *Regional Economic Growth; Theory and Policy.* Scranton, PA: International Textbook.

Siegel, P. B., J. Alwang, and T. G. Johnson. 1995. "Decomposing Sources of Regional Growth in an Input-Output Model: A Framework for Policy Analysis." *International Regional Science Review* 18(3): 331–53.

Smith, D. (with P. McGuigan). 1979. "Towards a Public Balance Sheet." Washington, DC: National Center for Economic Alternatives.

Smith, D. A. 1979. *The Public Balance Sheet: A New Tool for Evaluating Economic Choices.* Washington, DC: Conference on Alternative State and Local Policies.

Smith, M. P. 1989. "The Uses of Linked-Development Policies in U.S. Cities." In *Regenerating the Cities: The UK Crisis and the US Experience,* ed. M. Parkinson et al., 85–99. Glenview, IL: Scott Foresman.

Squires, G. 1989. "Public-Private Partnerships: Who Gets What and Why." In *Unequal Partnerships: The Political Economy of Urban Redevelopment in Postwar America,* ed. G. D. Squires, 1–11. New Brunswick, NJ: Rutgers University Press.

Sridhar, K. 1996. "Tax Costs and Employment Benefits of Enterprise Zones." *Economic Development Quarterly* 10(1): 69–90.

State of Florida Department of Community Affairs. 1983. *A Distress Atlas.* Office of the Secretary, Tallahassee, Florida, July.

State of Florida Office of the Auditor General.1993. *Review and Evaluation of the Enterprise Zone Program.* Program Audit Division: Report No. 12003, February.

Stein, R. 1991. *Urban Alternatives.* Pittsburgh: University of Pittsburgh Press.

Stokey, E., and R. Zeckhauser. 1978. *A Primer for Policy Analysis.* New York: Norton.

Stone, C. N. 1987. "The Study of the Politics of Urban Development." In *The Politics of Urban Development,* ed. C. Stone and H. Sanders, 3–22. Lawrence: University Press of Kansas.

———. 1989. *Regime Politics: Governing Atlanta.* Lawrence: University Press of Kansas.

Storm, S. 1997. "Domestic Constraints on Export-led Growth: A Case-Study of India." *Journal of Development Economics* 52(1): 83–119.

———. 1999. "Foodgrain Price Stabilisation in an Open Economy: A CGE Analysis of Variable Trade Levies in India." *Journal of Development Economics* 36(2): 136–59.

Subramanian, S., and E. Sadoulet. 1990. "The Transmission of Production Fluctuations and Technical Change in a Village Economy: A Social Accounting Matrix Approach." *Economic Development and Cultural Change* 39(1): 131–74.

Swanstrom, T. 1988. "Semisovereign Cities: The Politics of Urban Development." *Polity* 21: 83–110.

———. 2000. "The Costs of Economic Segregation and Sprawl." Draft Manuscript. University at Albany, SUNY. March.

Tao, J. 1995. "City Influence in Florida's Enterprise Zones: Measuring the Limits." Paper presented at the Midwest Political Science Association Annual Meeting,, Chicago, April.

Tao, J. L., and R. C. Feiock. 1999. "Directing Benefits to Need: Evaluating the Distributive Consequences of Urban Economic Development." *Economic Development Quarterly* 13(1): 55–65.

Taylor, J. E., A. Yunez-Naude, and G. Dyer. 1999. "Agricultural Price Policy, Employment, and Migration in a Diversified Rural Economy: A Village-Town CGE Analysis from Mexico." *American Journal of Agricultural Economics* 81(3): 653–62.

Taylor, J. E., A. Yunez-Naude, and S. Hampton. 1999. "Agricultural Policy Reforms and Village Economies: A Computable General-Equilibrium Analysis from Mexico." *Journal of Policy Modeling* 21(4): 453–80.

Tendler, J. 1987. *What Ever Happened to Poverty Alleviation?* New York: Ford Foundation.

Thorbecke, E. 1998. "Social Accounting Matrices and Social Accounting Analysis." In *Methods of Interregional and Regional Analysis*, ed. W. Isard, I. J. Azis, M. P. Drennan, R. E. Miller, S. Saltzman, and E. Thorbecke, 281–331. Aldershot, UK: Ashgate.

Thorbecke, E., and H. S. Jung. 1996. "A Multiplier Decomposition Method to Analyze Poverty Alleviation." *Journal of Development Economics* 48(2): 279–300.

Tiebout, C. 1962. *The Community Economic Base Study*. New York: Committee for Economic Development.

Tietz, M. B. "Neighborhood Economics: Local Communities and Regional Markets." *Economic Development Quarterly* 3 (1989): 111–22.

Townsend, R. F., and S. McDonald. 1998. "Biased Policies, Agriculture and Income Distribution in South Africa: A Social Accounting Matrix Approach." *Journal for the Study of Economics and Econometrics* 22(1): 91–114.

Treyz, G. 1993. *Regional Economic Modeling: A Systematic Approach to Econmomic Forecasting and Policy Analysis*. Boston: Kluwer.

Tribe, L. J. 1972. "Policy Science: Analysis or Ideology." *Philosophy and Public Affairs* 2.

U.S. Congress, House of Representatives. 1993. Hearing before the Committee on Banking, Finance and Urban Affairs, *The Administration's Empowerment Zone and Enterprise Community Proposal.* 103rd Cong., 1st sess., May, June.

———. 1994. Hearing before the Committee on Public Works and Transportation. *1993 Empowerment Zone and Enterprise Community Program.* 103rd Cong., 2d sess., February.

———. 1994. Hearing before Committee on Ways and Means. *Empowerment Zone Provisions of the Omnibus Budget Reconciliation Act of 1993.* 103rd Cong., 2d sess., March.

U.S. Congress, Senate. 1993. Hearing before the Committee on Small Business. *Hearing on Enterprise Zones.* 103rd Cong., 1st sess., June.

U.S. Department of Commerce, Bureau of the Census. 1980. *Characteristics of the Population: General Social and Economic Characteristics—Florida.* PC80–1-C11.

———. 1982. *County and City Data Book.*

———. 1990a. *General Population Characteristics: Florida.*

———. 1990b. *Social and Economic Characteristics: Florida.*

U.S. Department of Housing and Urban Development, Office of Policy Development and Research. 1995. "Empowerment: A New Covenant with America's Communities." President Clinton's National Urban Policy Report, Washington, DC, July.

U.S. Government Accounting Office. 1988. *Enterprise Zones: Lessons from the Maryland Experience*. Washington, DC: U.S. GPO. GAO/PEMD-89–2.

Vietorisz, T., and B. Harrison. 1970. *The Economic Development of Harlem.* New York: Praeger.

Wassall, G., and D. Hellman. 1985. "Financial incentives to industry and urban economic development." *Policy Studies Review* 4: 626–40.

Waters, E. C., D. W. Holland, and B. A. Weber. 1997. "Economic Impacts of a Property Tax Limitation: A Computable General Equilibrium Analysis of Oregon's Measure 5." *Land Economics* 73(1): 72–89.

Watson C. J. 1974. "Vacancy Chains, Filtering, and the Public Sector." *Journal of the American Institute of Planners* 40: 346–52.

Weale, M. 1991. "Environmental Multipliers from a System of Physical Resource Accounting." *Structural Change and Economic Dynamics* 2(2): 297–309.

Webster, D. 1979. "A Regional Development Application of Employment Shifting Concepts: DREE's Alberta Special Area Program." *Plan Canada* 19(3): 226–36.

Weimer, D., and A. Vining. 1999. *Policy Analysis: Concepts and Practice.* Upper Saddle River, NJ: Prentice Hall.

Weiss, C. H. "Nothing as Practical as Good Theory: Exploring Theory-Based Evaluation for Comprehensive Community Initiatives for Children and Families." In *New Approaches to Evaluating Community Initiatives,*Ecircumflexed. A. Kubisch. Washington, DC: Aspen Institute, 1995.

West, G. R., and R. W. Jackson. 1998. "Input-Output + Econometric and Econometric + Input-Output: Model Differences or Different Models?" *Journal of Regional Analysis and Policy.* 28(1): 33–48.

White H. C. 1970a. *Chains of Opportunity: System Models of Mobility in Organizations.* Cambridge: Harvard University Press.

———. 1970b. "Matching, Vacancies, and Mobility." *Journal of the Political Economy* 78(1): 97–105.

———. 1971. "Multipliers, Vacancy Chains, and Filtering in Housing." *Journal of the American Institute of Planners* 37(2): 88–94.

Wiese, A. M., A. Rose, and G. Schluter. 1995. "Motor Fuel Taxes and Household Welfare: An Applied General Equilibrium Analysis." *Land Economics* 71(2): 229–43.

Wiewel, W., B. Brown, and M. Morris. 1989. "The Linkage Between Regional and Neighborhood Development." *Economic Development Quarterly* 3: 94–110.

Wilkinson, T. J. 1999. "The Effects of State Appropriations on Export-Related Employment in Manufacturing." *Economic Development Quarterly* 13: 172–82.

Williamson, T., D. Imbroscio, and G. Alperovitz. 2002. "Democracy Community, and Economic Viability in the Global Era." Draft Book Manuscript. National Center for Economic and Security Alternatives.

Wilson, W. J. 1987. *The Truly Disadvantaged.* Chicago: University of Chicago Press.

Wolman, H. 1988. "Local Economic Development Policy: What Explains the Divergence between Policy Analysis and Political Behavior?" *Journal of Urban Affairs* 10: 19–28.

———. 1996. "The Politics of Local Economic Development." *Economic Development Quarterly* 10: 115–50.

Xie, J. 2000. "An Environmentally Extended Social Accounting Matrix." *Environmental and Resource Economics* 16(4): 391–406.

Yao, S., A. Liu, and R. Greener. 1996. "Agricultural Trade Liberalization in a Computable General Equilibrium Framework for the Philippines." *Economic Systems Research* 8(1): 3–14.

Zyblock M., and Z. Lin. 1997. "Trickling Down or Fizzling Out? Economic Performance, Transfers, Inequality and Low Income." Business and Labor Market Analysis Division, Statistics Canada, Ottawa (unpublished).

CONTRIBUTORS

VIRGINIA CARLSON is associate professor in urban planning at the University of Wisconsin–Milwaukee. Carlson has seventeen years' experience in industrial and employment research and applications. She has worked with the Federal Reserve Bank of Chicago, the University of Illinois Center for Urban Economic Development, the Chicago Urban League, and World Business Chicago, among others. Her latest publications include "Ladders to a Better Life" (*American Prospect*, June 19, 2000). Her current areas of interest include labor market restructuring, family support policies, and economic linkages between new economy and legacy industries.

MARGARET DEWAR is professor and chair in the Urban and Regional Planning Program at the University of Michigan. She also directs the Detroit Community Partnership Center. She does research in the area of economic development planning with particular interest in urban revitalization. Her current research relates to the effectiveness of Empowerment Zones, the redevelopment of brownfields, and the reuse of tax-foreclosed land in cities.

DAVID FASENFEST is associate professor of urban affairs in the College of Urban, Labor and Metropolitan Affairs. An economist and sociologist, his research focuses on the nature of economic transformations as they affect local economic development; the formation and implementation of local development policies; the structure of income inequality; and the impact of recent regulatory changes on the social economy. He is the editor of *Community Economic Development: Policy Formation in the U.S. and U.K.* (St. Martin's), and recent publications appear *in Economic Development Quarterly, Policy Studies Journal,* and the *International Journal of Urban and Regional Research.* His current research includes a regional examination of workforce development, and an evaluation of local economic development planning.

RICHARD C. FEIOCK is professor of public administration and political science at Florida State University. He directs the DeVoe Moore Center Program in Local Governance. His work on local economic development has appeared in a number of scholarly journals, including *American Journal of Political Science, Public Administration Review, Urban Affairs Review, Journal of Politics,* and *Journal of Pubic Administration Research and Theory.* He has also co-authored (with James Clingermayer) *Institutional Constraints and Local Government: An Exploration of Local Governance* (SUNY), and edited *Decentralized Governance: Government Organization in Metropolitan Areas* (forthcoming from Georgetown).

DANIEL FELSENSTEIN is assistant professor in the Department of Geography and director of the Institute of Urban and Regional Studies at the Hebrew University of Jerusalem. He specializes in regional economic development and impact analysis and has co-authored three books in these areas. His recent research has focused on the regional employment and welfare impacts of public assistance to small firms, and estimating local externalities arising from public subsidies to business. Current research issues include modeling and estimating the "trickle down" effects associated with employment creation in local labor markets, and investigating the dynamics of regional earnings disparities in small countries.

DAVID L. IMBROSCIO is associate professor of political science and urban affairs at the University of Louisville, where he teaches courses in the fields of urban political economy and public policy. He is author of *Reconstructing City Politics* (Sage, 1997) and, with Thad Williamson and Gar Alperovitz, *Making a Place for Community* (Routledge). His recent work has appeared in *Polity, Policy Studies Journal, Review of Policy Research, Journal of Urban Affairs, Good Society,* and *Urban Affairs Review.* He currently serves on the editorial board of the *Journal of Urban Affairs.*

JOHN C. LEATHERMAN is an associate professor in the Department of Agricultural Economics at Kansas State University, and a local government specialist with Kansas State University–Extension. He is the director of the Office of Local Government, an extension program providing educational outreach and technical assistance services to local governments in Kansas. His research and writings span diverse interest areas, including regional economics and economic development policy, local public finance, and natural resource management and land use.

DAVID W. MARCOUILLER is an associate professor of urban and regional planning at the University of Wisconsin–Madison and also serves as a resource economist with joint appointments in the Department of Forest Ecology and Management, the Institute of Environmental Studies, and the Center for Community Economic Development. His work focuses on the linkages between natural resources and rural economic development with a particular interest in the mechanisms behind income generation and distribution to rural households. His work has been published in the *Journal of Planning Literature, Society and Natural Resources, Land Economics, Tourism Economics, Economic Development Quarterly, Growth and Change, Forest Science, Canadian Journal of Forest Research, Northern Journal of Applied Forestry, Review of Regional Studies,* and the *American Journal of Agricultural Economics.* Along with Steven Deller, he serves as co-editor of the *Journal of Regional Analysis and Policy.*

JOSEPH PERSKY is professor of economics at the University of Illinois at Chicago. His research has focused on distributional implications of urban and regional economic growth. He and Wim Wiewel recently published a book, *When Corporations Leave Town,* on the costs and benefits of metropolitan employment deconcentration. Persky has written extensively on the logic and evaluation of state and local economic development efforts and has worked closely with several states and cities. He has a long standing interest in the economy of the southern U.S. including a book, *The Burden of Dependency.* Persky also writes an occasional feature, "Retrospectives," on the history of economics for the *Journal of Economic Perspectives.*

LAURA A. REESE, a political scientist, is a professor in the urban planning program and a fellow in the Fraser Center for Workplace Issues, College of Urban, Labor and Metropolitan Affairs, at Wayne State University. She has published articles on urban politics, local economic development, comparative urban policy, and public personnel management in *Urban Affairs Review, Economic Development Quarterly, Journal of Politics, Review of Public Personnel Administration, Publius: Journal of Federalism,* and the *International Journal of Urban and Regional Research.* Her most recent books are *Approaches to Economic Development* (with John Blair), *Implementing Sexual Harassment Policy* (with Karen Lindenberg), and *The Civic Culture of Local Economic Development* (with Raymond Rosenfeld) all with Sage. Her current research interests focus on further exploration of local civic cultures in the United States and Canada, comparative studies of urban consolidation and metropolitan governance, and identification and implementation of effective sexual harassment policy.

JILL L. TAO is an assistant professor of public policy in the Department of Political Science at the University of Oklahoma in Norman. She received her Ph.D. in Public Administration from Florida State University in 2000. Her research and teaching interests include comparative and development administration, community and economic development policy, implementation theory, policy analysis, and urban politics and administration. She has a chapter in a forthcoming volume with Georgetown University Press, "Social Capital Misconstrued: Regionalism, Fragmentation, and the Politics of Cooperation in Metropolitan Areas" with Richard Feiock, and a forthcoming article in the *International Journal of Economic Development.*

JORDAN S. YIN is a faculty member in the urban and regional planning program in the Department of Geography at Western Michigan University, where he teaches courses in neighborhood development and urban planning with an emphasis on community outreach and student service learning. He received his Ph.D. in city and regional planning from Cornell University and has worked broadly in the field of community economic development.

INDEX

www.ingramcontent.com/pod-product-compliance
Lightning Source LLC
LaVergne TN
LVHW010355080826
844660LV00016B/973/J
* 9 7 8 0 8 1 4 3 2 9 0 0 9 *